THE
KNOWLEDGE
OF
GOD
IN
ANCIENT
ISRAEL

BY THE AUTHOR:

The Holy Scriptures—A Survey
Preface to Old Testament Theology
A First Reader in Biblical Theology
The Apocrypha—Bridge of the Testaments
The King and His Cross

THE
KNOWLEDGE
OF
GOD
IN
ANCIENT
ISRAEL

Robert C. Dentan

 THE SEABURY PRESS • NEW YORK

Copyright © 1968 by The Seabury Press, Incorporated
Library of Congress Catalog Card Number: 68-11593
Design by Nancy H. Dale
596-368-C-3.5
Printed in the United States of America

To
Bernard Cromley Newman
and
Arthur Lester Middleton Worthey✝

לאוהב אמונה אין מחיר
ואין משקל לטובתו

—SIRACH 6:15

החוט המשלש לא במהרה ינתק

—ECCLESIASTES 4:12

PREFACE

ALTHOUGH THIS BOOK is a treatise on Old Testament theology, it does not attempt to deal with the whole subject as ordinarily defined, but only with one basic aspect of it: the Old Testament doctrine of God.[1] This limitation is due partly to the fact that there are already many works dealing with Old Testament theology as a whole, some of them well-nigh exhaustive in scope,[2] and it would seem pointless merely to add another title to the list; but more important is the conviction that the Old Testament doctrine of God is in reality the heart and crux of the subject and therefore deserving of special and concentrated attention.

As I have said elsewhere, all other aspects of the normative religion of ancient Israel "have their center in a distinctive doctrine of God (theo-logy)."[3] This doctrine is the pole around which all the other topics normally included in treatises on the theology of the Old Testament—ideas about the nature of man, sin, salvation, ethics and cultus—should properly be organized. But it is difficult to realize this ideal if the doctrine of God is treated simply as one doctrine among many others, as must be the case in any comprehensive survey of the subject. It seems at least possible that a treatise dealing with this single doctrine in isolation, to the exclusion of peripheral matters, however important, might do greater justice to its central position in the theological structure of the Old Testament, and enable the reader to see more clearly that it was the character of Israel's God that set the distinctive stamp on every aspect of her religion. That is at least the hope with which this book was written.

It will be obvious to students of the subject that this view is markedly different from that of Walther Eichrodt[4] or Gerhard von Rad,[5] the two modern authors who have written most extensively in this field. Although the titles of Eichrodt's separate volumes (*Gott und Volk, Gott und Welt, Gott und Mensch*) indicate his keen awareness of the centrality of the idea of God in Israelite thought, he regards the idea of the "covenant" as the distinctive and unifying principle. To me at least, the idea of the covenant seems much less dominant in Old Testament literature than Eichrodt would have us suppose, even if the term be defined rather loosely. The term is scarcely found, for example, in the eighth-century prophets,[6] and their concern with the idea is at least debatable; while the complete absence of covenantal terminology from the Wisdom Literature is notorious. This is not to deny the importance of the covenant idea in the Old Testament, but only to assert that the existence of the covenant seems to me a far less central, distinctive and determinative fact in Old Testament religion than does the character of the covenant God.

In contrast to Eichrodt, von Rad in effect denies even the possibility of an Old Testament theology in the usual sense of the term. For him, the God of Israel has no special character. Israel tried to understand what her God was like, but never succeeded, and grew increasingly baffled in the process. Consequently one cannot expect to find in the Old Testament any unified "theology" at all. Theological discourse in Israel was limited, von Rad believes, to a discussion of how God "acts"— what he had done in the past and what he could be expected to do in the future—but even here there was no general agreement except in certain circles and at certain times. The character of

God and the meaning of his acts were, for all practical purposes, a profound mystery until they were unveiled in the coming of Jesus Christ. Von Rad's skepticism seems to me far greater than the evidence warrants. Among all the changes of emphasis in different periods, resulting from cultural evolution and adaptation, and the inevitable differences of opinion from book to book and thinker to thinker, the character of Israel's God seems to me, in its most striking features, remarkably constant, especially when one keeps his attention fixed on the really basic contrast, which is not that between one biblical book and another, but between Israel and her pagan neighbors. Israel's religious development does not impress me as one of growing bafflement but, rather, as one of increasing understanding; and the New Testament seems to me less like a key to a long-locked door than like a keystone placed on an arch that had been long in building. These are very large questions that cannot be argued here at length. But the book that follows is, in some sense, part of the argument, since it attempts to present the Old Testament doctrine of God as a relatively consistent and organically developing whole.

The first two chapters are preliminary. Since the subject is "the knowledge of God in ancient *Israel*," it seemed desirable first of all to try to define what we mean by "Israel." In biblical thought God and Israel are interdependent; the most basic affirmation of Old Testament religion is that Yahweh is the God of Israel, and Israel is the people of Yahweh. To deal with the doctrine of God in the Old Testament without a serious study of both subject and predicate in these clauses would stultify the whole endeavor. Even in the New Testament the God of Jesus is still the God of Israel, and the New Testament gives no support to the idea that religion is an individual enterprise that a man can pursue outside the community of Israel as reconstituted in Christ. Chapter 1, "The Mystery of Israel," is an at-

tempt to give the reader some conception of the nature and
vitality of the remarkable community that produced the doctrine with which the rest of the book is concerned.

The second chapter deals with "the knowledge of God," considered as an almost technical term for what would now be called
the "theology" of Israel. Biblical theologians have always advocated using biblical terminology wherever possible rather than
terms derived from some alien source. "Theology" is, of course,
a word of Greek origin meaning "rational (or scientific) thought
about God," while the phrase "knowledge of God" is purely,
and characteristically, Hebrew. It has much the same meaning,
however, as the Greek term, and has therefore been used in the
title of the book. The terms are functionally equivalent, but the
Hebrew is far richer than the Greek and, for this reason, a special chapter is devoted to an exploration of its meaning.

The titles of the remaining chapters are self-explanatory.
Three of them (3, 4 and 9) have to do with the "action" of God
(and I am glad to acknowledge my debt to von Rad and G. E.
Wright[7] for this approach, while recognizing the extent to which
they would dissent from some of the ways in which I have used
it); two chapters are concerned with the nature and character of
God (where my debt to Eichrodt and many others who have
written at length upon these matters will also be obvious).

Two briefer sections are entitled "digressions" because they
deal with themes which, though important, are not central to
the main argument of the book. If one might think of Old
Testament theology as a single long sentence, these would be
only subordinate clauses. They treat of subjects that are integral
to the developed structure of Old Testament faith, but not to
its vital essence.

Any work on biblical theology is bound to have a certain
subjective element in it, especially in the choice of topics and
assignment of priorities. Unless the tendency is kept carefully
in check, a book may reflect the mind of the author as much as

it illuminates his sources, and become more a confession of faith than a historical essay. Although I have consciously tried to minimize the subjective factor, I would readily acknowledge its presence, to some extent, in the work that follows. It is hardly likely that any particular individual in ancient Israel would have thought about his God in just the way this book describes; the portrait it presents is, rather, that of the God of the Old Testament as he appears to me after many years of involvement with the records of his people in both private study and public teaching. Nevertheless, I believe that the picture given here is not inconsistent, in any essential respect, with the view of God contained in the Hebrew Scriptures; I have made an honest effort to see him through the eyes of ancient Israel and not simply through my own. The mood of the book is not meditative, confessional or hortatory, except in the final chapter, where it seemed reasonable to allow the question of the contemporary relevance of the biblical idea of God finally to intrude.

I should hope that, in intention at least, this book would seem acceptable to Jews as well as Christians. Most books on "Old Testament theology" have an explicit, and quite proper, concern to relate their discussion immediately to New Testament issues. The present book endeavors to look at the Hebrew Bible strictly within its own limits and on its terms. The argument in Chapter 1, "The Mystery of Israel," makes clear enough my belief in the relevance of the subject to Christian thought, as do several other books that I have written,[8] but I have deliberately tried to keep any specifically Christian point of view out of the chapters that follow. This is partly because of a profound respect for scientific method, but also because I believe that genuine theological conversation between Jews and Christians, joint heirs to "the knowledge of God in ancient Israel," is one of the important *desiderata* of our times. I should be happy if this book might be understood as an attempt to explore and evaluate our common theological heritage and might contribute in some way to a deepening of understanding and friendliness between the two historic communities that look to ancient Israel as their common mother.

For the benefit of the general reader, for whom this is intended even more than for the scholar, technical terms and notes have been kept at a minimum. For the same reason, I have not attempted to cover every conceivable topic even within this rather limited field; it seemed better to keep the main outlines clear rather than clutter the pages with too great a profusion of detail. To anyone who knows the literature of the subject, it will be evident that there is little that is original in this book; my debt to others is obvious in every chapter. If the book possesses any value as an original work, it lies only in the treatment of some minor aspects of the general theme, in the over-all arrangement of the material and, I hope, in a certain measure of simplicity in treatment and style.

Quotations from the Bible are generally from the Revised Standard Version of the Bible (with the permission of the National Council of Churches in Christ), except that I have frequently substituted the proper name "Yahweh" for the pious surrogate "the Lord" in order to bring out better the original flavor of the text. Where other versions are used the fact is noted.

ROBERT C. DENTAN

General Theological Seminary
New York, N.Y.

CONTENTS

1
THE MYSTERY
OF ISRAEL

Israel is my first-born son.

THE CENTRAL FIGURE of the Bible is a community
called Israel. The Bible is also, of course, a book
about God, and one might accurately say that God
is its hero; but in fact we know and see the God of the Bible
only through the mind and eyes of Israel—as he is known, proclaimed, worshiped, and obeyed, or disobeyed, in the life of the
elect community.

This is obviously true of the Old Testament; but even in the
New Testament, which announces that the divine word has
taken flesh and come to dwell among us, Jesus Christ is first
of all a citizen of Israel, with a message directed primarily to
his fellow citizens. The genealogy that stands at the beginning
of the Gospels makes this transparently clear when it lists Jesus
as the last and greatest of the sons of Abraham and a member
of the royal family of David (Matt. 1:1–17). It is reported that
Jesus himself said he "was sent only to the lost sheep of the
house of Israel" (Matt. 15:24), and he promised his disciples
that they would one day "sit on twelve thrones, judging (i.e.,

3

ruling over) the twelve tribes of Israel" (Matt. 19:28). Nathan-
ael, described as "an Israelite worthy of the name" (New
English Bible), hails him as "the king of Israel" (John 1:47, 49),
and it was Jesus' claim, or supposed claim, to this title that was
the immediate cause of his death (Mark 15:32; Luke 23:2f.).

Israel's Priority in the Bible Story

Difficult as it may be for the average reader to accept the fact, the Bible (the Christian Bible, that is, not merely
the Old Testament) begins and ends as the story of Israel. Although it is true that neither Israel nor her special ancestors
are mentioned in Gen. 1–11, this does not mean that the Bible
at its beginning is concerned simply with general problems of
a cosmological and anthropological nature. Israel, at least in
her early days, had little interest in matters of this kind; her
major concern was to trace her own origins and antecedents, and
the first part of Genesis has the function of taking that story
back as far as it is possible to go. The opening chapters of the
Bible are not intended to provide universal answers to universal
questions, but to set the stage, and provide a suitable prologue, for the great drama of Israel's history which begins explicitly in Gen. 12.

Even in these early chapters the unprepared reader may be
shocked by the sudden interpolation of narrowly Israelite
themes, as when the creation story comes to its climax, not in
some event of general human significance, but in the establishment of the Sabbath (Gen. 2:3), or when the story of Noah's
flood is made to eventuate in the imposition of the first of the
dietary laws (Gen. 9:4). While it remained for a much later
writer to say explicitly that God created the universe for the
sake of Israel (2 Esdras 6:55; 7:11), the point of view in Genesis
is not substantially different.

The creation stories and the primeval history were, as a matter of fact, the last ingredients to be added to Israel's canonical traditions. As we shall see later, the first traditions to attain definitive status were those that told how Israel came to be a nation—the stories of the exodus, the Sinai covenant and the conquest of the Promised Land. Subsequently these were supplemented by prefixing to them stories about Israel's remoter ancestors, Abraham, Isaac and Jacob. Only after these first two stages in the development of the tradition were finished did a final compiler add to the beginning of the story an account of the creation of the world and its inhabitants, thus providing the necessary backdrop for seeing Israel's call in its ultimate relation to the physical universe and God's purpose for other nations. The "priestly" account of creation (Gen. 1:1–2:4a), with its breathtaking cosmic vistas, is the final form in which this backdrop was conceived.

The faith of Israel did not begin with the conviction that there was a God who had created the world and had, incidentally, chosen the people of Israel as his own. Israel's faith began with a direct, immediate, historical experience of a God who had chosen her to be his people. Only later did she move on to realize that it was this same God who had created the world— or, at least, to realize the full implications of the fact. To put the idea in more technical language: Israel's election faith preceded her creation faith.[1]

The opening chapters of Genesis are conceived on a grand scale, but how quickly the magnificent vision narrows down from the sun, moon and stars to the earth, to the people on the earth, then to a particular segment of those people, and finally to *one nation* among them all. Gen. 1 is not primarily the majestic overture to world history, but to Israel's history.

In the last book of the Christian Bible—the Book of Revelation—Israel is still in the center of the picture. This is strange, because the official New Testament view is that the people of ancient Israel had forfeited God's favor by rejecting the Messiah, and their place had been taken by others who constituted a new, purely spiritual, international society, the Christian Church. Yet Revelation, looking forward to the end of the Bible story, represents the finally redeemed, for whose triumph the whole of previous history had been a preparation, as members of *the twelve tribes of Israel*, 12,000 from each, making 144,000 in all (Rev. 7:4–8). The following verses explain, of course, that the saved are not Jews by race or nationality, but men "of every nation, from all tribes and people and tongues" (v. 9).[2] Through the coming of Christ, Israel's constitution and external appearance had changed, but, for the writer, her continuity and spiritual identity were still intact. The Christian Church was, quite simply, the authentic community of Israel in a new, reconstituted form.

The exact development of thought in this chapter of Revelation may not be entirely clear, as is frequently the case in this difficult book, but what is significant for our argument is simply that the author could not conceive the last event of cosmic history except as the crowning incident in the story of Israel. Just as the world was created for the sake of Israel, so history to its very end was to be centered upon her. As the first act of the biblical drama culminated in Israel's call, so the last act ended in her victory. The curtain actually comes down with the descent from heaven of the New Jerusalem, surrounded by her twelve resplendent gates, inscribed with "the names of the twelve tribes of the sons of Israel" (Rev. 21:2, 12).

For modern readers these facts are embarrassing. It seems to them that a book which purports to be the sacred Scriptures of a universal religion ought not to concentrate in this way upon the fortunes of a particular people. It has, of course, often been pointed out that general truth must begin as particular truth, that even God cannot deal with man in general but only with particular men, and that God's ultimate concern for all nations is demonstrated first by the conviction of one nation that God

was concerned with *it*. For the moment, however, we are not
interested in justifying this peculiar characteristic of the biblical
approach to God, but only in pointing out what it is. If we
would understand the "knowledge of God" in the Bible, we
must see it first of all as *Israel's* knowledge of God. We cannot
somehow get Israel out of the picture and content ourselves
with isolating a set of universally valid propositions about God.
As the whole Bible presents it, the knowledge of God comes
to men through Israel, and when the phrase "knowledge of
God" is separated from the noun "Israel" it loses its specific
biblical quality, which is to say it loses its definiteness and existential urgency.

The knowledge of God in the Bible is not based primarily
upon rational speculation or discursive thought, but upon experience, and experience is always definite, local, temporal and
particular. The particular community that underwent the experience of God in the Bible was the community of Israel; and,
in biblical thought, the continued existence of this community
is essential to the continued existence and validity of the knowledge of God that it received. It is this particularity and specific-
ity of biblical thinking that makes it necessary for the student
of Old Testament theology to face the question of what men
have called "the mystery of Israel."

The Mystery of the Name

The phrase "the mystery of Israel" can be understood in several senses and most of them are relevant to the
present discussion. It can be used, for instance, in the Pauline
sense of mystery, which would see the existence of Israel as
part of the eternal purpose of God, made known to men only
at a specific juncture in their history. This is the sense in which
the phrase should ultimately be used, for both the Christian
and the Jew would regard this idea as in some way central to

their system of faith. But for the moment we shall be using the phrase in a more prosaic, untheological sense to indicate that there are certain mysterious elements in the character of Israel that puzzle anyone who considers the fact of her existence at all. There is, first (and least) of all, the mystery of the very name "Israel"—its origin and meaning; then there is the mystery of the variety and seemingly unstable character of the forms in which her existence has clothed itself throughout her long history; and finally, and most profoundly, the mystery of her persistence through the ages in spite of pitiless enemies who have assaulted her from without and disintegrating forces that have been constantly at work within—the mystery, that is, of her perennial vitality.

The first mystery is that of the name: Where did it come from, and what does it mean? In the Old Testament it appears first not as the name of a society, but as the name of a man, the name of one of the three patriarchs, Abraham, Isaac and Jacob —the last of whom was also called Israel (Gen. 32:28; 35:10). It is significant that the name appears first as a man's name, since this personal quality clings to it down through history. Israel, in her particularity, has never been just an ordinary society, but is, so to speak, the lengthened shadow of a particular man.

In the Old Testament one is not always sure whether the writers, when they speak of Jacob or Israel, are speaking of the man of the second millennium or the nation of the first. In the patriarchal narratives this confusion (if it can be called that) is already evident. In Gen. 27:18–29, when Jacob deceives his father, Isaac, and receives the blessing intended for Esau, it is obvious that vv. 18–27 refer to the man of the ancient folk story, but when, in v. 29, Isaac prays,

> Let peoples serve you
> and nations bow down to you,

it is equally obvious that he is not speaking about an individual *man* Jacob or Israel, who was never more than a half-settled shepherd, ruling only over flocks and herds, but rather about the later *nation* of Israel, which, under David and Solomon, ruled over a great empire. From a much later time we have a remarkable passage in Hosea (12:2–4), where the prophet declares that "Yahweh . . . will punish Jacob according to his deeds," the context making it perfectly clear that "Jacob" here means the contemporary eighth-century nation of Israel, and yet the next verses go on to say: "In the womb he took his brother by the heel. . . . He strove with the angel and prevailed. . . . He met God at Bethel," where the reference is quite as unambiguously to the patriarch of many centuries before.

This restless shift of meaning from community to individual and back to community is, of course, a particular example of the general phenomenon discussed in several works by the late H. W. Robinson and concisely described by him as the concept of "corporate personality," [3] an ancient, partly primitive and partly very sophisticated belief that groups do, in some sense, have a metaphysical and moral personality. In the case of national groups like Jacob-Israel or Esau-Edom, the founder thus appears to be genuinely immortal, possessing a continuing existence that transcends time and space; he continues to live in his descendants as they once lived in him; their sins and virtues are his, and his are theirs. This remarkable sense that Israel is not merely an organization, a society composed of numerous discrete individuals associated together in a purely external way, but is, rather, something like a person, vibrant, alive, with a character of its own, is an aspect of "the mystery of Israel" that must be taken seriously, and not dismissed as mere poetic metaphor. It has, incidentally, a certain analogy in the New Testament conception of the church as "the body of Christ" (Eph. 4:12; 5:30), although there seems to be no direct connection between the two ideas.

It is remarkable, also, that Israel is identified not only with a historical character, but with such a disreputable one. The patriarch Israel was notoriously unscrupulous, a despicable son who deceived his father, robbed his brother (Gen. 27:35f.); and self-righteously took advantage of his father-in-law (who, admittedly, had taken advantage of him! [Gen. 30:31–43; 31:19f.]) His alternative name, Jacob, is interpreted in the Bible to mean simply "supplanter" or, less politely, "cheat" (Gen. 27:36). One story says that he wrestled even with God and won a victory over him (Gen. 32:24–29). Whatever may have been the original sense of this curious tale, it certainly does not mean that he merely "wrestled with him in prayer," but that he actually got the better of him in physical combat, winning a blessing by force, not by merit.

Israel has never been tempted to idealize either her founder or herself. She was not, and is not, a society solely of right-thinking, good-living men and women, as the witness of the prophets bears abundant testimony. Men like Jeremiah (Jer. 2:10f.) and Malachi (Mal. 1:11) thought the heathen were better people and had more sense than the people of Israel. The Book of Jonah pictures the idolaters of Nineveh as responding instantly to the preaching of the prophet (Jonah 3:5), whereas Israel, as Jesus said, had always persecuted the prophets who were sent her and rejected their message (Matt. 23:37). This again is part of the mystery of Israel, that she is not composed of specially fine human material, sensitive and refined, attuned in some unique way to the mind of God, endowed with an unusual genius for religion. According to her own story she did not choose Yahweh, but Yahweh chose her, and the choice was an act of pure, unmotivated grace. It was out of such unpromising materials as the patriarch Israel-Jacob and his rebellious children of later generations that Yahweh made a sturdy, indestructible vehicle for bringing the knowledge of God into the world.

The literal meaning of the name "Israel" is part of the mystery, for no one can be sure even of its etymology. Scholars have expended considerable ingenuity on explaining it, but without arriving at any sure conclusion. In the Bible the name is said to have been given to Jacob after his wrestling match at the river Jabbok and is apparently understood to mean "one who strives with God" (Gen. 32:28), but this is an artificial, *post factum* explanation that has even less to commend it than most similar etymologies. The name contains the divine element *el* (that is, god) plus a verb-form indicated by the consonants YSR, but one can only guess at the meaning, and none of the guesses is very convincing. One cannot even be sure whether the name originally belonged to the patriarch and was later transferred to the community, or whether it belonged to the community and was later transferred to the patriarch. In other words, why Israel was called Israel is a question that no one can answer.[4]

The Origin of Israel

Far more important than the mystery of the name is the mystery of Israel's origin. Where and how did the community called Israel come into existence? There are at least three answers to this question. The first is the answer the Bible itself gives in the Book of Genesis, which is that the nation Israel originated with the patriarch Israel, that in fact the nation was simply composed of his physical descendants, his twelve sons being the ancestors of the twelve tribes of later times. A further refinement of this vew is that "Israel" in fact originated in the promise given to the patriarch Israel's grandfather, Abraham, whom God called out from his heathen background and to whose descendants he pledged his special favor (Gen. 12:2; 17:4–8; 22:17, etc.). But all this, of course, is simply an ancient way of thinking, one that is responsible also for the list of the nations in Gen. 10, where every nation in the world is represented as having a similar origin, the Hamites being the descendants of Ham, the Egyptians the descendants of Egypt, the

Canaanites the descendants of Canaan, and so forth. Everyone knows today that nations do not begin in this fashion. The fascinating stories of the patriarchs and their children, wherever they may have first been told and whatever their original meaning may have been, in their present form are simply part of an artificial scheme by which Israel attempted to rationalize her own diverse and complex ancestry. However attractive this scheme may be and however many elements it may contain that are beautiful, striking, and morally and theologically suggestive, the scheme itself is clearly factitious, based upon the assumptions of a world that had not yet begun to think scientifically.

If, then, Israel did not originate from the expanding family of the patriarch Jacob, where and when did she originate? This is a strictly historical question, directed at scholars, but unfortunately scholars are by no means agreed as to the answer. One hypothesis, based on the traditions preserved in the Book of Exodus, says that Israel became a community as the result of a compact made by certain Semitic tribes who had escaped from slavery in Egypt. Under their leader Moses, they entered into a solemn compact, at Mt. Sinai or some other desert shrine such as Kadesh, with Yahweh, a god previously unknown, who was believed to have delivered them. According to this view, the new tribal union was so vigorous that within two generations it had conquered the land of Canaan and made it the land of Israel. This theory would make Israel's early history very similar to that of Islam, in which the adoption of a new god by a group of previously separate tribes led to an even greater conquest in an even shorter space of time. This is the view which is perhaps most widely held today; it is advocated, for example, with much learning, by John Bright in his popular *A History of Israel.*[5] From the standpoint of critical scholarship, it is a fairly conservative position, since it regards the traditional story of Israel's departure from Egypt and her subsequent experiences in the desert as a relatively dependable account of the formative and determining events in her history, even though it is recognized that the basic narrative, as we now have it, is considerably distorted by the views of later times and greatly overgrown with legend. This view also takes seriously the many passages in later Hebrew literature, such as Pss. 106, 114, 136, that testify to the central importance of the exodus experience in the formation of the community.

A third and more radical view of the origins of Israel is that represented by Martin Noth in his *History of Israel*[6] and by Gerhard von Rad in a series of critical studies of ancient Israelite tradition.[7] Both these German scholars regard the traditions preserved in the Book of Exodus as artificial in their present form and sequence, though perhaps more definitely rooted in some kind of history than the patriarchal traditions of Genesis. They do not believe that a community of Israel existed before the arrival of the separate tribes in Canaan. The events reflected in the stories of the patriarchs, the exodus, the wilderness wanderings, the "conquest" of Canaan, may well have happened in some fashion, they think, to certain of the tribes or tribal groups that later became a part of Israel; one group, for example, may have had a tradition that told of a miraculous escape from Egypt; another may have had traditions of adventures in the southern desert, or of battles with the Canaanites; yet another may have told how its forebears came to Canaan from Mesopotamia with a tribal hero named Abraham or Jacob; but none of these traditions had anything to do with an entity called Israel. Israel was a confederation of tribes formed in the land of Canaan, composed of tribes and groups of tribes of heterogeneous origin, united by their regular worship at a central sanctuary, which belonged to them all and provided the only basis for their unity. In the course of time, according to this view, the various tribal traditions were consolidated, and almost unconsciously men began to think of all the separate stories as records of the common experience of the

new community. Events and personalities originally quite unconnected were now integrated into a single, common, "Israelite" tradition in which incidents and persons followed each
other in a pseudo-logical and pseudo-chronological succession.
According to these scholars "Israel" was not created at Sinai,
Horeb, Kadesh, or any other place in the desert, but at the
sanctuary of Shechem in Palestine, and nothing that happened
before that time can truly be called "Israelite" history or tradition at all.

There is here neither space nor occasion to criticize this view.
Just to show that it is not purely subjective, it is sufficient to
point out, as do Noth and von Rad, that certain presumably
authoritative, and possibly early, forms of Hebrew tradition,
which tell of the exodus and "conquest" make no mention at
all of a pact at Sinai (Deut. 6:21–25; 26:6–10; Josh. 24:2–13).
The German scholars find this inexplicable if the Sinai experience had the significance now attributed to it in the Book
of Exodus. For them the story of the Sinai covenant is merely
the "cult-legend" of a regular covenant-renewal ceremony at
Shechem. It must be said that this theory has been, and continues to be, warmly debated and that weighty arguments can
be brought against it as well as for it.[8]

On the whole it seems better to take the more conservative
view which places the origin of Israel in the period of desert
wanderings rather than in Canaan. But it must be emphasized
that the sources are of such a character that this, or any other
view, can never be more than a probable hypothesis and that
the details of the process have, in any case, been lost in the mists
of legend. There is no real history in Israel before the time of
the monarchy. Much that von Rad and Noth have to say about
the nature and development of the older traditions is certainly
correct, irrespective of their opinion that Israel originated at
Shechem rather than at Sinai, and at a later point we shall depend very largely on their analysis. For the moment, however,

our concern is simply to note that the mystery of Israel extends even to her origins. Despite the fact that she, along with Greece, Rome and the rest of the ancient Orient, was a primary creative factor in the formation of the world we live in, and despite the fact that she alone continues a vigorous existence to the present day, we know neither the meaning of her name nor precisely how she came into being.

The Tribal Confederation

The rest of our discussion will be concerned in the main with yet another mystery, though one that is not quite so elusive as the others, viz., the mystery of Israel's nature.

What, after all, is she? Is she a family, a race, a nation or a church? Or is she none of them? Or is she all of them in some new, unprecedented combination? In various periods Israel has been given every one of these names. The form of her existence has altered radically from time to time, and yet the vigor of her life has persisted undiminished. It is as though Israel was not so much a society as an *idea,* a spiritual concept capable of expressing itself in many forms, but neither defined nor limited by any of them.

If we look at the subject historically, we can see that Israel was successively a tribal confederation, a kingdom and a church. As a church, she appears in two forms, the one founded on ties of blood and centered in the observance of the Law (Judaism), the other founded only upon a common faith and centered in devotion to a Redeemer-Messiah (Christianity). If we prolong the historical line to our own day, we shall have to add that Israel has now manifested herself in yet another new form, that of a modern, secular nation of the Middle East.

One must also remember that Israelite legend pictures Israel as emerging first of all as a *family,* the sons and later descendants of Jacob-Israel. While this view has no historical value, it is important for her self-understanding and has permanent spiritual significance for both the Old Israel and the New. The "brotherhood" of Israel's members is a basic presupposition for regulating relationships within the group (Lev. 19:17; Mal. 2:10; 1 Cor. 8:13; 1 John 2:9–11).

From the standpoint of critical scholarship, Israel first emerges in the light of history as a confederation of tribes bound together by loyalty to a common God. It makes little difference whether this confederation originated at Sinai or in Palestine. Though Bright and Noth may differ in their books on the history of Israel as to when her common life began, they are united in their understanding of the character of the Israelite community. Noth, following in the footsteps of Max Weber, calls early Israel an "amphictyony," borrowing a technical term from the Greeks. In ancient Greece and Italy there are several examples of tribal confederations, most notably at Delphi, sometimes composed, like Israel, of exactly twelve tribes, organized for the service of a common sanctuary. The number twelve is explained by the fact that each tribe was assigned responsibility for the sanctuary for one month of the year. Since the organization of the earliest Israel is something of a puzzle in the biblical record, the only explicit descriptions of it being from the postexilic P-document which obviously reflects the opinions of a later time, it is tempting to find in these amphictyonic organizations of the classical world an analogy by which to understand it. It should be remembered, however, that the belief that Israel was actually an amphictyony is only an inference—a scholarly guess—and possibly a bad one.[9]

Our only direct evidence for the history and character of Israel before the rise of the monarchy comes from the books of Joshua and Judges, the former of which contains a great amount of material from a much later period and the latter of which tells us little about anything except tribal leaders and tribal wars. Nevertheless, *some* of the prerequisites of the amphictyony can be found. There were separate tribes, theoretically twelve in number, apparently united only by some kind of common cult or common faith; like other amphictyonies, we sometimes find the united tribes engaging in a common war, although the union seems nonpolitical and loosely organized. The crucial element that seems to be lacking in the picture from Joshua and Judges is the common sanctuary, which is of the very essence of the amphictyonic idea in the Greek sense of the word. There were many Israelite sanctuaries, of course— Shiloh, Gilgal, Bethel, Mizpah, and Shechem—but none of them seems to be central and unique in the sense required if Israel were truly an amphictyony. A common solution to this difficulty is to suppose that the sanctuary—and the sacred ark, which presumably was the focus of the cult—was moved at different periods, so that, for reasons we are no longer able to discern, the amphictyonic center, which was first at Shechem, was later transferred to Bethel and then, finally, to Shiloh. Some scholars insist that only Shiloh was ever the central sanctuary, the other shrines having had merely local or occasional significance. But, in any event, there is no evidence that caring for a central sanctuary was ever one of the functions of particular tribes at particular times. So it may be better to avoid the use of the term "amphictyony" entirely, and simply to describe Israel as a tribal confederation united, for mutual support, by a shared religious loyalty and some kind of common cult, although not necessarily at a *central* shrine. There is no precise parallel to this kind of confederation, and therefore no simple technical name can be given it, but, since ancient Israel was unique in so many other respects, it may well be that she was unique in her basic sociological structure also.[10]

Certainly some kind of common agreement bound the tribes together even in the time of the judges—Deborah's reproaches to those who failed to "come to the help of Yahweh" at the battle of Taanach are evidence of that (Judg. 5:15b–17, 23)—

and the basis for the agreement was obviously not secular, but religious; the cement that held the tribes together was not primarily fear of common enemies, but devotion to a common god. On this point there is no disagreement in the sources: all the tribes are loyal worshipers of Yahweh and their wars are fought in his name. Gideon's warriors do not fight for hearth and home, or even for "Israel," but carry "a sword *for Yahweh and for Gideon*" (Judg. 7:20). An early document, now lost, was even called "The Book of the Wars of Yahweh" (Num. 21:14). The unifying factor, in both war and peace, seems to have been Yahweh himself, and not his shrine.

It is probable that the confederation was held together by periodic meetings of the tribes. It is, furthermore, likely that these meetings were held at some Yahweh sanctuary. Two interesting passages in Joshua and Judges actually describe such tribal assemblies, both of which, however, have been suspected of being the creation of later times, although Noth and his followers have taken at least the Joshua passage to be ancient, and use it as one of the principal supports for their theory about the amphictyony. Without committing ourselves to any particular view as to the authenticity of the narratives, we may at least use them to recreate imaginatively some of the chief features that would have characterized a meeting of the tribal confederation.

In Josh. 24 we see the tribes assembling at the shrine of Shechem, which certainly played an important though now somewhat obscure role in early Israelite history, for the purpose of declaring their loyalty to Yahweh. A regular "renewal of the covenant" may conceivably have been an element in the cult in this early period.[11] The account in Joshua represents the leader as standing before the tribes and rehearsing the story of Yahweh's mighty works in the past on their behalf, and his gift to them of the land in which they live (vv. 1–13). The historical recital ends with an exhortation to the worshipers to pledge him their allegiance and forsake the service of other gods (vv. 14f.). The congregation then replies in a formula that summarizes the retrospective historical survey and concludes with the words: ". . . we also will serve Yahweh, for he is our God" (vv. 16–18). The challenge and response are repeated twice more in different and ever shorter form, and at last the leader affirms the existence of a covenant (v. 25), and declares that the stone set up in the sanctuary under the sacred oak tree will henceforth be public testimony to the oath of allegiance that had been taken (vv. 26f.).

The other story, from Judg. 20, is concerned with a different type of tribal assembly, one that took place not at regular periodic intervals but on the occasion of a particular crisis. The crisis in this instance was not an attack on one of the tribes by an external foe, which must have been the most common occasion, but the scandalous and depraved behavior of one of the confederated tribes, the tribe of Benjamin. The other tribes are pictured as gathering for consultation, with each other and with Yahweh their God (vv. 18, 23, 27). The assembly took place at a sanctuary, but the story wavers as to whether it was Mizpah (v. 1) or Bethel (v. 18); in any event, it was not Shechem or Shiloh. The parley finally determined that the other tribes should make war on Benjamin, since it refused to punish its guilty members, and the tribe of Judah was selected by the oracle to march at the head of the army (v. 18). The following chapter tells of the measures that had to be taken afterward to prevent Benjamin from being exterminated and thus decreasing the number of the federated tribes. The problem was solved in a rather complicated manner which involved both the savage punishment of a distant community, Jabesh-Gilead, that had failed to send any representative to the tribal assembly (21:1–15)—which was called "coming up to Yahweh" (v. 5)—and the seizure of girls, for brides of the Benjamite men, at the Shiloh vintage festival (vv. 16–24). In this way the confederacy preserved its moral and its physical integrity.

One must repeat that both these accounts have been suspected of being imaginative constructions of later times, and the second almost certainly contains a large meaure of fictional embellishment. Neither of them belongs in the same class with the magnificent early stories that make up most of the Book of Judges. Nevertheless, both are useful in helping us to visualize how the ancient Hebrew tribal confederacy may have operated. Even if the stories are entirely fanciful, which is most improbable, the imagination of the ancient Hebrews is likely to be closer to the realities of such situations than ours. Before the rise of the monarchy, this must have been the *kind of* community Israel was; this was the first form in which the idea of Israel became incarnate. What is most notable, if this view is correct, is that Israel was a religious community from the first, however strange the form of that community may seem to us. The history of Israel is not to be pictured, as was often done by scholars of an older period, as a development from secular tribal life to secular kingdom, and finally to spiritual community or church. From the very beginning Israel was more like a church than anything else. The impetus that begat it was not secular but religious; wherever it originated, at Sinai or in Palestine, the motive that led to the confederating of the tribes was, if not the care of Yahweh's sanctuary, at least an almost fanatical devotion to Yahweh himself— a type of devotion for which Islam provides the most obvious parallel in later times.

Monarchical Israel

The tribal confederacy was only the first of the forms that Israel was to take. The next incarnation of the idea was in the monarchy of Saul, David and Solomon. The Philistine invasion of the high country of Palestine made it necessary for the tribes to form a more tightly knit organization in order to meet this new threat which might easily have ended in the extinction of the Israelite community. In the ancient Near

East the only form available for the creation of a political state was that of kingship. Under the vigorous military leadership of Saul and his son Jonathan, the Philistine invaders were challenged, and Saul became the first king of the new Hebrew monarchy. Actually the monarchy of Saul was of an elementary sort, simple in structure and lacking most of the external paraphernalia of kingship. It differed from the organization that existed in the time of the judges chiefly in the fact that the leader was permanent and the succession hereditary.

But once the principle of monarchy had been introduced, it was bound eventually to develop into a much more elaborate institution, which would incorporate both the external forms and the religious ideology of oriental kingship. This happened in the subsequent reigns of David and Solomon. The beginning of the process appears in David's choice of a new capital, Jerusalem, which henceforth stood apart from the tribal structure as the private possession of the royal house, and the establishment there of a new center for worship in the old Canaanite city shrine. A fund of mystical sentiment also began to gather about the king and his relationship to Yahweh, such as is expressed in the oracle of Nathan (2 Sam. 7:4–29) and ancient "messianic" hymns like the so-called "Last Words of David" (2 Sam. 23:1–7). But the necessity for continual fighting on many fronts kept these tendencies somewhat in check at the beginning, and it was not until the long, peaceful, prosperous reign of Solomon that orientalizing tendencies were able to transform Israel into a monarchy of the common ancient type. The construction of a mammoth complex of palace buildings (1 Kings 7:1–12), the assembly of a huge harem (1 Kings 11:1–8) and the erection of a permanent temple for Yahweh (1 Kings 6ff.) were among the most important external symbols of this development.

By the time of Solomon the external structure of Israel had changed completely. No longer a loose federation of uncultured tribes, united only for war and worship, she was a nation like any other nation; in actual fact she was an empire that existed for a short time as one of the great empires of the ancient world. She tended to be a monolithic state with absolute power in the hands of the king. The old tribal organization had largely disappeared, its place having been taken by a new division of the state along convenient territorial lines, with twelve districts organized to support the luxurious life of the court and the great army of functionaries needed to sustain it (1 Kings 4:1–28). A major part of the energies of the state was spent in the mere collecting of taxes and the organization of forced labor, something unheard of in the old Israel (1 Kings 4:6–28; 5:13–18). External relations were no longer confined to occasional wars against an aggressor from outside, but were the subject of treaties (1 Kings 5:12), embassies and political marriages arranged by the royal chancellory (1 Kings 10:1–13; 3:1; 11:1). Instead of the simple figure of the charismatic judge or leader who stood at the head of the community in war, or on the rare occasions when the tribes met together for consultation or worship, there now stood permanently at the head of the nation a king who owed his office to inheritance and divine right, who was separated from the sphere of common life by the sacred oil of his consecration, and was considered to be a semidivine figure, a "son" of Yahweh 2 Sam. 7:14; Ps. 2:7; 89:26f.), if not some kind of "god" himself (Ps. 45:6, RSV margin?).[12] There were, of course, always circles that opposed these tendencies, recalling nostalgically the life and standards of former days, but, with slight modifications, this remained the type of kingship down to the days of the Babylonian exile. Jehoiakim, who stands near the end of the line, was obviously cut from the same piece of cloth and to the same pattern as a Solomon or an Ahab (Jer. 22:13–15, 18).

Two pictures from Scripture will help us to visualize the character of the Israelite community at this period of her existence. The first picture is that of Solomon presiding at the consecration of the temple he had just finished. The temple it-self represented an obvious break with older traditions, and Nathan the prophet had assured David that Yahweh was the kind of god who lived in a tent and had no need of a permanent dwelling (2 Sam. 7:6). But now he had been enshrined in a building constructed with all the art that money could buy, a temple deliberately made like the temples of other great peoples of the ancient world. Once more, as in former days, the whole of Israel gathered together, at least in theory, but now as citizens of a great state, the subjects of a king who stands as a priest and father-figure before them (1 Kings 8:2). The magnificence of the sacrifices was an expression of the magnificence of the court—22,000 oxen and 120,000 sheep (1 Kings 8:62f.). "Israel" was no longer assembled as a loose association of tribes, pre-cariously holding onto a foothold in the land of Canaan, but represented the citizens of an empire that extended from the Euphrates River to the border of Egypt (1 Kings 4:21), and as they went back to their homes they had less thought for God's goodness in bringing them up out of the land of Egypt than for "the goodness Yahweh had shown to David his servant" and to his son after him (1 Kings 8:66).

The other picture specially worth remembering from these times is that of Rehoboam, Solomon's son, waiting at Shechem to receive the homage of the men of the north, hearing their complaint at the burden of taxes, now grown too heavy to bear, and arrogantly threatening them with even heavier burdens if they did not submit (1 Kings 12:1–15). This, of course, resulted in the revolt of the northern tribes and the creation of two kingdoms where before there had been only one.

Later history showed this rebellion brought no amelioration of the problem, since the new kings of the north behaved ac-cording to the same oppressive pattern as their predecessors in the south. The monarchical system, with all its practical advantages, inevitably tended to move in the direction of tyranny. But it is not our purpose here to enter upon a critique of ancient monarchy. Our only purpose is to reflect upon these two scenes and try to visualize the glory and the peril of the new form of common life with which Israel clothed herself in this second period of her existence, and which lasted for over four hundred years—down, that is, to the beginning of the Babylonian exile.

Spiritual Israel

The third form in which the idea of Israel became incarnate was that of a spiritual community, a "church." This was the form of life that was thrust upon her during the Babylonian exile and took concrete shape on her return to Palestine. While the new structure had real affinities with the ancient tribal confederacy, in that it made of Israel a purely religious community with no necessary pretensions to secular power, it was actually something *sui generis,* a new kind of community formed to meet the peculiar conditions of a new age, a unique form of common life without any real analogy among the communities of the ancient world.

The most striking characteristic of the new community was its freedom from territorial limitations. While Palestine continued to be pre-eminently the Land of Israel—the Holy Land —the people of Israel became increasingly dispersed among other nations, carrying the reality of Israel within them wherever they went. They continued to dream, as they would for all their later history, of the re-establishment of the old monarchy under the rule of an ideal, future, "messianic" king, a descendant of the royal house of David, but this was not a belief of any great significance for ordinary life, since the dream could be realized only when God chose to bring it about. For all practical purposes they were content to turn the conduct of secular

affairs over to the particular kings under whom they happened
to be living, in Egypt, Babylon, Asia Minor, Greece or Rome.
All they asked was to be left in peace to cultivate their own
spiritual life, which they had learned to think of as no longer
tied up inextricably with residence on the soil of Canaan, but,
rather, with observance of the law of God.

The idea of law had always been prominent in Israel. The ancient confederation had probably been based in large part upon
the recognition of certain moral and cultic norms that Yahweh
imposed upon his people, and these norms were very likely
publicly proclaimed and reaffirmed at the regular tribal assemblies (Exod. 24:7; Deut. 5:1; 27:11-26; 31:10f.; Josh. 8:34f.).
And no doubt, under the monarchy, one of the functions of the
king was to maintain the law of Yahweh as received by Israel
at its birth (Deut. 17:18f.). But in the Israel of the confederation and monarchy, the idea of law (*torah*) had been only one
of the elements in the structure of the community. Now, of
necessity, it became the basic and essential thing, because it was
only through emphasis upon the law that Israel could learn to
transcend her former geographical limitations and become a
worldwide society. By emphasis upon "the Torah," much of
which could be observed as well in Babylon or Alexandria as
upon the soil of Palestine, Israel became a community of the
spirit, which was able to exist and flourish wherever its people
might be.

The laws of sacrifice could be observed, of course, only in
Jerusalem, but, with the passage of time, common sense rele-
gated such laws to a secondary position, and when at last Titus
destroyed the temple, and sacrificial worship ceased forever, its
passing left little impression on the basic character of Israel.
For Israel had learned to live already by other parts of the law.
The emphasis was placed upon the laws concerning circumcision, diet, and Sabbath observance, all of which were independent of particular places. This new type of society, centered

on the Torah, acquired also new leaders and a new mode of worship. Priests were useless in the diaspora and quickly sank into insignificance. What the community needed was men versed in the Torah, who could quote and expound it whenever need arose. So there gradually emerged the figure of the scribe, the lawyer, the rabbi of later times. And, since sacrifice could not be practiced in the diaspora, worship became simply the reading and study of the Torah, accompanied by appropriate prayers and hymns. Eventually the synagogue was created to provide a place where this might be done.

Several scenes from the Old Testament have helped us to visualize the form that Israel took in her two previous incarnations. Another will serve a similar purpose here. In the eighth chapter of Nehemiah there is again an account of an assembly of "all Israel," this time neither as a collection of militant, half-civilized tribes, nor as the proud citizens of a great empire, but merely as a small remnant of exceptionally devout men and women who had returned to Palestine after the exile and settled in the immediate neighborhood of Jerusalem. Militance and pride were gone; they now thought of themselves as the humble, the poor, the meek—who might hope some day fully to possess the land (Ps. 37:11), but certainly had not done so yet. Ezra the scribe, who in his secular capacity was an official of the Persian empire, stands up on a wooden pulpit built for the purpose, and from morning to noon reads to them from the Book of God's Law that he had brought with him from Babylon (Neh. 8:1-8). There stands with him a group of other men whose function is to explain the law so that the congregation will understand the reading (v. 8). At the end of the service the people eat and drink, and rejoice in their knowledge of the law (vv. 9-12).

This is an accurate picture of the form and spirit of the third Israel, the Israel that was known to Jesus and Paul, and which, under the name of Judaism, has continued her existence and preserved her vitality to the present day.

Universal Israel

But there is still a fourth form under which the idea of Israel has manifested itself, and which also must be considered here—the new Israel that we call the Christian Church. While the term "new Israel" does not occur in the New Testament, the idea that underlies it obviously does. We have already noted that Jesus chose twelve apostles so that they might be rulers over the twelve tribes of Israel. Whatever we may conceive this to mean, there can be no doubt that he was thinking in terms of continuity between the little society of which he was the center and the older Israel into which he had been born. And Paul, who seems to have been responsible for the physical breach between the old Israel and the disciples of Jesus, had no doubt that this new society of which he was a member was the new and true Israel of God. He says, for example: ". . . if you are Christ's, then *you* are Abraham's offspring, heirs according to the promise" (Gal. 3:29), speaking, of course, to the Christians of Galatia. And again, ". . . *we* are the *true* circumcision, who worship God in spirit and glory in Christ Jesus" (Phil. 3:3). The Epistle of James, who is called "a servant of God and of the Lord Jesus Christ" is addressed "to the twelve tribes in the dispersion," meaning scattered Christians (Jas. 1:1). The First Epistle of Peter is also addressed "to the exiles of the dispersion" (1 Pet. 1:1) and claims for Christians the words with which Yahweh characterized the Israelites assembled at Sinai: the disciples of Jesus are now the "chosen race, a royal priesthood, a holy nation, God's own people" (2:9; cf. Exod. 19:5f.). We have already noted the twelve-tribe motif in the Book of Revelation (pp. 5f.), where it refers unambiguously to the redeemed in Christ, those who have washed their garments in the blood of the Lamb (Rev. 7:14).

This is not the place for discussing the validity of this interpretation of the idea of Israel, a validity that would naturally be affirmed by Christians and denied by Jews. Our only concern here is to call attention to the amazing vitality of the idea itself, which, in the form of the Christian Church, legitimately or illegitimately, has created still another society and one which exhibits a different structure from any of the societies that preceded it. Its most striking characteristic is evident when it is compared with the third Israel—the one we have called the "spiritual" society. Whereas that Israel emancipated itself from limitations of place, making possible its existence and the practice of its religion anywhere in the world, the new Israel emancipated itself also from the limitations of blood and physical descent, opening its membership to men of all races and nations. Still a further characteristic differentiates it sharply from the other Israel: whereas the older Israel, formed in the postexilic period and continuing to the present day, finds its center and animating principle in the observance of a written law—the Torah—the new Israel of the Christian Church is centered in devotion to a person.

Having looked at certain congregational scenes from the Old Testament that helped us to visualize the nature of the older Israel in various stages of its existence, we need to look at least briefly on one scene that can bring before us with equal vividness the nature, and common life, of the new Israel. As it happens, there are not many such scenes in the New Testament, but the picture of the Lord's supper in 1 Cor. 11:17–34 will serve better than any other, particularly since its testimony to the presence of gross selfishness and even drunkenness at the sacred meal (v. 21) shows so clearly the intractability of the human material through which the idea of Israel tries to make itself known. The assembly is, of course, a local one, since under the new conditions a gathering of "all Israel" according to the Old Testament pattern is no longer possible. From 1 Cor. 12–14 we learn much about these regular occasions of public assembly, and, in particular, that there would be opportunity for individual members to edify the congregation with hymns, prayers, "speaking with tongues" and instructive discourses (14:26). But central to everything else was the common banquet—similar to some of the sacrificial feasts of the older Israel (e.g., Exod. 18:12; 24:11; Deut. 14:26f.; Neh. 8:10–12)—in which the members had fellowship with their common Lord through receiving bread and wine which they identified with his "body" and "blood," and, while proclaiming the fact of his death on the cross, looked forward joyfully to his second coming into the world (1 Cor. 11:23–26). As the older Israel, in all the centuries that followed, continued to express its character through the weekly assembly for the reading and study of the Torah, so the new Israel has continued—in the majority of its local forms—to center its life around the regular, often weekly, celebration of the communion meal, evidencing its solidarity through an act of devotion to the person of its crucified, risen and coming Lord. In both Israels, as both Old and New Testaments eloquently reveal, the deficiencies of the human constituents have frequently threatened to overwhelm the creative idea (see, e.g., Isa. 1:10–17; 28:7f.; Jer. 7:1–15; 1 Cor. 11:17–22).

It should be noted finally that the vitality of the idea of "Israel" has found a new incarnation in our own day in the establishment of the Zionist state in Palestine. Whether this is a valid expression of the idea or not is a question that cannot be answered here. Many would say that it is not, that it is a betrayal of a spiritual concept; others would feel very strongly that it represents an indispensable precondition for expressing the idea of Israel in its final and perfect form.[13] Since our purpose here is not to discuss the validity or invalidity of the various forms in which the idea of Israel has become incarnate, but only to take note of the mysterious vitality of the idea itself, we need only remark on the almost incredible fact that the idea of Israel, born so long ago and productive, as we have seen, of so many different forms of life, is capable of producing a new form—that of a modern secular republic—in our own lifetime. When one considers how dead are all the other cultures and nationalisms of the ancient world—Assyria, Babylon, Egypt, Rome and even Greece—most of which would have seemed so much more viable from a purely objective standpoint, the miracle and mystery of Israel seem almost overwhelming.

Our purpose in this chapter has been merely to emphasize the miracle and the mystery. On the level of historical science the existence of Israel can be accepted only as a datum, an inexplicable fact to be included among all the other irreducible phenomena with which history is abundantly provided. Why the name and the concept of Israel have persisted is a question that the historian can answer no more satisfactorily than he can that other famous puzzler, "Why did Yahweh the God of Israel become the universal God, rather than Chemosh the god of Moab?"

But at least there is nothing to prevent those who share the biblical faith from continuing to give the biblical answer: The idea of Israel has persisted and shows such inexhaustible vitality because it comes from God and not from man. At the beginning of the discussion, we observed that the word "mystery" is ambiguous; it can have either a secular or a theological sense. In connection with Israel both meanings are present. If the secular historian must look on Israel's continuous, though protean, existence as a mysterious fact of human history, the religious Jew and the Christian can only regard it as a mystery in the New Testament sense of the term, a part of the eternal purpose of God made manifest in the history of our race.

What Is Israel?

Finally, some attempt needs to be made to define the idea of Israel a little more closely, to express it at least in terms of some lowest common denominator. This is not difficult to do, for "Israel" is, in all its forms, the name of a society that believes itself to stand in a special, intimate relationship to God, and which believes that that relationship is not the result of its choice but of God's. There can be no comprehension of biblical religion, faith, theology—or whatever one chooses to call it—without the idea of "Israel," for at every stage that idea stands at the very center, and biblical faith is inconceivable without it. The faith of the Bible is not the faith of individual Israelites, but the faith of the community of Israel. The individual shares in that faith only insofar as he shares in the life of the community. From this point of view, the present book is really misnamed, for what we are about to discuss in detail is not "knowledge of God *in* ancient Israel," but the knowledge of God *of* ancient Israel, the knowledge of God that was indeed the constitutive factor of her existence.

2
THE NATURE OF ISRAEL'S KNOWLEDGE

Is not this to know me?

IT IS A frequently noted paradox that the nation that gave the Western world its religion had no word for "religion." It goes without saying that it had no word for so intellectual a concept as "theology." In the later development of the Hebrew language a time would come when a special word for religion would seem necessary; the Jews then began to use the word *dat* for this purpose, an Aramaic word that originally meant simply "law." The Hebrews of the biblical period, however, were still in an early stage of intellectual development, and felt no need for the technical words and precise distinctions that are so essential for logical thinking in a scientific age.

While we must guard against romanticizing the deficiencies of Hebrew language and logic and attributing them to some special quality in the Hebrew soul, this lack of precision undoubtedly had certain compensations. Modern scientific logic tends to divide life into a multiplicity of separate compartments and reduce every living whole to an infinite number of abstract and lifeless elements. It is refreshing from this point of

view to read the Bible, where thinking always tends to be syn-
thetic rather than analytic, and where men seem always to be
aware that the whole is something greater than the sum of its
parts. In biblical thought, God is simply God and cannot be
subjected to the scalpel of the critical intellect; man also is a
unitary being, not an amalgam of body, soul and spirit, under
the control of a variety of faculties; and the life of man is a
single reality—open to God at every point—which cannot be
divided into separate, opposing spheres called the religious and
the secular.[1] When all of life is religious, there is no need for
any special word for religion.

Hebrew Terms for "Religion"

Having said this—and it is important that it should
be said—we must then go on and acknowledge that even the
Old Testament exhibits signs of an awakening tendency toward
logical thought, especially in the Wisdom Literature; and that
there are two phrases, current in Hebrew from early times,
which have a functional meaning very close to our word "religion." These are "the fear of God" (*yir'at 'elohim*) and "the
knowledge of God" (*da'at 'elohim*).

In Gen. 20:11, Abraham excuses his apparently unethical
conduct toward the king of Gerar by explaining, "I thought,
There was no fear of God at all in this place, and they will kill
me. . . ." Transposing his thought into modern terms, one
can see that he meant it was a very *irreligious* community which
probably could not be expected to observe the norms of behavior common to *religious* men of whatever persuasion. Even more
frequent than the phrase "the fear of God," which means religion in general, is "the fear of *the Lord* [Yahweh]," which
means specifically the religion of Israel. There are many places
in the Old Testament where the substitution of the word "religion" (or "Israel's religion") for this phrase immediately
clarifies the meaning of a sentence and gives precision to a

thought that would otherwise seem vague, as in Ps. 19:9, "the fear of the Lord is clean, enduring forever"; Ps. 34:11, "I will teach you the fear of the Lord"; or Prov. 1:7, "The fear of the Lord is the beginning of knowledge." In all such passages "the fear of the Lord" means something considerably more than "being afraid of the Lord"; it means, rather, an attitude of awe and reverent submission to Yahweh, the God of Israel, involving an acceptance of the whole complex of beliefs and practices that was incumbent on his worshipers; it means, in other words, all that we mean by the word "religion" or "the religion of Israel."

The other phrase, "the knowledge of God," occurs less frequently, but has much the same force, as can be seen by the parallelism in the two following passages from Proverbs:

> My son, if you receive my words,
>   and treasure up my commandments with you,
>
> . . . .
>
> then you will understand the fear of the Lord
>   and find the knowledge of God. [PROV. 2:1, 5]

> The fear of the Lord is the beginning of wisdom,
>   and the knowledge of the Holy One is insight. [PROV. 9:10]

The most familiar occurrences of the phrase are two in the book of Hosea,

> There is no faithfulness or kindness,
>   and no knowledge of God in the land [HOS. 4:1]

and

> I desire steadfast love and not sacrifice,
>   the knowledge of God, rather than burnt offerings. [HOS. 6:6]

Although the passages from Proverbs show that the two phrases can have a similar functional use, the two passages from Hosea show that there could be a real difference of nuance between them. While both refer to man's total relationship to God, the phrase "fear of God" seems to lay primary emphasis on an *attitude,* whereas the phrase "knowledge of God" attaches priority to the *act of understanding.* Both Hosea passages emphasize that true religion involves the understanding and is not merely a matter of superstitious practices and crude emotion. Hos. 4:2 goes on to say that the land is full of "swearing, lying, killing, stealing, and committing murder." It is no coincidence that these are all crimes specifically forbidden in the Ten Commandments and therefore part of the basic ethical code of Israel, regularly taught in her public assemblies, and presumably familiar to every member of the community. Yahweh had explicitly forbidden acts of this kind and a genuinely devout Israelite would *know* that this was so. The second quotation insists that what Yahweh desired above all else was not a people engaged in a thoughtless, mechanical round of sacrifices and burnt offerings, but rather a nation that knew God's nature and will, and performed the ceremonies of his cult as an expression of fidelity to him and his covenant rather than as a magical *opus operatum.* According to Hosea, what Yahweh required was not the mindless practice of ceremonial religion, but a genuine understanding of who, and what kind of God, Yahweh was, and an intelligent grasp of the ethical implications of worshiping him.

If, then, "the fear of God" can be understood to mean "religion," there is a very real sense in which "the knowledge of God," that is, knowing who God is and what he expects, can be taken as the Old Testament equivalent of "theology"—a word that means, etymologically, "the knowledge (or science) of God." [2]

The Hebrew Conception of "Knowledge"

We must now go on to examine a little more closely what "knowledge" means in the Old Testament. What has just been said may suggest that knowledge in ancient Israel, as in the modern world, was simply a function of the intellect. That is, of course, the primary sense of the word, just as in every other language. The verb "to know" (*yada'*) refers basically to what we should call intellectual, cognitive activity, as the context of the first quotation from Hosea clearly shows, and, since the wise men who produced the Book of Proverbs were the intellectuals of ancient Israel, it is probably for this reason they gave the *knowledge* of God, rather than the *fear* of him, the climactic position in the two passages quoted above from Proverbs.

But, though the Hebrew word refers primarily to the operation of the intellect, it has a range of meaning that gives it other and far richer connotations than the English word. This richness of connotation is a result of the Hebrew inability to think in analytical terms. There is no special faculty of the intellect or reason in Hebrew psychology. The word most commonly used for "mind" in Hebrew is simply the common word for "heart" (*lev;* 1 Sam. 9:20; Isa. 46:8, etc.). The heart is regarded as the seat of the intellect, but it is also regarded as the seat of the will and the emotions as well. This illustrates the well-known principle that the men of ancient Israel thought in terms of wholes rather than parts. Occasionally they may speak as though the different functions of the human psyche are situated in specific organs of the body, but, disconcertingly, other passages can usually be adduced to show that most of the functions are elsewhere assigned to still other important organs. The ancient Hebrew did not, in fact, suppose that men thought with their minds, felt with their emotions, and made decisions with their wills, but that all these activities were carried on by the whole person, every function involving the others also.

"Knowledge" has an important emotional as well as intellectual aspect. Even in English, "to know" can take on an emotional coloring when it is used in connection with persons; we are aware that to know a person is something quite different from merely knowing a fact. But in Hebrew the emotional aspect of the verb "to know" is sometimes so strong as to make it practically equivalent to the verb "to love." The most striking evidence of this is the occasional use of the word to denote sexual intercourse, as when it is said "Now Adam knew Eve his wife, and she conceived and bore Cain" (Gen. 4:1); here it is apparent that "knowledge" means personal familiarity of the most intimate kind. But elsewhere, "to know" is used in a number of passages where it obviously also means something much closer to "love" than "to know" in the merely intellectual sense of the word. When, for example, Amos represents Yahweh as saying, "You only have I known of all the families of the earth" (Amos 3:2), the idea of intellectual knowledge makes nonsense of the passage and seems almost entirely absent from it. The plain meaning is that Yahweh had entered into a uniquely intimate personal relationship with Israel; in other words, that he loved her. A familiar verse of the First Psalm lends itself to the same interpretation and to no other,

> For the Lord knows the way of the righteous,
>   but the way of the wicked shall perish.   [Ps. 1:6]

There is also a passive form of the verb "to know" (*meyudda'*), which the KJV translates literally "acquaintance," but which actually refers to a much warmer and more intimate kind of relationship, as one can see from Ps. 55:13 (Heb. 14),

> But it is you, my equal,
>   my companion my *familiar friend* [RSV],

and from Ps. 88:18 (Heb. 19), where it is set in parallelism with other words meaning "lover and friend." [3]

So when the men of ancient Israel spoke of "the knowledge of

God," they were not talking merely of *information concerning* God, but of an intimate personal attachment to him. The Old Testament does not depreciate intellectual knowledge; it stresses over and over again the importance of knowing certain theological facts: that Yahweh is the God of Israel (Deut. 29:6; 1 Sam. 17:46; Ezek. 6:7; etc.), that he is the only God there is (Deut. 4:39), that he has a definite moral character (Ps. 119:75; Jon. 4:2), that he has done certain mighty acts for his people (Judg. 2:10; Ps. 78:4; Mic. 6:5), and that his will has been revealed in formulas that can be learned (Pss. 78:5f.; 119:125). But, for Old Testament man, this kind of second-hand knowledge of mere facts about God is no substitute for the personal confrontation with God himself that Martin Buber describes, with classic brevity, as the relationship of "I and Thou." The "knowledge of God" is not simply the absorption by the mind of accurate theological information, but the involvement of a person with a Person.

There is still a third dimension to the idea of knowing God. If it includes the emotions as well as the activity of the cognitive intellect, it also includes the will, for the true knowledge of God always issues in ethical behavior. This aspect of knowledge is expressed in striking form by the prophet Jeremiah in his diatribe against King Jehoiakim (Jer. 22:13–17). Following the reign of the devout Josiah, who had been notable for the justness of his rule and his meticulous concern for Israel's traditional social morality, Jehoiakim, his son, reverted to the absolutist policies of Solomon and Ahab, using tax money for the ostentatious decoration of himself and his court. The intolerable climax was reached when he built a great palace "with spacious upper rooms," "paneling it with cedar and painting it with vermilion." Jeremiah says to him

> Do you think you are a king
> because you compete in cedar?

> Did not your father eat and drink
> and do justice and righteousness?
>
> . . . .
>
> He judged the cause of the poor and needy;
> then it was well.
> Is not this to know me?
> says the Lord.   [JER. 22:15f.]

In ancient Israel, knowledge that did not issue in appropriate action was not true knowledge at all; genuine knowledge involved the whole of a man's personality—his mind, his feelings, and his deeds.

It is this concern for wholeness that gives Old Testament thought in all its aspects its peculiar and appealing existential quality. The biblical Hebrews—unlike the Greeks of the Periclean age—made little use of discursive reasoning; they had no understanding of scientific analysis and were acquainted with the principles of logic only in the most elementary and pragmatic way. Like other men of the archaic world, the ancient Hebrew thought not only with his mind, but with his emotion and his will, with the conscious participation of his entire being, and, likewise, he thought of his world in terms of totalities, not of complex mechanisms to be analyzed into ever smaller and smaller components. He saw life simply and saw it whole.

Modern men cannot return, nostalgically, to this ancient way of thinking, or even completely understand it, but they can appreciate to some extent its validity, and may perhaps find that a seasoning of something like it may still be useful. Certainly, science has a place for synthesis as well as analysis, and many scientists have testified that intuition, imagination, excitement—perhaps even a kind of love for the object in view —may be as important in the discovery of truth as rigorous laboratory experiment and analytical reasoning.

For modern man, with his possibly too rigid devotion to pure scientific method, it can be a stimulating and even liberating experience to renew acquaintance from time to time with the less logical but more completely human world of Homer, the Gilgamesh Epic, and the Bible. It is valuable to be reminded occasionally of what the ancient world knew so well—that the most important truths are those that are apprehended not with the mind only, but with the total being of a man. Above all, it must be repeatedly emphasized that, whatever may be the situation in other branches of learning, there is no true knowledge of *God* that does not involve the whole of a man's personality. A man's "theology" should engage his passions as well as his thoughts, and must call forth not only the response "I understand," but "I love" and "I will."

The Limitations of This Book

In the following chapters, unfortunately, we shall have to content ourselves largely with discussing the purely intellectual aspect of Israel's "knowledge of God"—her "theology." Although this impoverishes the idea, it is unavoidable, since all that we can expect to do here is to try to understand the framework of *thought* within which the men of the Old Testament lived their religious lives. If one would get the fullness of the knowledge of God as they apprehended it, one must read the books of the Old Testament itself, with all their prosy listing and cataloguing, wild poeticizing, vehement emotion, hortatory fervor, passionate irrationality, careless disorder, irritating redundancies and overwhelming immediacy. A book on the theology of the Old Testament can never be a substitute for the Old Testament, nor is it intended to be.

The most that can be hoped is that a book such as this will show in some sense what the Old Testament is all about, and give the reader some kind of conceptual background—not found in the Bible itself—that will make it easier for him to understand individual books, passages and ideas when he encounters them. What he will find in the chapters ahead is nothing more than the intellectual skeleton without which Israel's "knowledge of God" might seem an amorphous mass of only vaguely related ideas and violent but obscurely grounded emotions.

The present chapter should have made it clear that the knowledge provided in the rest of the book must still be clothed with the flesh and blood of actual religious life as one finds it in the pages of the Bible, a need only partly met by the illustrative quotations given in the text. The full knowledge of God in ancient Israel is not to be learned from formulas. It is to be found only in the witness borne by the total dedication of her prophets, wise men, saintly priests and humble devotees, to Yahweh, the God of their people—a dedication rooted in understanding, but issuing directly and continuously in awe, wonder, love and obedience.

3

GOD IN THE PAST

What has God wrought!

MUCH RECENT DISCUSSION in Old Testament theology has centered on the views of the Heidelberg professor, Gerhard von Rad, whose basic thesis is that Israel's theology consisted only in statements about the *acts* of God. He maintains that Israel was not committed to any particular beliefs about God's nature and moral character, but only to certain assertions about what he had done, especially in establishing and preserving the Israelite community. Later, we shall argue that this is an oversimplified view, based on an unnecessarily narrow definition of theology, and the arbitrary exclusion of much biblical evidence that would be relevant by other definitions. For the moment, however, we must acknowledge that the oversimplification is a brilliant one which serves a useful purpose in directing attention to an aspect of ancient Israelite thought that is undoubtedly central and characteristic. It is undeniable that many of the basic statements about God in the Old Testament, particularly those from earlier times, have nothing to say about God's nature, but speak only of his actions; they are rich in verbs and poor in adjectives. The main concentration of Israel's thought was undoubtedly, in theology as in other areas, upon act rather than essence.

It must be recognized, of course, that this emphasis is partly due to the relatively primitive, prephilosophical if not actually prelogical, character of the ancient Hebrew mind, which naturally expressed itself in terms of act rather than of thought, and found itself more at home in the concrete than the abstract. And it must not be overlooked that in later times, even in Israel, there were growing tendencies toward abstraction and systematization, and even a hesitant approach to philosophical ideas. It is not reasonable to exclude, as von Rad does, these tendencies from the "theology" of Israel, especially when one's concern is with the totality of Israelite thought and not simply with its earliest manifestations. But, as a starting point, there can be no doubt that von Rad is right and any account of "the knowledge of God" in ancient Israel must *begin* with a discussion of what Israel believed her God had done. Israel's theology was not, at least in origin, the product of general reflections on the meaning of life, but grew out of specific reflection on her own historical experience.

The creed of earliest Israel—if she had had one—would not have begun, like the Christian creed, with a series of descriptive words indicating God's unity, paternal nature and omnipotence (The Nicene Creed runs: "I believe in *one* God, the *Father Almighty* . . ."), nor would it have gone on to say that he had created heaven and earth. It would have begun simply with the statement that somewhere, somehow, Yahweh (a particular god, not just God in general) had revealed himself to the community of Israel, saved them from a powerful enemy, and invited them to be his own people. Israel made no attempt at first to define this god any further, except to identify him with "the god of the fathers" (Exod. 3:6), the mysterious deity (or deities) who had been worshiped by the tribal ancestors.[1] There were certainly no statements as to the metaphysical nature of Yahweh; there was no absolute, necessary conviction that he was the only god that existed; and it was not even clear that his actions were always good, at least as men understand goodness. He was reported to have tried once to kill Moses, without reason (Exod. 4:24), and he was inclined to send terrifying and disproportionate punishments—fire and earthquake for disagreements about questions of ecclesiastical polity (Num. 16:31–35), and poisonous snakes for petty grumbling (Num. 21:5f.). Early Israel could have said, with even more justification than Second Isaiah, centuries later, "Truly, thou art a God that hidest thyself" (Isa. 45:15), meaning that Yahweh's character and ways were often incomprehensible to his people.

At the beginning—and for long afterward—Israel was not certain what her God was like. What she could not doubt was that he was *her* God, whoever and whatever he might be, that he had met her in the desert and chosen her for his own. He had said to Israel, ". . . you shall be my own possession among all peoples . . . a kingdom of priests and a holy nation" (Exod. 19:5f.).

This God had a name, Yahweh, which helped to individualize him and distinguish him from the gods of other peoples. Some later attempts were made, as we shall see, to give this name a theological or metaphysical significance, but in fact its meaning was as mysterious to the ancient Hebrews as it is to us today, and served only to identify Israel's God, not to define him.

Basic Conceptions: Election, Covenant, Torah

The first article of Israel's faith—the assurance of her election—does not appear explicitly in any of the ancient confessions; indeed, the abstract noun "election," which comes so naturally to the lips of the English-speaking commentator, occurs nowhere in the Old Testament, and even the verb "to choose" or "to elect" (*bachar*) was not used in a theological sense before Deuteronomic times.[2] The idea, nevertheless, is basic from the earliest period, since the story of God's dealings with Israel, which is the whole content of her basic theology, makes no sense without the conception that Yahweh, for mysterious reasons of his own, had "chosen" her to be the object of his special favor (Exod. 6:7).

The explicit formulation of the doctrine of election belongs to the prophetic age and appears in its most attractive form in certain poetic, imaginative passages in the books of the later prophets. It is best to consider it first in the terms in which the prophets express it, since they saw the doctrine in its full theological depth; for them the election of Israel was not a dry fact recorded in some ancient chronicle, but the most important fact of Israel's continuing existence. Israel's election had, of course, occurred at a point in time, but the consciousness of *being* elected was what made Israel in every age different from other nations. It was on this consciousness that the prophets based their message, both to arouse Israel to a consciousness of sin and to inspire her with hope for the future.

The profound emotional force and basis of the doctrine appears in the prophets' choice of poetical images rather than prosaic historical language to describe the event. Ezekiel, for example, tells how Yahweh, in the guise of a traveling prince, found Israel as an abandoned child in the desert, adopted her, and raised her up to be his bride (Ezek. 16:3–14). Jeremiah, using terms coined long before in the school of Hosea (Hos. 2:15), speaks of Israel's marriage to Yahweh in the wilderness, and the love she showed in their early days together (Jer. 2:2). Amos seems to speak in less emotional language when he represents Yahweh as saying, "You only have I known of all the families of the earth" (Amos 3:2), but we have already seen that "knowing" in a context like this never refers to mere intellectual cognition, but to a warm and intimate relationship between persons. Even a nonpoetic book like Deuteronomy, which is largely a collection of laws, can describe Israel's election in terms almost equivalent to falling in love (Deut. 7:7f.).

Earliest Israel had no such language at her command; she could only speak objectively of what Yahweh had done. There

is no reason, however, to suppose that her sense of emotional
and spiritual involvement with her God was any less real and
vital. There may have been some difference in the nature of
her emotion, but certainly none in the intensity with which
she felt it. The prophets did not originate this sense that Israel's
election had created a relationship in depth; they merely gave
it articulate expression.

But if the basic doctrine in Israel's faith was that of her own
election, the doctrine in which it found its structural shape
was that of the covenant. Her unique relationship with Yahweh,
which was a continuing fact of her life, had its beginning in an
act of election; but it was preserved by the covenant. So the
ideas of election and covenant are inseparable, and the discussion of one leads inevitably to a discussion of the other.

The word "covenant" might be defined as "an accepted tie
of enduring relationship." The adjective "accepted" is necessary because covenants always have to do with voluntary relationships, not with those that are inherent in the natural order,
and the adjective "enduring" is equally necessary since it excludes all relationships, however deep, that are merely casual
and temporary. The Hebrew word for "covenant" (*berit*) covers
a considerably wider field of meaning than the English word.
In English the word belongs almost exclusively to the realm of
jurisprudence and is seldom used outside of legal documents.
For this reason one can easily miss the full range of its theological significance in the Bible.

The legal meaning is, of course, common in the Old Testament also. *Berit* can mean a treaty between nations (1 Kings
5:12, Heb. 26), or a legal compact between individuals or groups
(Gen. 26:28; 31:44), and the covenant between Yahweh and
his people is often interpreted in this sense, especially in the
literature associated with Deuteronomy. Some recent studies
have attempted to relate the covenant between Yahweh and
Israel to the forms of international treaties that were in use

during the second millennium B.C. In this period, treaties imposed by a suzerain upon his vassal kings, as exemplified in surviving Hittite documents, contain the following elements, which it is alleged are also found in the Israelite covenant with Yahweh: the self-identification of the suzerain (cf. Exod. 20:1a); a historical prologue, reciting the benefits that the vassal has received from the suzerain (Exod. 20:2b); a consequent demand on the vassal for observance of a list of stipulations (Exod. 20:3–17); an insistence upon exclusive loyalty to the suzerain (Exod. 20:3); a warning against altering the terms of the treaty (Deut. 12:32); curses on disobedience (Deut. 27:15–26; 28:15–68); the invocation of heavenly witnesses (i.e., the gods, for the pagans; but cf. Isa. 1:2; Ps. 50:4).

Although this view of the Israelite covenant as merely a particular instance of a widespread international-covenant form is probably accepted by a majority of scholars today, and though the parallels are impressive when set forth in a diagrammatic form like that above, there are still some to whom the evidence seems less than convincing, at least so far as it applies to the ancient "Mosaic" covenant rather than to later interpretations of it. These scholars feel that Israel in the tribal period is not likely to have borrowed the basic forms of her religious life from the field of faraway imperial politics, and are inclined to think that the parallels are due to factors inherent in similar situations rather than to any direct historical influence. There can be no doubt, however, that the study of the Hittite, and also the later Assyrian, treaties helps to illuminate the psychological development of Israel's later understanding of the covenant, and provides a possible explanation of some of its peculiar features.[3]

If the Hebrew word for covenant is often used to denote a purely legal relationship of the treaty type, it can also be used for relationships of a much simpler and nonjuridical kind. Most impressive is its use in connection with friendship. In the story of David and Jonathan, for example, it is said that "Jonathan made a covenant with David because he loved him as his own soul" (1 Sam. 18:3; cf. Ps. 55:20). The word can also be used of the marriage relationship (Ezek. 16:8; Mal. 2:14; Prov. 2:17), where, although there is, of course, a legal aspect, the sense of personal responsibility and loyalty is primary. The covenant God made with Abraham, according to the Yahwist's version (Gen. 15:18)—the covenant which created the intimacy between God and Abraham that is so characteristic a feature of the Abraham stories and led to his being called *par excellence* the "friend" of God (Isa. 41:8)—is obviously of this character. One can see by the accounts of Israel's election quoted above, from the great prophets, that they, too, preferred to think of the covenant between Yahweh and Israel in nonlegal terms; for them the covenant was basically a personal, friendly relationship, founded, so far as Israel was concerned, on love and gratitude. She had undertaken certain formal obligations toward her God, as she was perhaps reminded in regular covenant-renewal ceremonies, but the motive for respecting them was not the legally binding character of the compact, but her own sense of loyalty to a generous friend and benefactor.

Israel's obligations under the covenant were contained in a body of laws—some of which were peculiar to herself and some simply particular expressions of ancient Near Eastern common law—which tended to grow ever more complex with the increasing complexity of her culture and social life. These were variously called "commandments," "testimonies," "statutes" and "ordinances" Deut. 4:40, 45), and they defined the divinely ordained mode of life that Israel voluntarily took upon herself in response to Yahweh's generosity in choosing her and delivering her from slavery in Egypt. For those scholars who accept the suzerainty-treaty analogy, these laws are to be understood as corresponding to the detailed prescriptions imposed by an ancient oriental emperor upon his subject kings in recognition of favors conferred. Whatever may be decided ultimately as to the validity of this comparison, there can be no doubt that the relationship it describes is, from one side at least, a correct one: Yahweh was Israel's sovereign and benefactor, and she had a corresponding obligation to obey his will as defined in his laws. Nevertheless, we have noted that Yahweh's relationship to his people could also be described in quite a different way from that of sovereign and subject—as a more human, intimate, personal kind of relationship—and it is important to note that all the separate legal ordinances of the covenant were eventually subsumed under the general name of *torah,* a word that is customarily translated "law," but actually means something more like "direction," "teaching," or "instruction." The image it calls up in Hebrew is that of an understanding friend or wise parent or, perhaps, a learned priest at a shrine, graciously imparting wisdom, rather than that of a despotic monarch laying down arbitrary rules. This is, for example, the precise and only sense in which the word is used in the canonical Wisdom Literature (e.g., Prov. 1:8, "your mother's *teaching,*" cf. KJV).[4]

Unlike the word "law" (Latin *lex,* Greek *nomos*), which tends to be abstract and impersonal, *torah* is a relationship word; it calls to mind the image of a particular torahgiver—a teacher —and implies a personal tie between the instructor and the instructed. Whereas disobedience to "law" results in punishment, disregard of *torah* breaks a relationship. Israel's obedience to the *torah* was a sacramental sign of her continuing fidelity to a relationship that Yahweh had freely offered and she had freely accepted. Obedience was not so much an attempt to assure the good will of an inflexible and possibly testy ruler as an expression of loyalty toward a trustworthy lord, a demonstration of gratitude to a wise and powerful saviour who had generously made known the rules by which his people could live in health and peace before him.

In trying to avoid a too legalistic view of the covenant relationship, one must naturally be careful not to sentimentalize it.

The God of earliest Israel was certainly not the God of the New Testament, of Second Isaiah or some of the psalms; his character reflected the sternness of the times. He was, and long remained, the God of armies (1 Sam. 1:3; Ps. 24:10), the exalted Lord (Exod. 24:10; Isa. 6:1–5), the "Fear" of Isaac (Gen. 31:42), the Mighty One of Jacob (Gen. 49:24; Isa. 49:26), the Rider on the cherubim (Ps. 18:10; Ezek. 11:22), the mysterious power whose presence was manifest in earthquake and thunderstorm (Judg. 5:4; Hab. 3:3–6); and Israel's relationship to him is often pictured as that of a slave to his master (Ps. 123:2; Mal. 1:6), a subject to his royal lord (Ps. 44:4; Isa. 6:5), a mortal man to his immortal creator (Isa. 64:8). But more basic than any of these, more central to Israel's developed theology and more satisfying to her deepest feelings, was the conception of the covenant relationship as that of a person to a Person (Exod. 33:11, 14f.; Isa. 63:9), of a friend to his benefactor (Deut. 2:7; Mic. 6:3f.), of an orphaned child to its adoptive father (Exod. 4:22; Hos. 11:1; Jer. 31:9), of one beloved to her lover (Hos. 2:16; Isa. 54:5).

Israel's Earliest Creed: Exodus, Sinai, Promised Land

Underneath the present elaborate structure of the Hexateuch (Genesis through Joshua) lies implicitly the earliest of Israel's "creeds," a simple confession that Yahweh had delivered his people from slave labor in Egypt, entered into a covenant relationship with them at Sinai, and given them the land of Canaan. This, in essence, is the story that is told in Exodus through Joshua. The Genesis narratives, falling into two parts—the primeval history (Gen. 1–11), and the patriarchal sagas (Gen. 12–50)—seem to have been added later as a kind of preface, and represent two further, successive stages in the development of the tradition. The heart of the Hexateuch, and the heart of the faith of early Israel, lies in the story of the exodus and its necessary continuation in the account of the Sinai covenant and the settlement in Canaan.

The evidence that the exodus, Sinai and settlement narratives, in their organized form, are the oldest elements in the canonical traditions of Israel, and therefore first among her articles of faith, is set forth in important studies by G. von Rad and M. Noth.[5] It is impossible to reproduce the arguments here, since they are part of a comprehensive analysis of the entire Hexateuchal tradition. But even the ordinary reader cannot help but notice the weight and centrality of the exodus story among the narratives of the Hexateuch. It constitutes a single unit occupying the whole of Exod. 1–15, rising to a climax with a great hymn of praise addressed to the God who, in destroying the hosts of Pharaoh, "triumphed gloriously" (Exod. 15:1–18). Except for the Joseph story (which, in its present position, merely explains how the Israelites happened to be in Egypt), no other episode in the Hexateuchal history receives anything like the same amount of attention either in extent or in detail. The patriarchal stories (except for Joseph) are episodic and anecdotal, while the apparent unity and coherence of the remaining Hexateuchal narrative in Exodus through Joshua is due simply to the fact that it relates the series of events that inevitably followed after the exodus, and is therefore really a part of the exodus story.

A similar concentration on the exodus and the events that followed is apparent in prophetic literature (Amos 2:10; 5:25; 9:7; Hos. 2:15; 9:10; 11:1, 5; 12:13; Jer. 2:6, etc.) and in the psalter (Pss. 78; 106; 114; 136), whereas references to God's dealings with Abraham and his descendants are rare and late (e.g., Ps. 105:6, 9, 42; Isa. 41:8; 51:2; Neh. 9:7). It seems clear that the developed patriarchal traditions, and *a fortiori* the primeval history, were not part of the canonical story of earliest Israel, and only gradually attained a relative importance in her developing theological structure. We shall consider them in detail at a later stage.

Von Rad believes he has found additional, and more direct, evidence of the earliest form of Israel's theological traditions in the shape of several brief passages that he considers to have performed the function of "creeds." One of them is found in Deut. 26:5–10, a liturgical formula prescribed for recitation by one who brings the first fruits of his harvest to the sanctuary. The worshiper is instructed to say:

A wandering Aramean was my father; and he went down into Egypt and sojourned there, few in number; and there he became a nation, great, mighty, and populous. And the Egyptians treated us harshly, and afflicted us and laid upon us hard bondage. Then we cried to the Lord the God of our fathers, and the Lord heard our voice, and saw our affliction, our toil, and our oppression; and the Lord brought us out of Egypt with a mighty hand and an outstretched arm, with great terror, with signs and wonders; and he brought us into this place and gave us this land, a land flowing with milk and honey. (And now behold, I bring the first of the fruit of the ground, which thou, O Lord, hast given me.)[6]

While it seems doubtful that this formula is a "creed" in any meaningful sense of the term, and the present formulation of it almost certainly took place in a comparatively late period of Israel's history, it may well preserve the shape of an ancient manner of thinking and speaking. What is striking at first glance is its concentration on the exodus and the settlement of Canaan, with only a scant allusion to a patriarchal prehistory, and no mention of creation or primeval history at all. It is quite possible that, in the days of the tribal confederacy, if anyone had been asked to characterize in the briefest possible terms the God whom he and the community worshiped, his answer would have been in some such language as this. Whatever may be the date and origin of the passage, it is valuable in helping us visualize the nature of Israel's faith when stripped down to its basic and nuclear elements.

The form- and tradition-critics of the von Rad-Noth school make much of the fact that this formula, like a number of others (Josh. 24:2–13; Pss. 78; 105; 135; 136), contains no mention of the covenant at Sinai; von Rad concludes, therefore, that the story of the covenant at Sinai did not constitute a part of the basic theological tradition of Israel, but was merely the "cult legend" (or "historical" explanation) of the covenant-renewal ceremony (pp. 18f.), which the Yahwist himself was responsible for incorporating into the canonical history. Much has been written in opposition to this opinion, and one can only say here that it does not seem really tenable. There are, of course, difficulties in the usual view, geographical as well as form-critical, and these have often been pointed out, but the difficulty of separating the traditions seems even greater. Certainly the traditions of the exodus and of the covenant would appear to be complementary rather than independent or alternative, the covenant being the logical climax to the drama of the exodus, an act of fealty and gratitude in return for an act of deliverance. The absence of any mention of the Sinai covenant in Deut. 26:5–10 is likely due to the fact that this is not a creed at all, but a liturgical prayer meant to be recited in connection with the symbolic giving to Yahweh of the fruits of the land. What is included is only what is immediately relevant to the fact that Yahweh brought his homeless people out of a foreign land, which belonged to others, into a land that would belong only to them. The absence of the covenant tradition in the other formulas can probably also be explained on grounds that are inherent in the occasion for which they were composed rather than from any deficiency in the tradition itself.

If, then, we attempt to analyze this earliest form of Israel's knowledge of God and reduce the formula to the simplest possible terms, we shall come up with something like this: in the first stage of her existence Israel, without committing herself to any further statements about the character of Yahweh, believed that he had met her as a people somewhere at a definite point in her history, had redeemed her from slavery in Egypt, had made her his own by some kind of solemn ceremony in the desert, had given her a way of life to live—his *torah*—and a land in which to live it. At this point in its development, the "creed" of Israel did not reach back substantially beyond the exodus (although it included Jacob's descent into Egypt, which was the indispensable prelude), nor forward beyond the conquest. It was a simple, satisfying creed for the times, which found deity not in the skies or in the regularities of nature, as did most Near Eastern "creeds," but firmly set amidst the realities of human history and in a context of human relationships. Knowledge of God in oldest Israel was not based upon a process of rational thinking, but upon what she conceived to be the fact of *meeting*—upon her belief that she had had a decisive historical encounter with him. While all the implications of this earliest creed were realized only at a much later time, one can note by way of anticipation even at this stage that the God of Israel was primarily and essentially a loving, redeeming and gracious God, for he loved his people, had redeemed them out of Egypt and graciously given to them a law and a land.

The Creed Expanded: The Patriarchs

In the long run Israel could not be satisfied with this simple statement of her first encounter with Yahweh. The bare bones of her basic creed were elaborated with historical traditions and legends from many sources, and with codes of law developed in later situations, which were woven together to form the present complex structure of the Hexateuch. Thus the simple early creed developed into a lengthy and variegated historical narrative.

The creed was elaborated not only in depth, but in length and compass. Israel's historical origins were thrust ever further back. The formula in Deut. 26 speaks only vaguely of a single "father" (Jacob), a "wandering Aramean" who went down into Egypt, but some of the individual tribes had popular stories that told of the adventures of other "Arameans" who had been connected with the land of Canaan in the distant past, some of whose descendants eventually joined the Israelite confederation. These stories could not be directly interwoven with the events of the exodus, since they seemed to tell the story of another "exodus" (from Mesopotamia rather than Egypt), of covenants with other gods whose original names were certainly not Yahweh (Gen. 31:42, 53; 49:24; Exod. 6:3), and of a previous settlement in the Promised Land (Gen. 13:14–18). The only way in which these stories could become a part of Israel's canonical tradition was by giving them a chronological setting in an earlier stage in the story of her dealings with God, treating them as incidents in the lives of the ancestors of those who took part in the exodus. The basic creed was thus extended backward, so that it now began with Abraham, the most impressive of the ancient heroes, but also included Isaac, an important figure in the saga of some particular tribal group, and Jacob, the one name that belonged to the tradition from the very beginning. The presence of the two former figures in the canonical narrative could be rationalized by regarding Abraham as the father and grandfather, respectively, of Isaac and Jacob. This stage in the development of the tradition is represented by the opening verses of another of the so-called creeds, the one found in Josh. 24:2ff.:

Your fathers lived of old beyond the Euphrates, Terah, the father of Abraham and of Nahor, and they served other gods. Then I took your father Abraham from beyond the River and led him through all the land of Canaan, and made his offspring many. I gave him

Isaac; and to Isaac I gave Jacob and Esau. And I gave Esau the hill country of Seir to possess, but Jacob and his children went down to Egypt.[7]

In this brief outline it is easy to see that we have a real parallel to the story of the exodus and Sinai. There had already been an exodus, not from slavery in Egypt, but from heathenism in Mesopotamia; the land had been promised to Abraham, and, in effect, he had already taken possession of it. The only way in which the two traditions could be joined was by supposing that the descendants of Abraham, who had already settled in the land of Canaan, had been forced by circumstances to emigrate to Egypt, from which they must once again emerge and once more take possession of the land. The awkward seam that joins together these two forms of the tradition is evident in one of the later documents (the Priestly source of the Hexateuch), which states that Israel's ancestors lived in Egypt for over four hundred years, although it fails to mention a single name or event from that period (Gen. 15:13; Exod. 12:40).

Eventually this new first paragraph of the creed, this new preliminary chapter in the history of Israel's encounter with God, was elaborated like the story of the exodus and took literary form. In its final shape, which includes the lengthy novelistic account of the career of Joseph, it is found in Gen. 12–50. This stage of the tradition is by no means as neatly unified as was the first stage, for the account in Exodus through Joshua moves forward with a certain inevitable logic from the deliverance from Egypt, which stands at the beginning, to the conquest of Canaan, which stands at the end. But the stories in Gen. 12–50, with the exception of the Joseph story, which has a literary history all its own, have no such unity. This section of the Pentateuch is, for the most part, simply a collection of separate tales strung loosely on a string, many of which could be told about anybody, and several of which are, as a matter of fact, related to different persons in different contexts. The story of the man with the bride who was also his sister, and who passed her off on a heathen king, is related no less than three times with different *dramatis personae* on each occasion (Gen. 12:10–20; 20; 26:6–11). Isaac is a shadowy figure and the principal stories told about him are also told elsewhere about someone else. Jacob is presented in greater depth, but even he has two names, probably because he represents the amalgamation of two quite different personages. Abraham is, on the whole, the most attractive of the three patriarchs, but even he can appear somewhat inconsistently as a coward and liar (as in the story of the sister-bride mentioned above). One story depicts him also as a military chieftain (Gen. 14), although the dominant picture is that of a devout and peaceful owner of flocks moving majestically through an almost empty landscape. Inconsistent and unharmonized as the patriarchal tradition is, it is in many respects the most fascinating in the Pentateuch, with its many colorful and appealing stories, its interesting all-too-human characters, and its frequent revelations of spiritual insight and deep theological conviction.

The one entirely new element that the patriarchal traditions introduced into the original faith of Israel was the idea of "promise and fulfillment," a theme of tremendous significance for the development of Old Testament thought in later times. The belief that "the God of the fathers" had promised the land of Canaan to Abraham was deeply embedded in some of the patriarchal stories, but, since Israel's canonical tradition fixed the actual settlement of the land in the time of Moses and Joshua, the two traditions could be reconciled only by supposing that Abraham's settlement in Canaan was temporary and provisional, while the true fulfillment of the promise came in the time of his descendants several generations later. In this way there entered subtly into Israelite thinking the seminal idea of a divine "promise" whose "fulfillment" might be long post-

ooned. This pattern of promise and fulfillment would later be
applied to the covenant with David and to the eschatological
hopes that were to be such an important element in the fully developed theology of the exilic and postexilic period. Israel would
find it easy to believe that the God who, according to her tradition, had so magnificently fulfilled his promise to Abraham
(Josh. 23:14) would also certainly fulfill the promises made,
through his prophets, to the people of later days.

The acceptance of the patriarchal traditions, most of which
were originally only of a local and popular character, into the
main stream of Israel's thought must also have had the effect of
enlarging her mental horizons. For one thing, the vistas of her
thinking began to open toward a distant past in which she
could see that God had already been at work long generations—
perhaps even centuries—before the exodus; and the chronological framework of her creed was extended to include this
remoter period. For another, there was significant enlargement
in her geographical and cultural landscape also, for she had to
begin thinking of her God as active in far away Mesopotamia
as well as in Canaan and nearby Egypt. This helped to give a
new and profounder dimension to her faith. If God had been
at work over so long a time and in so great an area, it must have
become increasingly clear to Israel that her election was not the
result of a momentary divine impulse, but part of some consistent, meaningful plan, however imperfectly she might understand it. Her later theological history demonstrates the growing strength of this conviction.

The sense of history, which is so characteristic an aspect of
Israel's mature intellectual life, may have been born in this
period when the development and complication of her tradition
forced her to conceive of God's work as involving many nations
and as spread over a long period of time. In the exodus-Sinai-
conquest story, which covers the span of only two generations,
everything important seems to occur at a particular point or

period, but when this is seen only as the climactic chapter in a series of events possibly spread out over several centuries, something like a sense of history begins to emerge—a feeling for human life as being involved in a sequence of events stretching backward on a line that vanishes in the remote past and forward into a future that is unforeseeable, though causally linked with the present as the present is with the past.

Probably because the patriarchal narrative consists of stories about individuals rather than about groups, one finds in this part of the tradition a deeper sense for the richness and infinite variety of human character, a deepened appreciation of the value of individual life. In the exodus tradition only Moses is a fully realized human being, and even then one has to search to find him, since the center of interest is on what he did rather than what he was. But in the stories of the patriarchs, despite the occasional admixture of extraneous elements, the characters of Abraham, Jacob and Joseph at least are deeply etched. To what extent this is the result of a later imposition of stereotypes upon the older materials we are no longer in a position to know —in the case of Joseph one can clearly see the hand of the literary artist at work—but the point is not particularly important. The fact is that the tradition at this stage provided something with which the imagination could work, characters that existed in their own right and were capable of artistic amplification. In any event, in these traditions we can look more deeply into the soul of Israel and see something of the qualities in human life that she admired, and believed to be characteristic of her people. Here we find Abraham, the man of faith, who, seeing himself as living under the secret guidance of God, trusts himself implicitly to God's care; we see Jacob, the charming and successful rogue whom God forces into his service and compels to become the man of destiny; and here we find Joseph, the most attractive figure of all, who has the faith of Abraham, the charm and gift for success of Jacob—without the roguery—

and whose dominant qualities are love for his family and for-giveness for his enemies.

So the prefixing of the patriarchal stories to the basic tradition of the exodus did not result in mere mechanical addition, but achieved a real deepening in the quality of Israel's faith by giving her a sense of "promise and fulfillment" as one of the characteristic modes of action of her God. It also had the effect of extending her geographical and chronological perspectives so as to evoke for the first time a genuine sense of history; and, by giving her a keener appreciation of the interest and variety of individual human life, helped to lay the foundation for the more "humanistic" and "secular" kind of thinking that began to emerge in the early days of the monarchy.[8]

The Creed Expanded Further: Creation and Primeval History

The opening of her historical vision made inevitable the third stage in the development of Israel's basic creed, the one that provides the last essential element in the completed structure of the Hexateuch. This consisted in adding as a preface to the story of Israel a collection of traditions about the history of the primeval world, reaching backward from the time of Abraham to the creation of man and the universe. When once Israel's sense of history had developed to the point where she could look back, as through a long tunnel, and see, diminishing in the distance, the figures of Moses, Joseph, Jacob, Isaac and Abraham, she was bound some day to ask what happened *before* Abraham, since plainly history did not begin with him. And where did Israel stand with reference to this previous history? And what was Yahweh doing then? Was any part of his purpose evident even in those distant times?

Israel, as has been noted, had no great natural interest in stories of origins, in cosmology or cosmography. That is not to say that no one in Israel was ever concerned with such matters, for there must have been as many curious minds in early Israel as in any other ancient people, but as a nation her predominant and obsessive concern was with history, not with nature.[9] The chief interest among most peoples of antiquity was in the mysterious natural world which visibly surrounded them and on which their lives depended. Their basic questions were: What —or who—makes the crops grow, and how can they be made to grow again? Where does the rain originate? Where does the sun come from when he rises, and where does he go when he sets? And who is the sun anyway? And what about the stars, and the moon? What brings about the alternation of the seasons? And why are some years wet and others dry? Where in fact does everything come from? What are the rules that govern the natural order and how can we so integrate our lives into that order that we may be happy and prosperous? [10]

Whatever the reason may be, early Israel seems to have had little interest in such questions; at least she did not see them as particularly relevant to her basic religious faith. Her concern was with human relationships, with the forces that knit man to man in social structures, with the laws that govern a human society and with the events that produce it. This is a somewhat sophisticated way of expressing the idea; if we had to put it more crudely, we would have to say that her God was a tribal or "national" God, or at least a God of the group—a God whose laws determined the character of social life, who showed his power chiefly in war, in the conflict of one human group with another, and in the protection of his people against their enemies rather than in his control of the forces of nature. He could use natural powers when he chose, but it was almost always the storm, the volcanic eruption, earthquake, fire or flood. He could come, as in the Song of Deborah, on the wings of the storm to rescue his people in battle (Judg. 5:4f.), or he could rain down hailstones on their enemies (Josh. 10:11), but in all this he was still the God of the group and of its battles rather than the God of the storms. His use of the powers of nature was only incidental to his main function and he was rarely associated in this early time with the regularities of nature, with its benign and life-giving functions. For this reason his worshipers turned readily, when they came into the land of Canaan, to the Baalim and the Ashtaroth, who were gods of nature and of the land, and could be helpful in the production of the crops (Judg. 2:13).

Ultimately, as we shall see in a later chapter, Yahweh became the Lord of nature also; and the Bible as we now have it begins with a cosmogony, an account of how the God of Israel created heaven and earth, and which obviously implies that he still sustains them by his power. But this is the *latest* addition to the Hexateuchal tradition. In its elaborate, priestly form (Gen. 1:1–2:4a), it was added to the Hexateuch during or after the Babylonian exile; and even the simple Yahwistic story (Gen. 2:4bff.) was not a part of the canonical tradition before the early years of the monarchy.[11]

Furthermore, Israel arrived at her creation faith through her meditations on history, not through the contemplation of nature. The story of creation did not arise because of Israel's attempt to penetrate the secrets of the natural world around her in order to discover the source of its mysterious powers, but through her attempt to trace back through history the meaning of her own historical existence. Her backward historical glance could not be satisfied until she had traced all the events she knew to their final origin. Back beyond Abraham, she finally came to believe, lay the figures of Shem, Ham and Japheth; their father Noah; the dimly perceived antediluvian patriarchs, Cain and Abel, Adam and Eve; and then at last the thought of Israel reached the *ne plus ultra:* "In the beginning God created heaven and earth." So, out of her meditation on history and the fact of her own existence, Israel finally came to have a cosmology and cosmogony. The purpose that lay behind this latest addition to her creed was not to answer the question "Where do *things* come from?" but "Where do *we* come from?"

One indication that this element in the creed is of late origin is that it is not a part of any of the formulas we have examined, which, whatever their date, undoubtedly testify to the basic "shape" of Israel's early theology. Its absence is particularly notable in the formula of Deut. 26:5–10, where an expression of the creation faith would seem so natural and appropriate on the lips of a worshiper who is bringing the first fruits of his crop to offer them to the Lord of nature. But nothing is said of God as the giver of natural products. The crop is not offered to him as the Creator, but only in grateful remembrance of the fact that he delivered his people out of the land of Egypt and brought them to the Promised Land. In whatever period of history the formula was composed, it is striking that this is the shape it takes.

Although the presence of a creation story in the J document of the Hexateuch—compiled sometime during the early years of the kingdom, perhaps in Solomon's reign or shortly afterward—is evidence that creation faith was in some sense already a part of Israel's theology then, it does not seem to have become a really vital element until the time of Second Isaiah. At least he is the first to draw frequent, unmistakable, and far-reaching conclusions from it. One finds suggestions of creation faith in Amos and Hosea, but some of the references (such as the hymnic passages in Amos: 4:13; 5:8–9; 9:5–6) are suspected of being later interpolations, and others, such as those in Hos. 2:8–9 are only incidental and rhetorical. These facts merely underline the observation that Israel's basic way of thinking was always historical rather than cosmological. For centuries after she had received the primeval history as a part of her theological inheritance, it still seemed more natural to think in terms of history and "covenant," and it was only in the long run and almost with reluctance that she at last accepted the full implications of a doctrine of creation.[12]

But when finally this reluctance was overcome and a prophet appeared who moved in the realm of creation theology as his native habitat, the result was the most impressive body of theological discourse we possess in the Old Testament. It can be said of Second Isaiah that with him, for the first time, the belief in God as creator of heaven and earth became the *first* article of Israel's creed. The story of creation had long stood at the beginning of her historical traditions; it was now to become the point of departure for her thought as well. Here are some of the passages in which this faith finds classical expression:

> Lift up your eyes on high and see:
>   who created these [i.e., the stars]?
> He who brings out their host by number,
>   calling them all by name;
> by the greatness of his might,
>   and because he is strong in power
> not one is missing.   [ISA. 40:26–27]

> I form light and create darkness,
> I make weal and create woe,
> I am the Lord, who do all these things.   [ISA. 45:7]

> For thus says the Lord,
> who created the heavens
>   (he is God!),
> who formed the earth and made it
>   (he established it;
> he did not create it a chaos,
>   he formed it to be inhabited!):
> "I am the Lord, and there is no other. . . ."   [ISA. 45:18]

These passages from Second Isaiah represent the most exalted level attained by theological reflection in the Old Testament.

The earliest form of the primeval history, as contained in the Yahwistic parts of Gen. 2:4b–11:32 is naturally far more primitive in its theology than Second Isaiah or the great Priestly creation story of Gen. 1:1–2:4a. Gen. 2:4b–6 simply states, without elaboration, that Yahweh was the creator of the earth and the heavens and then goes on immediately to describe in naïve and picturesque language how the first man was formed out of a clay doll into which Yahweh breathed the force of life. The story of the Garden of Eden that follows is of enormous psychological and moral interest but belongs, rather, to ancient Israelite views about the nature of man than to Israel's knowledge of God. The rest of the primeval history is concerned with man's expulsion from the garden, the murder of Abel, the succession of worthies before the flood, then the account of Noah and God's first judgment upon mankind, followed by the division of the world into its present three ethnic groups, with the attention of the narrative now focusing upon Shem as the ancestor of Israel. Finally the story of Babel and the Tower forms the immediate background for the call of Abraham and the beginning of the patriarchal history.

This rapid survey of the contents of the traditions belonging to the third stage in the development of Israel's creed reveals immediately two facts about them: first, their completely legendary character, and second, their foreign derivation. In a general way the exodus traditions belong to actual history, and the patriarchal traditions only somewhat less so. That is to say, the escape of Israel from Egypt was a historical event that took place in the reign of a certain Pharaoh, although it is no longer possible to be absolutely certain just who he was or what the precise circumstances were. Similarly, the settlement of Canaan, whether by rapid conquest or gradual infiltration, took place during a particular historical epoch, although its exact limits can no longer be defined because of the paucity of historical records from the period. When one moves back to the period of Abraham and the other patriarchs, the historicity of the personages and events is much less certain, but one is still dealing with characters who probably once existed and may even have done some of the things that tradition ascribes to them. At least the patriarchs have a definite historical milieu which can be defined within a span of two or three centuries and which can be partly correlated with information derived from such historical documents as the Nuzi and Mari tablets.[13]

But there is obviously no such historical background for the stories in the primeval traditions. There was a city of Babel, better known to us as Babylon, and, like all great Mesopotamian cities, it had a tower, a ziggurat. But there the connection with history ends. That the tower was built for the purpose of reaching heaven is obviously an anti-Babylonian libel, and the idea that the languages of the earth originated in the frustration of the attempt is not even within the realm of discussion. So it is with the lists of individuals who "begat" the various nations of the world, with the flood, and the ark which contained samples of all the animals, with the supernatural beings who impregnated the daughters of men, with Adam and Eve, the fruit of knowledge, and the talking snake.

These are legends, even though the ancient Israelites used them as history. Israel had a passion, one might say, for history, and these stories were the only materials she had available for extending her historical narrative backward from Abraham to creation. It is significant, though, that these materials were not of her own devising. The mind of Israel was not adept at the making of myths and legends. For this kind of tradition, she had to turn to her neighbors, especially to Babylonia. This is not the place to discuss these borrowings in detail. It is sufficient to mention again that the Tower of Babel story is connected with Babylon, that the flood story is only a version of another found in various versions in cuneiform, mostly notably in the Gilgamesh Epic, and that the stories of creation and the fall contain elements that can be also paralleled in Mesopotamian sources.[14]

That fact that Israel had to borrow these stories to fill up the inevitable gap in her historical memories is, as we have said, a remarkable tribute to the antimythological, one might almost say prosaic, cast of her mind, for, unlike most other races, she seems to have had no store of fantastic stories about primordial times on which to draw. But, even more remarkable is the use she made of them, once they were incorporated into her sacred traditions. As could easily be demonstrated in detail, none of them is any longer just a good story, or told just for the sake of satisfying idle curiosity about the origin of things. All the basic ones, at least, have been reshaped in a distinctive Israelite mold that makes them vehicles of psychological insight and of moral and theological truth. This is strikingly evident in the flood story, where a tale about the unmotivated peevishness of the Babylonian gods has become a parable of the sinfulness of man and the judgment of a righteous God.

At this point the basic structure of Old Testament faith, as preserved in the general outline of the Hexateuch, is complete. Israel's history of how God had dealt with her now runs without a break from creation to the settlement in Canaan. The main articles in her faith may be summarized in these words: creation, election, redemption (i.e., the exodus), and promise fulfilled (the gift of the land). Of course it needs to be said again that this logical order is the reverse of the order in which the articles were formulated, for Israel's faith in election, redemption and Promised Land was prior to her faith in creation. Israel did not begin with belief in a universal God of creation, who then elected her: she began with a God whom she had come to know as *her* God, and only later came to acknowledge him as the universal God, creator of heaven and earth. This order gives to Israel's faith an unspeculative, existential character that it otherwise would not have.

Having made this point, and made it emphatically, we must then go on to say that in its final and mature form, the faith of Israel—as expressed by Second Isaiah and the first chapter of Genesis—could also be expressed in the more conventional form in which we know it from the Christian creeds, where "I believe in God the Father Almighty, Maker of heaven and earth" is the first article. Making use of completely un-Hebraic language, one might say that while the doctrine of election is prior in the order of epistemology, the doctrine of creation is prior in the order of ontology, and hence, ultimately, of theological importance. If the doctrine of election gives the doctrine of creation an existential impact it would not otherwise have had, it is also true that in the long run the doctrine of creation, in the developed faith of Israel, gave to the doctrine of election a depth and breadth and universal relevance it certainly does not have at its first appearance. This latter point is made clear by the following passage from Second Isaiah:

> Thus says God, the Lord,
>   who created the heavens and stretched them out,
> who spread forth the earth and what comes from it,
> who gives breath to the people upon it
>   and spirit to those who walk in it:
> "I am the Lord, I have called you in righteousness,
>   I have taken you by the hand and kept you;
> I have given you as a covenant to the people,
>   a light to the nations;
>   to open the eyes that are blind,
>   to bring out the prisoners from the dungeon,
>   from the prison those who sit in darkness."   [ISA. 42:5-7]

Some interpreters have supposed these words to mean that Israel has a direct missionary obligation to the Gentile world, but this may be pushing the thought too far. What is perfectly clear, however, is that Second Isaiah, in the light of his creation faith, cannot conceive the election of Israel in terms merely of national or racial pride, or as aimed at the mere preservation of her national identity. The creator God could have chosen Israel only as a part of his whole purpose in creating the world. However tentatively Second Isaiah may have understood his own new vision, there can be no doubt that he saw the purpose of Israel's election as lying outside herself. She was not chosen simply because God loved her, but because he had a mission for her to perform; she was in some way to be the nucleus of a universal covenant, to bring light to other nations, to bring freedom and joy to those who were bound in slavery and darkness. When Israel's election was seen to be the work of a universal creator God, it became necessary to suppose that the purpose of her election was, in some mysterious way, as broad as creation itself.

The Creed's Final Expansion: Zion and David

There is still a fourth stage in the development of Israel's faith, but it is one that is more difficult to integrate into the general discussion, because it was never incorporated into the developed structure of the Pentateuch. This was the belief that Yahweh had chosen Jerusalem to be, in some sense, his dwelling place, and had chosen David, and his family after him, to play a crucial role in the life of the people. Although these articles of faith were finally rejected by the Israelites of the northern kingdom and were probably opposed by significant conservative groups in the south, their centrality in the developed faith of the only part of Israel to survive the disasters of the Assyrian period is shown abundantly by quotations from the Psalter and some of the prophets. Psalm 132, for instance, is a classic expression of the faith in David and Jerusalem:

> The Lord swore to David a sure oath
>   from which he will not turn back:
> "One of the sons of your body
>   I will set on your throne.

If your sons keep my covenant
    and my testimonies which I shall teach them,
their sons also for ever
    shall sit upon your throne."

For the Lord has chosen Zion;
    he has desired it for his habitation;
"This is my resting place for ever;
    here will I dwell for I have desired it. . . ."   [vv. 11–14]

Some passages from the Book of Isaiah may be added simply to confirm the basic importance of the idea. The first two are from the prophet Isaiah of the eighth century:

For to us a child is born,
    to us a son is given:
and the government will be upon his shoulder
  . . . .
Of the increase of his government and of peace
    there will be no end,
upon the throne of David, and over his kingdom,
    to establish it, and to uphold it
with justice and with righteousness
    from this time forth and for evermore.   [Isa. 9:6–7]

"Behold I am laying in Zion for a foundation
    a stone, a tested stone,
a precious cornerstone, of a sure foundation. . . ."   [Isa. 28:16]

Two brief quotations from Second Isaiah show how this faith persisted through the centuries. One of them, addressed to Jerusalem, depopulated and in ruins, speaks of it as the "holy" city, meaning the one that in a special way belongs to Yahweh:

    Awake, awake,
        put on your strength, O Zion;
      put on your beautiful garments,
        O Jerusalem, the holy city;

> for there shall no more come into you
> the uncircumcised and the unclean.   [ISA. 52:1]

The second is the allusion, in 55:3-4, to

> . . . an everlasting covenant,
> my steadfast, sure love for David.

which goes on to say,

> Behold, I made him a witness to the peoples,
> a leader and commander for the peoples.

From these and many other passages that will come readily to mind, it can be seen that, for certain circles at any rate, Jerusalem and David were just as significant theologically as the exodus, the Sinai covenant and the conquest. It is particularly striking that the term "covenant" is used in connection with both the exodus-Sinai and the Zion-David complexes of ideas.

The reason that the Zion-David tradition was the last to enter the structure of Israelite faith is, of course, the simple fact that the rise of the Davidic dynasty and the conquest of Jerusalem came comparatively late in Israel's history, when the canonical traditions that constitute the framework of the Hexateuch had already taken definitive form. The older theology of pre-monarchical days had regarded the historical work of God as ended with the conquest of the land. But Israelite faith could hardly disregard the manifest signs of God's favor shown in the career of David, who rose from a simple small-town youth to become the first real king of Israel (Saul having been much more like a "judge" than a king in the oriental sense), and who had transformed the people of Israel in his own lifetime from a loose confederation of culturally backward tribes into a great empire. The capture of Jerusalem from the Canaanites and its elevation into the capital of the kingdom, with the shrine of the ark at its center, could only seem the dramatic focus of the process.

Like the backward extension of Israel's creed into patriarchal times, this new act which brought it forward into comparatively recent times was difficult to harmonize with the basic faith that centered around the exodus. As a matter of fact it was more difficult than with the patriarchal materials, for they were after all only units of oral tradition which could be shaped and molded at will to eliminate the harsher contradictions, but the events of David's reign, in contrast, took place in the full light of history and were recorded in writing, so that any adapting could be accomplished only by means of shifting emphasis and new interpretation. The events of the patriarchal period could easily be regarded as preparing the way for the exodus, and foreshadowing the conquest, but no such conciliation was possible between the exodus-Sinai-conquest traditions and those about Zion and David.

As a matter of fact, no really satisfactory resolution of this conflict was ever achieved during the monarchical period, and both traditions continued to live side by side, each somewhat uneasily pursuing its own way. It is possible, as some suppose, that the two traditions were differently emphasized in different groups. Obviously the Zion-David tradition would have been the special property of the city of Jerusalem and the court. The prophet Isaiah, for example, has nothing to say about Moses and the exodus, but moves in the aura of the Zion-David traditions. The premonarchical traditions of the exodus and the Sinai covenant may have had a greater vitality in the countryside of Judah, for country people in general tend to be more conservative, and are likely to have an unfavorable opinion of city-folk and aristocrats. Isaiah's rustic contemporary, Micah, has no hesitation in predicting that

Zion shall be plowed as a field;
Jerusalem shall become a heap of ruins,
    and the mountain of the house a wooded height. [Mic. 3:12]

We have already noted that the Davidic covenant was explicitly rejected by the tribes of the north, who eventually formed themselves into a separate kingdom and declared

What portion have we in David?
We have no inheritance in the son of Jesse.   [1 KINGS 12:16]

It is entirely possible that the reform of Josiah, based upon the Deuteronomic law, where the king is very much reduced in stature (Deut. 17:14–20), represented a temporary victory of the exodus-Sinai party over the party of Zion and David. On the other hand, the Chronicler, who lived some centuries later, obviously lived by the Zion-David tradition almost exclusively. His whole work (I–II Chronicles, Ezra, Nehemiah) is a glorification of David, Jerusalem and the temple, with only a few passing allusions to Moses and the exodus.[15]

But, though tensions such as these undoubtedly existed, they should not be exaggerated, for probably the bulk of the people had no difficulty in holding to both forms of the covenant, seeing in the covenant with David only a new and special form of the covenant at Sinai, and seeing in the sanctity of Jerusalem only an intensification and concentration of the general sanctity of the Promised Land. The temple, built by Solomon, stood, of course, as a visible monument to the magnitude and magnificence of the Zion-David tradition. It was both the royal sanctuary and also the place where Yahweh the God of Israel had chosen to take up his earthly dwelling. But the presence of the ancient ark served to bring it into some kind of continuity with the traditions of older days, and it was possible to think of it as simply the last and greatest of those sanctuaries—Shechem, Gilgal, Bethel, Mizpah, Shiloh—where Israel had worshiped in the days of the tribal confederacy. Even the reform of Josiah, which as we have seen, quite possibly represented a kind of re-affirmation of the older traditions, actually helped—by emphasizing worship at the Jerusalem sanctuary—to give the Zion-David tradition, in a purified form, a canonical place in the fully developed traditions of Israel and in the structure of Israelite faith.

The process by which the Zion-David tradition became completely and comfortably assimilated to other elements in the developed faith of Israel was enormously accelerated by the fall of the kingdom, which meant that this circle of ideas could, to a large extent, be freed from association with politics. It was no longer possible to regard it as simply an ideology for the perpetuation of the ruling dynasty. It now became a purely transcendent, theological idea, untainted by politics. The new temple of Zerubbabel was a national, not merely a royal, shrine. Jerusalem was still "the city of the great king," but the king was Yahweh, not some fallible human being. Israel's God came more and more to be thought of as clothed in royal attributes and the idea of the coming "kingdom of God" began to assume shape. And somehow in that future time the promises once made to David would be realized and the "messiah" would come. But these are thoughts which belong to the realm of eschatology, and further consideration of them must be deferred until a later chapter. Here we are concerned to note only that by the end of the Old Testament period the complex of ideas which center around David and Zion had become an integral part of the faith of Israel.

Summary

By way of recapitulation, we may say that, while Israel actually had no creed, in any real sense of the term, her basic faith was expressed in her historical traditions, where she recorded the great things God had done for her in the past. These traditions are found in a developed form in the Hexateuch, in more compact form in certain liturgical formulas that

were used on cultic occasions, and in allusions scattered throughout the Psalter and the prophetic books. Israel's faith was not
the product of philosophical speculation or of curiosity about
the universe; it arose, in the beginning, out of her attempt to
face the problem of her own identity: who she was and where
she came from. The irreducible datum from which her thinking
started was the knowledge that she had once met the God whose
name was Yahweh and he had chosen her for his own. At the
first stage her election was associated exclusively with the exodus, with the covenant offered and received at Sinai, and with
the gift of the Promised Land. Later, however, these events
were seen as only the culminating act in a historical drama
which began with Abraham and the other patriarchs. And,
finally, these events were all seen as having emerged out of the
matrix of universal and, indeed, cosmic history, and the God
whom Israel had met in the wilderness was seen to be the one
God who had created heaven and earth and all that is in them.
The last article of the Israelite deposit of faith declared that
God's establishment of the Davidic dynasty and his choice of
Zion were the final proof of his election of Israel. Psalm 78
shows how this final article of faith could be integrated into
Israel's historical credo. Verses 5–66 are a recital of God's deal-
ings with his people in Egypt, in the desert and the early days
in Canaan, but the concluding verses are these:

> . . . he chose the tribe of Judah,
>   Mt. Zion, which he loves.
> He built his sanctuary like the high heavens,
>   like the earth, which he has founded for ever.
> He chose David his servant,
>   and took him from the sheepfolds;
> from tending the ewes that had young he brought him
>   to be the shepherd of Jacob his people,
>   of Israel his inheritance.
> With upright heart he tended them,
>   and guided them with skilful hand.   [Ps. 78:68–72]

This last article of faith, like the others, was the result of experience in the past and of meditation upon the historical records that preserved it. But, more than any other of the articles, it leads us on into Israel's understanding of God's work in the present and the future, because the events with which it is concerned had occurred *since* the formation of the old canonical tradition and showed that God was still at work. They had a contemporary flavor because they were recorded in written, reliable historical documents, accessible to all literate men, and were not derived from a shadowy oral tradition or ancient legend. And, furthermore, they spoke not of a God who was known only at Sinai, or Ur of the Chaldees, or at the day of creation, but of one who was still, in the living present, dwelling in his temple at Zion, and had given to David his servant the pledge of his covenant for the limitless future.

4

GOD IN THE PRESENT

I am doing a work in your days.

HABAKKUK 1:5

ALTHOUGH Israel's convictions about God's actions
in the past constituted the hard core of her faith,
and the recitation of his benefactions in days of old
was possibly at times a central feature of her worship, the belief
that he continued his work in the present was also integral to
the structure of her theology, and probably had more immediate significance for the ongoing life of the community.

Before we consider this aspect of her faith in any detail, we
must first speak of a factor that, unfortunately, tends to confuse
the picture and make it seem that, in this area at least, Israel
had no consistent doctrine. While it is obvious that her conception of God's work in the past was composed of many heterogeneous, divergent, and sometimes contradictory elements—the
traditions of various clans and tribes—all these elements in time
were rationalized, harmonized and systematized so as finally to
produce a unified body of canonical "truth." Israel's "creed,"
in its ultimate Hexateuchal form, is a smooth and harmonious
narrative that on first reading seems to move in a straightfor-
ward way from creation to the conquest, or, if we include parts
of the Deuteronomic history, from creation to the rise of the
monarchy and the building of the temple. There are no shock-

ing discontinuities or gross inconsistencies in the story. But there is no such unity, and little attempt to achieve it, in Israel's view of God's continuing activity in the present.

A Threefold View

There were three distinct groups engaged in instructing Israel about God's work in the contemporary world: the priests, the prophets and the wise men. Their conceptions of the way he operated were so different that many writers on the history of Israel's religion have tended to think of them as wholly incompatible and have even talked about separate "religions" of priests, prophets and wise men, as though these men were proponents of competing faiths, adherents of jealous and mutually exclusive churches or sects. Sometimes the wise men appear to encourage this view by slighting the importance of the cult; and prophets make matters even worse by seeming to disparage both wise men and priests.[1]

But the division among them is not so deep or fundamental as it seems. Modern scholars tend particularly to minimize the differences between priests and prophets. One school says that the prophets could not have had any basic antipathy to the cult, since they themselves were no more than cultic functionaries of a special kind.[2] While this is an extreme position, no one doubts that the prophets were more closely connected with the cult than was imagined a generation ago. A few scholars have also tried to show that the teaching of the wise men was closer to normative Hebrew tradition than used to be supposed. They point out, for example, that the Book of Proverbs, which seems at first glance to be utterly remote from Israel's peculiar theological tradition, is nevertheless careful almost always to refer to God by the "covenantal" name, Yahweh, rather than by one of the vaguer, more philosophical names (El or Elohim) that were readily available. There were also definite efforts on

the part of the wise men to bring their teaching, which was undoubtedly of foreign origin, into ever closer harmony with the
native Israelite tradition of cult and covenant.[3]

To the general reader, the differences in priestly, prophetic,
and "wisdom" points of view are evident enough. It would be
difficult, for example, to find three books that seem more totally
dissimilar in subject matter and basic philosophy than Leviticus,
Amos and Proverbs, each one a typical product of its "school."
And yet the differences are certainly not so irreconcilable as
they at first appear, and are more the result of the different purposes the books are intended to serve than of any theoretical
disagreement among their authors in respect either to theology
or philosophy of life.

In order to understand the relationship of these groups to
each other, we shall do well to forgo any elaborate investigation
of their pre-Israelite history, and simply try to look at them in
an objective, common-sense way as they appear to us in the
pages of the Old Testament. It will then appear that the underlying differences among them were not really differences of
theory or theology, but of sphere and function. The three
groups were not representatives of competing theological points
of view, but of complementary and parallel functions in human
society. All of them belonged to Israel and believed that Israel's
God was continually at work, but their individual concern was
to show how he worked in the particular spheres of life in which
they exercised their respective vocations. The priest was interested in showing how God's presence and power were manifested in the ceremonial and sacrificial cult; the wise man—a
teacher of the young—was concerned to show his pupils how
God was at work in everyday life through his control of the
moral order; the prophet was intent on demonstrating that God
was still active in the affairs of nations, just as he had been long
before.

There is, no doubt, some danger here of oversimplification

and of oversystematizing, but the picture seems basically correct. There were clashes among these groups, because each tended to overemphasize the importance of its own function and method, but it does not seem unreasonable to suppose that the normal member of each group recognized the legitimacy of the others' functions, and all felt themselves loyal members of the community of Israel and inheritors of its ancient faith. The average citizen would probably have been quite unconscious of any basic cleavage among them. In the course of a single morning, a good citizen of Israel might send his child to school at the wise man's academy, go himself to offer sacrifice in the temple with the help of a priest, and, while there, listen sympathetically to an impassioned address by a prophet on the inequity of Israel's social structure and the folly of her international politics. In all of this he would have felt himself still the member of a single political and religious society, dealing with other faithful citizens of Israel, each of whom was acting reasonably and competently within his own chosen sphere.

On the assumption, then, that we are dealing with points of view that are complementary rather than conflicting, we shall consider the theme of God's contemporary action, according to the faith of ancient Israel, under these three heads: in the cult, in world history, and in daily life, as seen respectively by priests, prophets and wise men.

The Cult and the Divine Presence

For the priest, as no doubt for the greater part of the populace, Yahweh's activity was especially manifest in the cultus, for the cult represents for most men the specifically religious aspect of life. Eventually the prophets would attack this tendency to identify religion and cult, this feeling that God was present only where his name was explicitly mentioned and was not concerned with ordinary life so long as men kept the

rules of the game in his temple. For the moment, however, our
interest is not in perversions of the cult, but only in the in-
dubitable fact that, from first to last, Israel's religion included,
as an essential element, public rites and ceremonies, under the
supervision of regularly constituted officials, in which God was
conceived to be objectively present and specially active. Control of these rites and ceremonies was mainly—and came to be
increasingly—a function of the priesthood, although "prophets," and perhaps even wise men, may have had occasional
minor roles to play.

Corresponding to the three stages in Israel's constitutional
history, which we have examined in a previous chapter, were
three stages in the development of the cultus: that of the tribal
confederacy, that of the monarchy, and that of the postexilic
temple. Unfortunately, we have detailed information only about
the last, the period of the Priestly Code, and must depend
largely on inference and hypothesis for the period of the tribal
confederacy and the monarchy. Nevertheless, there are interesting hints that deserve to be followed.

It is of the first period that we know the least—the period of
the settlement in Canaan and the tribal confederacy. We have
already seen that the principal means of expressing the unity
of Israel in this period was probably a formal assembly of the
tribes at some sanctuary either on certain regular occasions or
at times of special stress (pp. 18f.). We have also seen that one
feature of the regular assembly may have been the solemn recital of the acts of Yahweh in establishing and maintaining the
community (Josh. 24:1–15), followed by a formal renewal on
the people's part of their allegiance to him and to his covenant
(Josh. 24:16–27).

But along with this liturgical recitation of the "creed" and
the people's reaffirmation of loyalty, there would almost certainly have been the reading of the divine law, which they were
pledged to obey and which formed the basis of the tribal union.

Two different passages in Deuteronomy suggest how this may have been done, at different times or possibly at different sanctuaries. Deut. 31:10f. says: "And Moses commanded them, 'At the end of every seven years, at the set time of the year of release, at the feast of booths, when all Israel comes to appear before the Lord your God at the place which he will choose, you shall read this law before Israel in their hearing.' " The older critical view is probably right in regarding this passage in its present form as relatively late, connected directly with the reform of Josiah. But a plausible modern interpretation sees the work of Josiah as being in essence a revival of older traditions from the days before the monarchy, a rejuvenating of customs that had prevailed in the time of the tribal confederacy. So it is not at all impossible that we have, in the passage above, a reflection of a very ancient form of cult in Israel. The specific mention of the "seven year" period, which has no cultic significance elsewhere in Deuteronomy, points in this direction. Some commentators would go further and say that the mention of Moses here (as of Joshua in Josh. 24:1) indicates that the law was proclaimed by a particular appointed official who, for want of a better term, might be called "the covenant mediator." They suppose that each succeeding generation chose its own "Moses" or "Joshua" to perform this function.

Still another passage in Deuteronomy, 27:11–26, points to a ceremony in which the law was proclaimed in a quite different way. No one doubts that this passage, at any rate, has about it the atmosphere of a genuine ancient rite. It tells how the tribes, gathering in the neighborhood of Shechem, were divided into two groups, one of which was to stand on Mt. Gerizim for the pronouncing of blessings, the other upon Mt. Ebal, for the pronouncing of curses. The "Levites" were then commanded to "declare to all the men of Israel with a loud voice" (v. 14) a dodecalogue of laws, each sentence of which begins with the word "Cursed be . . . ." The laws have to do with such matters as image-worship, honor to parents, the moving of landmarks, etc., and conclude with a general curse upon everyone "who does not confirm the words of this law by doing them." It is not clear how the division of the tribes helped to facilitate the distribution of blessings and curses, nor is it obvious just what group in the days of the tribal confederacy would have corresponded to the "Levites" of this passage, since, in v. 12, Levi seems to be treated as just one of the secular tribes, but the ceremony does not sound like a mere invention in the days of King Josiah (cf. also Josh. 8:30–35, though it is clearly an interpolation in its present context).

Undoubtedly there were other rites and ceremonies common in those days. The offering of sacrifices must have played an important role, just as in later times, both on ordinary occasions at local shrines and at the formal assemblies of the confederacy. We read, for example, in some detail of the sacrifice of Gideon at Ophrah and the building of an altar there (Judg. 6:19–24), of the sacrifice of Manoah (Judg. 13:19–20), and of periodic sacrifices at Shiloh (1 Sam. 1:3f.; 2:13). Communal sacrifice was offered by Samuel (1 Sam. 9:12f.); "all Israel" is said to have offered sacrifices at Bethel (Judg. 20:26) and Shechem (Josh. 8:31), although both these passages are admittedly of dubious historical value. It is also significant that sacrifices are reported to have played an important role in the covenant ceremony at Sinai (Exod. 24:5). But in respect to these things, Israel was just like other nations, and the whole practice of sacrifice is probably an inheritance from the Canaanites insofar as it is not simply a part of tribal customs that go back to immemorial antiquity.[4] So we can safely leave any discussion of the philosophy of sacrifice to a later period when the sacrificial element had become more central to Israel's religion and had been reinterpreted in terms of her unique faith.

What was distinctive of Israel at this period was presumably the formal recitation of the acts of Yahweh and the reading of the law, with the accompanying blessings and curses for obedience and disobedience. In accordance with the mentality of ancient times, a cultic recital of this kind would not have been seen as a mere pedagogical exercise; the recounting of God's acts would not have been considered only a lesson in ancient history, nor would the recital of the law have been merely a declaration on behalf of an absentee deity. As Mowinckel has persuasively argued,[5] ancient cult was always realistic; it was not merely subjective in its effect, but was regarded as objectively efficacious. The recitation of God's acts in the past would have been considered an effective means of gathering up the present generation into full participation in those saving events; what had happened once now happened again and became contemporary with those who heard the recital (Deut. 5:2f.). So the proclamation of the divine law by his chosen representative would have been heard as actually proceeding from God's lips. The ancient worshiper did not approach the cultus primarily to feed his intellect or stimulate an act of mental recollection; his purpose was to achieve actual participation in the events portrayed and existential involvement in the blessings proclaimed.

What such a ceremony would have meant, therefore, was that Yahweh himself appeared in the assembly, performing once again the mighty acts that brought the community into existence and continually sustained it, proclaiming anew his *torah* —the way of life that he had ordained for it—dispensing the blessings and curses that were connected with its observance or nonobservance, and personally accepting from his priests the sacrifices that were offered in his honor and for his pleasure.

The second period in the history of the cultus was that of the monarchy, when the erection of a permanent temple, built and furnished according to foreign models and closely connected with the interests and fortunes of the ruling dynasty, provided a new focus for Israel's worship, and to some extent altered both its character and its spirit. Whether or not the recital of

Yahweh's mighty acts and the proclamation of his law—which, as we have seen, were possibly the most distinctive features of the cult in the days of the tribal confederacy—continued to be important elements in the temple cult is difficult to say, for lack of direct evidence. But it seems probable that they did continue in some form; and psalms like 50 and 81, with their dramatic picture of a divine theophany and proclamation, may reflect a temple ceremony of this kind, although their date, like that of most of the psalms, is uncertain. Many scholars think there continued to be a regular festival of "covenant renewal," [6] but this, if it existed at all, had certainly lost its significance by the time of Josiah, for the whole account of Josiah's reform suggests that the king was reviving a way of life and worship that had long been neglected (2 Kings 23:22). The natural tendency under the monarchy was in the direction of emphasizing the unity of the nation, and suppressing any reminders, cultic or otherwise, that Israel was merely a confederation of tribes.

Whatever ceremonies may have survived from the time of the tribal confederation, there can be no doubt that the construction of the temple and the growing importance of the complex of ideas connected with the Zion-David covenant caused the emphasis in the cult to shift from the recitation of saving history and the proclamation of law to three other features as the main centers of interest. There was, first of all, a new importance attached to the regular offering of sacrifice; then a new concern with the temple itself as the visible sign of Yahweh's dwelling among his people and the unique focal point from which his power ceaselessly radiated for the benefit of the nation; and finally a profound concern with the figure of the king as the mediator of Yahweh's saving strength.

The new importance attached to *sacrifice* is shown by the magnitude of the sacrifices said to have been offered at the dedication of the temple (1 Kings 8:63f.). One may assume that there were daily sacrifices, offered morning and evening, just as in the postexilic temple (Exod. 29:38–42), and that the essence of worship was seen to consist in the unfailing performance of this duty. The sacrifices were conceived to be pleasing to God and were regularly "accepted" by him at the hands of his priests. How important the routine of sacrifice had become can be seen from certain passages in the prophets which accuse the people of putting too much confidence in it. Isaiah represents God as saying to his people on some cultic occasion, "What to me is the multitude of your sacrifices? . . . I have had enough of burnt offerings of rams and the fat of fed beasts" (Isa. 1:11; cf. Ps. 50:8).

It is instructive to see that neither priest nor reforming prophet had any doubt that Yahweh was present and active during the temple cult. The priests believed he was there to accept the sacrifices complaisantly; the prophets declared that, in certain circumstances, he came only to repudiate them because of the unworthiness of his worshipers. Ps. 50, in prophetic style, pictures him as suddenly appearing during the temple ceremonies to reject the offerings of the congregation (vv. 8–13) and condemn the people for neglecting his ethical commands (vv. 16–21; cf. Isa. 1:12–17).

The *temple* itself was a central item in the cult of the monarchical period, because the temple was understood to be "the house of God" in a quite literal sense; as Solomon says in his dedicatory prayer, "I have built thee an exalted house, a place for thee to dwell in for ever" (1 Kings 8:13). Yahweh was now believed to have taken up residence in the midst of his people; he was immediately accessible to their prayers and was available to act on their behalf in times of emergency (Pss. 20:2; 46:4f.; 48:1–3; 134:3; 135:21). As we see from Jer. 7:4, this conviction was so strong that it degenerated into the superstition that Yahweh would always intervene to save Jerusalem simply because his house was there.[7]

And, finally, the period of the monarchy saw the *king* standing in a special way at the focus of the cult. He could sometimes act the part of a priest, as Solomon did. But most important was the fact that Yahweh was believed to have chosen him as his own agent—his "son" (Pss. 2:7; 89:26f.; cf. 2 Sam. 7:14)—to perform his saving acts. Every king was seen as potentially like David, who had delivered his people from Philistine dominion and made Israel a great nation by the power of Yahweh. The promise of divine favor, so brilliantly realized in David, was never again fulfilled, but throughout the whole monarchical period the king, in Judah, as David's legitimate descendant and bearer of an inherited *mana* which was confirmed at his consecration, stood at the head of the worshipers in the temple as a tangible sign of Yahweh's continuing favor and saving potency. All through this period touching prayers, like Ps. 72, were offered on the king's behalf, asking that he might be to his people "like the rain that falls on the mown grass, like showers that water the earth" (Ps. 72:6), and that the benediction emanating from his presence might support the nation and lead it to ever greater prosperity and power.[8]

The third period in the history of Israel's cult is that of the postexilic community and the rituals associated with the temple of Zerubbabel.[9] This is the period we know most about, for its regulations have been largely preserved for us in the priestly parts of the Pentateuch, in Exodus, Leviticus and Numbers. Most of the rituals are probably identical with those of the temple of Solomon, and the scribes of the exile have merely preserved and partly systematized them. The king, of course, was gone, and the mystical feelings that had formerly been connected with his person were more and more transferred to an ideal figure in the future. But the temple still was there and Yahweh had again taken up his abode in it, although men now preferred rather to speak of the presence of his "Glory" (Exod. 40:34f.; later, "the Shekinah") rather than to say crudely that *he* was there. Cut off from all association with political life now that the monarchy was gone, the temple became of even greater spiritual significance than it had been before the exile. Pilgrims came from all parts of the world to visit it (see e.g., Ps. 107:2f.) and offer their prayers (Isa. 56:7), and in the daily round of worship sacrifice was offered for the universal fellowship of Israel as well as for the needs of the local community.

The principal changes in the postexilic cult as compared with the days of the monarchy are probably these two: First, its rituals were infused with a more somber feeling, a new sense of the omnipresence of sin and punishment. The old cult had been basically a joyous one, as one can see from Deuteronomy (Deut. 12:12; 14:26, etc.), but the devastating experience of the exile had brought in an atmosphere of gloom, symbolized by a new emphasis on "sin-" and "trespass-offerings" (Lev. 4:1–7:7) and the elevation of the Day of Atonement to a climactic position in the liturgical year (Lev. 16). God's action was seen, therefore, with a new intensity, as directed primarily toward the removal of sin and its consequences from the life of the community.

The other, and much more significant, change, was the explicit incorporation of the priestly sacrificial system, with all its detailed regulations, into the covenant of Sinai. Whereas, before the exile, the laws of the cult had probably been for the most part simply traditional rules connected with a particular sanctuary and frequently inherited from pre-Israelite times, they were now regarded as part of the law that Yahweh had revealed to Moses on the sacred mountain. While in some ways this may appear an unfortunate development, since it seems to attach a disproportionate importance to a multitude of ceremonial minutiae, in other ways it represents enormous progress, because it deprives the whole body of ritual and ceremonial practices of magical significance. From this time forward, no priestly rite could be regarded as having efficacy or value in itself. Whatever power it had was not inherent in the act, but only in the will of God who commanded that it be done. The sacrificial system and all the incidental rites connected with it were now understood to be simply means of grace (to use the terminology of the Christian sacraments) which God had appointed to be used. Scrupulous attention to every detail of a ceremony, under this new way of seeing things, had nothing in common with the fear of the wizard that his trick might not work if he used unorthodox material or pronounced a word incorrectly; it was, instead, merely a symbolic act of obedience, inspired by gratitude and love. God had commanded that certain effects were to be achieved by the performance of certain rituals; obviously God was not compelled to do it that way, but since that was the way he chose to have it done, it was incumbent on those who served and honored him to pay meticulous attention to the rules he had given. While the priestly system presented obvious dangers and could under some circumstances lead to a picayune kind of legalism, the spirit that animated it was admirable and thoroughly in accord with both common sense and Israel's ancient faith.

The chief value of the cult in every period of Israel's history, however much the particular rites and ceremonies may have changed with changing times, was in maintaining the sense that Yahweh was no absentee deity, living in heaven or on some far-off mountain peak, or only active long ago in the saving events that created the nation. The presence of the temple and the constant routine of the cult were inescapable reminders that he was a living presence in the midst of Israel, still blessing the righteous, cursing the disobedient, and using contemporary means to save, strengthen and sustain his people. The continuing sense of God's daily activity in the cult provided a necessary background for the insistence of the prophets and the wise men that God was not only presently active in forms of worship, but in the interplay of secular forces as well.[10]

Prophecy and International History

It has been argued with considerable cogency that the prophets were also connected with the cult, at least in origin.[11] This is a very complicated question, particularly since one cannot be sure that the word "prophet" in the Old Testament always refers to the same kind of person. It is not impossible that its precise sense came eventually to be weakened so that it meant hardly more than "inspired religious leader." [12] But, without inquiring into the meaning of the name and how it was used, it is obvious that, while some prophets like Amos and Jeremiah seem to stand largely outside the cult and are critical of it, others, like the early prophets in Samuel, seem to be directly connected with it; and it seems likely, furthermore, that there is a real historical connection between these two groups, although the connection can no longer be traced in detail.

The earliest prophets were associated with sanctuaries, and by their ecstatic behavior showed themselves to be "men of God," possessed by his spirit and hence of his power (1 Sam. 10:5f., 10–13). Their chief social function was presumably that of pronouncing a blessing on the undertakings of the king and the people and a curse on their enemies (e.g., 1 Kings 22:6), such "blessing" and "cursing" being understood to have effective power and not to be merely an empty expression of good will or personal antipathy. These were the ancestors of the so-called false prophets of later times, though one must remember that the adjective is prejudiced and must be understood in the light of a particular historical situation; even the greatest of the prophets also sometimes functioned in this way, especially when they pronounced curses on Israel's enemies (e.g., Amos 1:3–2:3; Isa. 10:5–19). It may be that the line of demarcation between the professional, cultic prophets, and the great reforming prophets, is to be drawn at the point where some prophets within the cult began, like Micaiah (1 Kings 22:17) and Amos (Amos 2:6ff.), to pronounce curses rather than blessings upon Israel herself. This would lead, of course, to the alienation of these prophets from their fellows and, to some extent, from the cult. Since we know so little about the background of the re-forming prophets, such a view as this can be only hypothetical, but it seems more plausible than any which makes the reforming prophet an altogether different kind of person from the prophets of the sanctuary.

This brief account of the possible origins of classical Hebrew prophecy may be useful in providing a background for the discussion of the prophetic understanding of God's activity in the world of their day, since, if true, it would serve to minimize the gulf between the prophetic and the cultic. If the prophet, like the priest, originally functioned within the cult, then the new element in classical, reformist prophecy was simply the diversion of the power of God that was inherent in the cult primarily into the channel of cursing rather than of blessing. In any case, there can be no doubt that the belief that God was present and active in the temple cult prepared the nation to accept the assertion that he was also active on a larger stage and in a less comforting role.

Although the origin of classical prophecy may be found within the cult, the center of interest of the great prophets was certainly elsewhere. As we meet them in the pages of the prophetic books, they have become independent figures, active under the direct inspiration—as they believed—of God himself, concerned with the whole moral life of Israel and with her relationship to the larger world outside. That there should have been such a succession of religious and ethical teachers in one nation, lasting over a span of nearly three hundred years, is a miracle and mystery second only to that of Israel herself. In a sense it is only an aspect of the larger mystery, for the teaching of the prophets is Israel's most significant contribution to the thought of the world, the most striking manifestation of the intellectual vitality that, in every generation, proceeds from the spiritual vitality within her.

The prophetic sphere of interest was the political and social life of the nation. But the prophets' largeness of mind is shown by the fact that they were concerned not only with the life of Israel, but with the life of the world. However close their original connection may have been with the cult, and however much they may have used cultic language, and literary forms derived from Israel's covenant with Yahweh, it is evident that they had an incipient apprehension of the existence of a universal moral law under the dominion of a universal God. This point of view appears in striking form in the opening chapters of Amos—the first, chronologically, of the prophetic books—which contain a series of denunciations against various of Israel's neighbors, culminating in a denunciation of Israel herself. All of them are based upon an identical predicate, that God does not tolerate the inhuman treatment of men by men. The God who will punish Israel for her "three transgressions . . . and for four" is the same God who is going to punish the Syrians, the Philistines, the Ammonites and the Moabites for the same offenses.

Where the prophets got this breadth of vision is not entirely certain, but particular factors undoubtedly played a role. Perhaps most basic was the growing power of Assyria, the first real world empire, which helped to break down parochial viewpoints, and led thoughtful minds to begin thinking in world terms rather than purely national ones. The chronological coincidence of the growth of Assyria with the rise of the prophetic movement can hardly be purely coincidental. But one must not discount the growing importance also of the creation faith in Israel, which was certainly associated in a special way with the Jerusalem temple and its cosmic symbolism. Isaiah's temple vision, in which he saw "the King," whose glory fills "the whole earth" (Isa. 6:3–5), is relevant evidence in this direction. The sense of Yahweh's universal sway over the created order naturally led to an increased feeling for his concern with the life of *mankind* rather than merely the life of Israel, a point of view that becomes explicit in Second Isaiah, but was already present in germ in the earlier prophets. Another phenomenon that undoubtedly bore some relation to the rise of universalistic interests in the prophets was the spread of the Wisdom movement, which had begun in the time of Solomon, and no doubt became increasingly influential during the period of the later monarchy; as we shall see later in the chapter, this was a movement explicitly concerned with truths that were understood to be universal rather than merely national.[13]

However we explain the origin of the peculiar prophetic point of view, our chief concern here is with the remarkable fact that the classical prophets—from Amos onward—saw the present activity of God as chiefly evident in the movement of nations and their interlocking roles in the drama of world history. In this respect the prophets stand very close to the heart of Israel's theology, for her faith from the beginning had been centered in the thought that Israel's election was an act in history, a significant moment in a series of historical events. What the prophets added to this was the declaration that Yahweh's concerns are far larger than Israel's election faith might have led her to suppose. The fact is stated with brutal clarity by the first of the canonical prophets. It is true, says Amos, that Yahweh "knows" Israel alone out of all the families of the earth, but this concentration of his interest is no reason for self-congratulation, since it means merely that he is more alert to notice and punish Israel's iniquities (Amos 3:2). Furthermore, if he once saved Israel from Egypt and brought her to the Promised Land, is it not also true that he performed a similar favor for the Philistines in bringing them from Caphtor and for the Syrians by bringing them from Kir (Amos 9:7)? Although Amos is temperamentally more prosaic in style and more pragmatic in interests than Second Isaiah, the God of whom he speaks is already, in effect, the universal Lord of history, shaping the destiny of nations in accord with his own sovereign will.

In the time of the eighth-century prophets, Israel was already being forced to take an interest in the events of international history. It was the special service of the prophets to interpret the meaning of these events and show how they were all manifestations of the universal rule of Yahweh. If the analogy did not suggest the trivial, the prophets might be compared to newspaper, radio and television commentators of our own day, whose function is to set reported events in a larger context and interpret them in terms of the great movements of the age. The only basic difference is that the context of the prophets was a theological one and the interpretation was in terms of God's moral character and ultimate purpose. In a later chapter we shall see how this kind of interpretation led at length to a developed theory about the direction in which history was moving and the end it must finally attain. Perhaps there is more of this forward look in the prophets of the eighth and seventh centuries than has usually been conceded, but a superficial reading of their books certainly leaves the impression that their overwhelming concern was not with the eschatology of a remote future, but rather with contemporary events and conditions and with the future that would immediately grow out of them.

It was evident to everyone that the Assyrians were on the march, but it took an Isaiah to see that they were only "the rod of [God's] anger, the staff of [his] fury" (Isa. 10:5), and to assert that their advance against Israel was no historical accident, but part of a quite specific plan of Yahweh to punish her for the misuse of her privileges. The Assyrians, in their turn, were to be punished for the arrogance with which they discharged their mission (vv. 12–16). At a later date, another prophet would call Nebuchadrezzar, the Babylonian king, Yahweh's "servant," appointed by a divine decree to carry out the sentence of punishment against Jerusalem (Jer. 25:9). Jeremiah could even represent Yahweh himself as fighting alongside the Babylonian armies as they laid siege to the Holy City (Jer. 21:5).

Yahweh's control of history was not, however, merely to punish, but also to bless, when blessing was what the situation called for. This appears in classical form in Second Isaiah, where the prophet of the exile sees Cyrus, the founder of the Persian empire, as the "anointed" of Yahweh, called to free Israel from captivity in Babylon and to rebuild Jerusalem and the temple (Isa. 44:28–45:1). It was Second Isaiah who transformed the pragmatic belief that Yahweh controls significant historical events into a comprehensive philosophy of history, declaring that God has been using history from the beginning for the realization of a plan, and has revealed to his prophets the secrets of it:

> . . . I am God and there is none like me
> declaring the end from the beginning
>   and from ancient times things not yet done,
> saying, "My counsel shall stand,
>   and I will accomplish all my purpose." [Isa. 46:9f.]

It is impossible to exaggerate the importance of the prophetic expansion of Israel's belief in the continuing activity of her God. It was they, even more than the wise men, who showed that Yahweh's day-to-day activity is not restricted to the cult, the sphere of things narrowly called "religious," but is just as evident in the affairs of the so-called secular world, in the social life of nations, in wars and military alliances, and that it is he who determines the pattern to be formed by the interwoven political and military forces of national and international history.

Wisdom and the Moral Law

The third area in which the men of ancient Israel saw God presently at work was the daily life of individuals. Here for the first time we find an aspect of Israelite faith in which the concept of "Israel" is not central. By definition, the idea of Israel is corporate, and concern with the Israelite community in its corporate relationship to Yahweh is of the very essence of Old Testament theology. Yahweh's work in the past had been seen in the salvation and befriending of the community; the existence of the community was predicated on belief in its special relationship to a particular God who chose to be called "the God of Israel." In his present activity in the cult, it was the community which stood in his presence and toward which he condescended in instruction and blessing; and in the prophetic understanding of God's work his activity was seen in the employment of secular historical forces either to punish Israel for violating her obligations, or to open for her the path into a better future. Generally speaking, priestly and prophetic religion had little to say to *individual* Israelites about the conduct of their own lives, so long as they kept free of grosser violations of the moral law.

Since the major part of any man's life, in the ancient as in the modern world, is taken up with his relation to other men in ordinary social and economic life rather than in activities of the cult and international politics, it was fortunate that there was a group in Israel which asserted that God was active there also. This was the circle of the so-called wise men who produced the biblical books of Proverbs, Ecclesiastes and Job. But their books present a special problem. Their point of view is so different from anything else in the Old Testament that scholars have frequently looked upon them as a foreign entity that really had no place there. All that we have seen to be distinctive of Israel's religion—the sense of history, of community, the practices of the cult—is absent from the Wisdom books, and in its place is a concentration on the life of the individual Israelite—or better, the individual man—and the way in which he can attain his ambitions and find happiness in his personal life. Furthermore, the prescriptions that are given seem to owe nothing to Israelite thought, but are simply borrowed from foreign nations that had been thinking of these particular problems long before Israel was born.[14]

It would be a mistake, however, to think of the Wisdom Literature as really extraneous to the Old Testament. Something would be gravely lacking in the thought of ancient Israel if she had found nothing to say about the ordering of normal human life within the larger framework of the elect community. Faith in the election doctrine could sustain Israel's group life, and was no doubt a frequent source of pride and inspiration for individuals, but it was not sufficient to provide strength and guidance for the average Israelite in determining his personal goals, performing the small tasks and making the small decisions that are the major concerns of life as we know it. Instruction in these matters had to be given in Israel as in every other civilized society.

Israel, in the course of time, like ancient Greece, was to develop a system of education, her *paideia* (Heb. *musar*), and it was in the hands of the men who were called, collectively, "the wise." In the beginning, this system of education was only for the upper classes, as has been everywhere the case until quite recently, and was designed to prepare young men for service in the state and in large-scale commercial enterprise. But with the passage of time, the teaching of the wise men spread out from the schools and became to a considerable extent the property also of the common man; this process of "democratization" of Wisdom was probably more extensive in Israel than in any other ancient oriental country.

A brief survey of the early history of the Wisdom movement will help to show its position in the life and thought of the nation. It almost certainly began in the reign of Solomon, as tradition hints. Solomon's new imperial state had need for well-trained men to staff the bureaucracy that such a state requires, men who could read and write and who knew something at least of the elementary principles of statecraft. There were, of course, no such men in Israel, since the conditions of life in the old tribal confederacy did not require them, and even in the busy days when David's kingdom was taking shape, skill at arms had been still the principal requirement in a courtier. So Solomon had to go outside Israel to get teachers who could prepare his own young men to serve in a well-ordered, peaceful, civilized, "modern" state. Egypt, which was nearby and with which he had close personal ties, had a long tradition of culture and statesmanship, so it was to Egypt that he probably turned for help in developing his own schools for training secretaries, diplomats, and civil administrators, schools which, like their Egyptian models, were not limited to instructing their students in such basic skills as reading and writing, but were also interested in developing their personalities so that they might fit into the structure of a stable, conservative society without strain upon either themselves or others. Collections of maxims useful for this kind of instruction existed in Egypt (as also in Babylon) and some have survived to the present day.[15] They would have been copied by the students in order to develop facility at reading and writing, and at the same time would have been studied and memorized. Some of this material was brought to Israel in the days of Solomon, one may suppose, but down to the very end of the monarchy new collections probably continued to be introduced for reading and imitation.[16] Naturally, around this borrowed literature as a nucleus, there began to grow up a body of native Israelite "Wisdom" Literature which could be used for the same purpose and which dealt with more specifically Israelite conditions. It was from such collections as these that the typical Wisdom book, the Book of "Proverbs," eventually developed. For our present purpose we need consider only this one book, since Ecclesiastes and Job, although firmly rooted in the tradition of Wisdom, are eccentric in character and represent an intellectual reaction against some of its basic presuppositions.

The fact that Wisdom is a borrowed form in Israel helps to explain, of course, the fact that the Wisdom Literature seems so different from anything else in the Old Testament. But the fact that it is different does not mean that it is in any way incompatible with the rest. The rules that it teaches are, for the most part, simply the rules of cultivated common sense and are no more incompatible with the religion of Israel than with any other high religion. Certainly Christians do not feel that the Golden Rule and the principle that "whatsoever a man soweth that shall he also reap" are inconsistent with Christian theology just because they cannot be derived directly from it and are as a matter of fact included also among the ethical maxims of a number of other great religions. In the same way those who sat at the feet of the wise men and learned the basic principles of the moral life felt in no way alienated from Israel and its election faith.

In the long run, though, the wise men were not content to leave their teaching in this unassimilated form, forever unconnected by any vital link with Israel's historic faith. The gradual and deliberate "nationalizing" of Wisdom is the most significant phenomenon in the whole history of the Wisdom movement, and affords impressive evidence of the vigor and absorptive power of Israelite religion.

Even in Egypt, the teaching of the wise men was never limited to the communication of separate pragmatically useful rules of life. The separate rules were believed to be only partial manifestations of a universal order of *maat,* the order of the "right" and the "true," and the wise man was the one who had learned to conform his life in all particulars to this order.[17] In Israel, this universal order was simply called Wisdom, spelled—so to speak—with a capital letter, as in the many sayings in the Book of Proverbs where Wisdom by itself is commended or glorified without reference to any particular rules or sets of rules. So the sage can say:

> My son, eat honey, for it is good,
> and the drippings of the honeycomb are sweet to your taste.

> Know that wisdom is such to your soul;
>   if you find it, there will be a future,
>   and your hope will not be cut off. [PROV. 24:13f.]

But the Wisdom teacher in Israel ultimately went one step further and declared that this universal order of Wisdom had been created by Yahweh the God of Israel, and that it was his power that activated it. Sometimes this order was represented as acting in an almost impersonal way, bringing blessing and success to those who conformed to it and retribution to those who dared to oppose it, but this impersonal conception is probably just a reflection of the pagan source from which the idea was originally borrowed.[18] The wise men of Israel more characteristically represented Yahweh himself as directly active in the moral process, and in any case thought of him as the one who set the order in motion.

The most explicit statement of the view that Yahweh was the source of the moral order is the remarkable poem in Prov. 8:22–31, where Wisdom is represented as poetically describing her own origins.

> Yahweh created me at the beginning of his work,
>   the first of his acts of old.
> Ages ago I was set up,
>   at the first, before the beginning of the earth.
>   . . . .
>   then was I beside him, like a master workman;
> and I was daily his delight,
>   rejoicing before him always,
> rejoicing in his inhabited world
>   and delighting in the sons of men.

There is serious question as to whether the word translated "master workman" should not better be rendered "little child," thus attributing to Wisdom a merely passive role rather than an active one in the drama of creation,[19] but the discussion is irrelevant to our present purpose, which is merely to show how in later Hebrew thought Yahweh himself came to be regarded as the creator of the wise order by which the wicked are punished, the good rewarded, and the moral life becomes also the happy and successful one. This view is obviously an over-simple one, and came under the severe criticism of such rebel spirits as the authors of Ecclesiastes and Job, but it is certainly preferable even on theoretical grounds to the moral nihilism that is its opposite, and has the enormous practical importance of making men conscious of the relevance of moral values and belief in God to the entire conduct of life. Religion, in this view, shows men not only how to behave when they come into God's presence in the sanctuary, or how the total structure of their society should conform to a divine pattern, but also how they should conduct themselves day by day in the ordering of their business and social life.

The way in which the wise men conceived of God as active in the common life is shown by the following quotations:

> The eyes of Yahweh are in every place,
>   keeping watch on the evil and the good.   [PROV. 15:3]

> Yahweh's curse is on the house of the wicked,
>   but he blesses the abode of the righteous.   [PROV. 3:33]

> Do not rob the poor, because he is poor,
>   neither oppress the afflicted at the gate:
> for Yahweh will plead their cause
>   and despoil of life those who despoil them.   [PROV. 22:22f.]

> If your enemy is hungry, give him bread to eat;
>   And if he is thirsty, give him water to drink;
> For you will heap coals of fire on his head,
>   and Yahweh will reward you.   [PROV. 25:21f.]

Agree with God, and be at peace,
  thereby good will come to you.

. . . .

For God abases the proud,
  but he saves the lowly.
He delivers the innocent man;
  you will be delivered through the cleanness of your hands.

[ELIPHAZ in JOB 22:21, 29f.]

Trust in Yahweh, and do good;
  so you will dwell in the land, and enjoy security.
Take delight in Yahweh,
  and he will give you the desires of your heart.
Commit your way to Yahweh;
  trust in him and he will act.
He will bring forth your vindication as the light,
  and your right as the noonday.   [Ps. 37:3–6]

The finest expression of the wise men's philosophy in the Old Testament is the story of Joseph, which has been shown unmistakably to belong to the Wisdom Literature, even though it is now embedded in the narrative of Genesis.[20] Its hero is the ideal pupil of the wise men who, through his keen understanding of the course of events and the means necessary for dealing with them, attains to the highest administrative office in the state, sustained all the way by his purity, loyalty and patience, and by a spirit of forgiving love toward those who had wronged him. When, at the end, having come safely through many hazards and been reunited with his family, he speaks in the purest accents of the wise men when he says to his brothers, ". . . you meant evil against me; but God meant it for good" (Gen. 50:20). For the wise men, God's work was to be seen not only in his mighty acts of old, or in the splendor of the temple services, or in the clash of armies on the battlefields of history, but in his quiet control of the forces that are everywhere at work to frustrate the evil and promote the good. It was part of his wonderful work to give a full and satisfying life to those who sought after Wisdom and walked in her ways.

Israel's knowledge of God would have been seriously defective if she had not known that he was active in this way also.

Summary

At the beginning of this chapter an attempt was made to show that these three ways of understanding the present activity of God—those of the priests, the prophets and the wise men—were not three competing "religions" but simply the views of men who had different functions to perform in the community of Israel, and therefore naturally saw different aspects of the truth. This unity of faith is shown most clearly in the Psalter, a book of hymns compiled primarily for cultic use which, nevertheless, contains contributions from all three groups.

Ps. 37, for example, from which we have just quoted, is a pure Wisdom psalm from beginning to end. The whole psalm merely repeats in constantly varied language the thought of the opening verses:

> Fret not yourself because of the wicked,
> > be not envious of wrongdoers!
> For they will soon fade like the grass,
> > and wither like the green herb.
> Trust in Yahweh, and do good. . . . [Ps. 37:1–3]

Just a little later in the book come Pss. 42–43, actually a single poem in three stanzas, centered entirely on the temple and its cult, a psalm whose point of view is purely "priestly":

> These things I remember,
> > as I pour out my soul:

> how I went with the throng,
>   and led them in procession to the house of God,
> with glad shouts and songs of thanksgiving,
>   a multitude keeping festival. [Ps. 42:4]

The psalmist prays the God who dwells in the temple to command some guiding and protecting power to lead his faithful devotee to Jerusalem and the shrine:

> Oh send out thy light and thy truth;
>   let them lead me,
> let them bring me to thy holy hill
>   and to thy dwelling! [Ps. 43:3]

And yet a third psalmist, the author of Ps. 50, talks with the accents of a prophet and speaks, if not in terms of a God who operates through foreign armies, at least of a God who comes in judgment rather than to bless, a God who has no real need for the ordinances of the cult:

> For every beast of the forest is mine,
>   the cattle on a thousand hills.
>
>   . . . .
>
> Do I eat the flesh of bulls,
>   or drink the blood of goats? [Ps. 50:10, 13]

His God, like the God of an Amos or a Jeremiah, can say,

> What right have you to recite my statutes,
>   or take my covenant upon your lips?
> For you hate discipline,
>   and cast my words behind you. [Ps. 50:16f.]

The citizen of ancient Israel who habitually listened to the temple choirs singing such a variety of songs from the official hymnal certainly was not conscious of any basic incompatibility in the teaching of the wise man, the priest and the prophet. All were speaking of the same God, and they believed that he was a living God who was active still in every phase of his people's life, in the home and shop as well as in the temple, and in the strange, threatening movements of foreign armies.

5

DIGRESSION: GOD AND THE NATURAL WORLD

Who makest the winds thy messengers, fire and flame thy ministers.

PSALM 104:4

ANCIENT ISRAEL was chiefly concerned with God's action in history, that is in the world of human affairs, rather than with his relation to nature. This is indeed one of the most striking points of contrast between Israel and her pagan neighbors, since for paganism the activity of the gods in nature was the point of primary concern. The gods of Canaan were, to a large extent, gods of fertility who had control over the forces that make soil and herds productive; the prosperity of an agricultural and pastoral community was dependent upon their power and continuing good will. Religion consisted in offering to those gods gifts that would make them friendly, and in performing rites of sympathetic magic, particularly of a sexual nature, that were believed to increase the potency of the natural forces which the gods controlled and with which they were often identified.

The religion of Israel stood almost diametrically opposite to this whole complex of ideas and interests. Yahweh was not a god of nature, but a God of the human community—the God of Abraham, Isaac and Jacob. He was in no way identified with the world of nature, but was increasingly understood to be nature's Lord. When the Israelites first came into the land of Canaan, this kind of theology presented a real problem for them, since it was difficult for them to see the bearing of their communal faith on daily life, where they were more and more occupied with agricultural activities which, traditionally, were none of Yahweh's concern. Consequently, many Israelites simply accepted the cult of the fertility gods—the Baals and the Ashtaroth, as the Bible calls them (Judges 2:13, etc.)—who were the ancient gods of the land. They continued of course, to look to Yahweh as God of the Israelite community, and sought his aid especially in time of war or other national crisis. It was not for many generations that Israel learned that it was not the Baals, but Yahweh himself "who gave her the grain, the wine, and the oil" (Hos. 2:8), and that an accurate knowledge of the best methods of agriculture is not necessarily something alien to Israel's religion, but "also comes from the Lord of hosts" who "is wonderful in counsel, and excellent in wisdom" (Isa. 28:29).

Yahweh's relationship to the world of nature was, therefore, originally peripheral to Israel's main theological interests. As we have already seen, the principal question that Israel asked was not "Who created this wonderful world in which we find ourselves?" but "Who is the author of this unique community to which we belong?" It was not in the daily operation of the forces of nature that the Israelite primarily saw the hand of God, but in his wonderful works of old on behalf of his people. Nature was not a window through which one could see God at work, even though the heavens might tell his glory and the firmament his handiwork (Ps. 19:1); it was, rather, a wall that stood between man and God, a world of reality controlled by God but not identical with him nor inhabited by him. Although the Bible can say "the whole earth is full of his glory" (Isa. 6:3), one must remember that Yahweh's "glory" was simply the bright light that issued from his presence. Like the light of the sun that shines on the hills after the sun has set, the divine brightness the Israelite saw in the natural world was only the reflection of a reality that was itself beyond, and outside of, visible nature.

Nevertheless, as we have seen, Israel had moved on from the thought of Yahweh as the Creator and Lord of Israel to the conviction that he was also Creator and Lord of the visible world. She knew that he had a relationship to that world, and she had, or developed, means of expressing the nature of that relationship. For the most part there was nothing unique in Israel's understanding of the cosmos, and most of the theological conceptions she used to explain God's relation to it were part of an inherited pattern of ideas she shared with the rest of the ancient world. The ideas we are now going on to discuss are not so much essential and distinctive elements in the theology of the Old Testament as they are common ideas, drawn from a larger cultural milieu, which Israel adopted—and often strikingly *adapted*—to fill out some empty spaces in her own distinctive theological framework.

The Idea of Nature; Miracles

The word "nature," which we have used repeatedly and which can hardly be avoided in a discussion of this kind, is of course one that is foreign to ancient oriental thought, biblical or otherwise. In modern Western thought, "nature" is an autonomous realm of being that operates under the rule of automatic laws that do not depend directly and constantly on separate acts

of divine volition. Religious men think of nature as created by
God and dependent upon him, but, at least for practical purposes, they do not conceive of him as directly responsible for
the details of its operation. In a sense, nature is like a mechanism
that has been set in motion and must not be interfered with
afterward.

It is this conception of an independent world of nature that
creates many of the problems of the modern theologian, the
whole problem of the "miraculous" and the "super"-natural. If
nature is the kind of autonomous realm we implicitly assume it
to be, it is hard to believe that God would ever interfere with its
independent operations, and, if so, where, when, and *why?*
There was no such problem for men of biblical times, since
biblical man had no such conception as that of "nature." When
men of ancient Israel used the word "miracle," i.e., "wonder,"
as they frequently did (Exod. 3:20; Ps. 77:14; Dan. 4:3, etc.),
they were not thinking of acts that contravened the "laws" of
nature, but merely of acts that aroused a sense of wonder in the
eyes of the beholder, acts that seemed to show in a remarkable,
unmistakable way the power or character of God. Such acts
were often, but not always, unique or unusual; sometimes they
were quite normal occurrences that nevertheless seemed to
provide special evidence of God's concern for his people (e.g.,
Ps. 107:8f.). The ancient Hebrew believed that God operated
with unhindered freedom, directing the world and the events
in it along whatever line he might choose; though he might
ordinarily work in a particular way, he might at any time decide
to do things differently. There were no "natural laws" that he
had either to follow or else deliberately to set aside.

The men of the Old Testament were aware, of course, of the
regularities of the natural world. On occasion they could speak
in explicit language of its general dependability, as when Noah
was told that "While the earth remains, seedtime and harvest,
cold and heat, summer and winter, day and night, shall not

cease" (Gen. 8:22), or when Jeremiah remarked on the un-varying recurrence of the migration of the birds (Jer. 8:7) and of God's "covenant with day and night and the ordinances of heaven and earth" (Jer. 33:25). In such expressions there is obviously an approach toward a more scientific way of looking at the world than that of primitive man, but even here the em-phasis is on the divine will which established the "covenant" with nature, and the personal character of the "ordinances." There is never any idea of an inexorable law in nature that works impersonally and merely automatically. Even an advanced thinker like Second Isaiah found it difficult to conceive of the nightly rising of the stars except in terms of the direct imposi-tion of Yahweh's will,

> Lift up your eyes on high and see:
> who created these?
> He who brings out their host by number,
> calling them all by name;
> by the greatness of his might,
> and because he is strong in power
> not one is missing. [ISA. 40:26]

The Universe

The universe of Old Testament man was definitely arranged in three stories, with the heaven (meaning merely the sky, pictured as a solid ceiling, a "firmament," and the mysteri-ous world that lies beyond it) above, the earth in the middle, and, below the earth, the dark underworld of Sheol, the abode of the dead and of the forces of chaos. This tripartite world, with its inhabitants assigned to their proper spheres, is reflected in one of the psalms:

> The *heavens* are the Lord's heavens,
> but the *earth* he has given to the sons of men.

The dead do not praise the Lord,
nor do any that go down into the *silence*.   [Ps. 115:16f.]

It is notable in this picture that Yahweh seems to be excluded
from Sheol, and this interpretation is confirmed by other passages, such as Ps. 6:5 and Isa. 38:18; even in a book as late as
Job it is possible to speak, with poetic license, of the underworld as being under the dominion of "the king of terrors"
(Job 18:14). It was only in later times that Sheol, too, was added
to Yahweh's realm with the result that another psalmist could
say it is no easier to escape God's presence by making one's bed
in Sheol than by ascending up to heaven (Ps. 139:8; cf. Amos
9:2). The final subjugation of Sheol, like the world of agriculture (see above, pp. 110f.), to Yahweh's dominion is remarkable
testimony to the overwhelming power and "jealousy" of Israel's
God, which ultimately could not tolerate leaving any area of
life outside his control.

Above the "firmament," the blue dome that stands over the
earth, was a vast reservoir of water (Gen. 1:7), in which or on
which Yahweh had built his heavenly palace (Ps. 104:3). When,
from time to time, God opened the windows in heaven, the
waters, as anyone could see, came tumbling down (Gen. 7:11).
There was also water under the earth (Exod. 20:4), which
usually came forth in gentle springs to fructify the soil. Actually,
though, the underground water, along with the great ocean and
the Mediterranean Sea, represented the subjugated waters of
chaos, which, if not kept under control, could come rushing up
destructively. Man's life was continually threatened by this
dark, seething, subterranean chaos (Ps. 69:1f., 14; Jon. 2:5f.),
as it was by the turbulent sea that hemmed him in, but Yahweh
usually kept the rebellious waters under strict discipline. Once,
on the day of creation, the chaotic waters had burst forth from
their underground habitat, as they were to do again at the time
of the flood (Gen. 7:11, "the fountains of the great deep burst
forth"), but Yahweh attacked them, drove them back and

hemmed them in, and declared, "Thus far shall you come, and no farther, and here shall your proud waves be stayed" (Job 38:8–11). The foreign origin of these conceptions, though never in doubt, has become even clearer as a result of the discovery of the Canaanite tablets from Ras Shamra, which tell of a similar battle between the god Baal and Prince Sea (*yamm*).[1]

Providence

It is Yahweh alone, in the developed thought of Israel, who, having created the world in the beginning, now sustains it and everything on it. Second Isaiah speaks of Yahweh,

> who created the heavens and stretched them out,
> who spread forth the earth and what comes from it,
> who gives breath to the people upon it
> and spirit to those who walk in it. . . .   [ISA. 42:5]

while Psalm 104 describes at considerable length the thoughtful provision God has made for all his creatures, the birds, the wild animals, the creatures of the sea, and man himself:

> These all look to thee,
> to give them their food in due season.
> .   .   .   .
> When thou hidest thy face, they are dismayed;
> when thou takest away their breath, they die
> and return to their dust.
> When thou sendest forth thy Spirit, they are created;
> and thou renewest the face of the ground.   [Ps. 104:27–30]

The last verse suggests that Old Testament man did not make such a sharp separation between God's act of creation and his continuing acts of providence as we are inclined to do, but rather saw the provision of daily needs as a part of a permanent process of world creation.[2]

Mediatorial Agencies: Angels,
Cherubim, Seraphim

Since God is not himself a power of nature, but is
over and above it and utterly different from it, by what means
can he operate upon it and how can he act within it? Ancient Israel could, of course, see the difficulty and, in doing so, had become faintly aware of a basic philosophical problem: how the infinite can have any relationship with the finite, how the eternal
can be implicated with the temporal, how the One can establish
contact with the many, how it is possible for the Holy and
Eternal God to deal with his contingent and temporal creation
without diminishing or compromising his own being. Naturally,
the ancient Israelite did not express himself in philosophical
language of this kind, but he was perfectly conscious of the gulf
between God and his creation—as were other peoples of the
ancient Near East—and sought ways to bridge it. Often, of
course, the problem does not come to the surface and the ancient
author is content to say with reference to some event merely that
God caused it to happen, as when in the days of the exodus, it
is said that "Yahweh hardened the heart of Pharaoh" (Exod.
14:8) or that he "discomfited the host of the Egyptians, clogging
their chariot wheels" (Exod. 14:24f.).

But in many instances the writer is more explicit and speaks
of some particular agency through which Yahweh accomplished
his purpose. After all, God has at his disposal all the forces of
the universe and can use any of them as instruments.[3] By using
intermediaries of this kind Yahweh could keep a distance between himself and creation and thus avoid too intimate, and
possibly too demeaning, a contact between himself and the lower
world. The psalm we have just been quoting addresses him as
one

who makest the winds thy messengers,
fire and flame thy ministers. [Ps. 104:4]

Yahweh has at his disposal an army of angels who will do whatever he tells them. The Hebrew word translated "angel" is merely the ordinary word for "messenger," as in the psalm above. The "angels" of the Old Testament apparently have the appearance of men, and are indistinguishable from them unless they choose to make themselves known by performing some unusual act. Certainly they have no wings. Although they are always there, available for God's service, the Old Testament is remarkably reticent about them, probably because they are really survivals of a polytheistic pantheon, now demoted to the status of servants and subordinate counselors of the one who alone is God. Apart from the latest of the biblical books, Daniel, they have no names, no personalities, no permanent functions, except for the one who is called the "adversary" (Heb. *satan*) of man, who acts as a kind of prosecuting attorney (Job 1:6; Zech. 3:1) and near the end of the Old Testament story develops into "Satan," the cosmic adversary of God (1 Chron. 21:1). The army of anonymous, faceless, shadowy messengers or "angels" whom Yahweh has at his beck and call is to be sharply distinguished from so-called "angel of the Lord" (Judg. 13:3 etc.), who is not an angel at all, but a transparent disguise for Yahweh himself (see below, p. 149).

Besides the "angels," the Old Testament also knows of other beings of the supratemporal world such as the cherubim, who sometimes have the function of standing guard over things that are *tabu* (Gen. 3:24; 1 Kings 6:23–28), and at other times act as a throne or means of celestial transport for Yahweh (1 Sam. 4:4; Ezek. 10:1–11:22). The cherubim, unlike the "angels," do have wings, and in their function of heavenly chariot are probably a personification of the storm wind (Ps. 18:10).[4] The Book of Isaiah also mentions the seraphim, who likewise have wings and are probably half human, half dragonlike in form (Isa 6:2); they are obviously survivals from Canaanite mythology. Both cherubim and seraphim are striking examples of how bits of harmless, undigested pagan conceptions could survive within the religion of Israel and enrich the texture of its imagery.

In the latest Old Testament period and to a far greater extent in the intertestamental period, the world of the angels about which the older literature had so little to say, became a center of interest for its own sake. Angels proliferated in number (note, for example, the 10,000 times 10,000 of Dan. 7:10) received proper names (Gabriel and Michael: Dan. 8:16; 10:13) and were given fixed hierarchical functions. This development was partly due to an increasing sense of the transcendence of God, who was thus connected with his world only by a chain of subordinate beings; it probably owed something also to foreign (specifically Persian) influence.

The Spirit

Of far greater theological importance than the idea of angels are three conceptions of a more abstract, philosophical character that also had their analogues in the theological ideas of other sophisticated nations of the ancient Near East: viz., the Spirit of God, the Word of God, and Wisdom.

The Spirit of God is a figure who appears in all stages of Israelite thought from the earliest to the latest. Since the Hebrew word translated spirit (*ruach*) is identical with the word for "wind" and with one of the words for "breath," it is evident that the conception of "Yahweh's Spirit" is ultimately based upon the simple physiological observation that a man's breath is a means by which he can operate at a distance (as, for example, in blowing dust off a tabletop); one then supposes that the storm-wind is simply the breath of an immensely stronger being, a god, which makes it possible for him to achieve the most powerful effects, such as blowing down trees and buildings, without moving from his place. This is not to suggest that the Spirit of God in the Old Testament is ever conceived quite so crudely as this, but simply to indicate the original source of the image, and to underline a significant and recurring fact—the association of the phenomena of the Spirit with wind and breath—in various passages concerned with the gift of the Spirit even in the New Testament (John 20:22; Acts 2:2-4; cf. Ezek. 37:9f., 14). The image of the Spirit—the wind or breath of God—provided the men of ancient Israel with a convenient, easily understood means of expressing certain modes of the divine activity, especially when there was a desire to introduce the thought of God's partial, but not exhaustive, communication of power in a particular situation for a particular purpose.

The essential note of the Spirit is the note of power. The Spirit of Yahweh comes upon men to enable them to do things that they otherwise could not do, like tearing a lion in pieces (Judg. 14:6), killing a thousand men (Judg. 15:14f.; cf. 3:10; 6:34, etc.), executing works of specially skillful craftsmanship (Exod. 31:3-5), or, in later times, exhibiting unusual steadfastness and strength of moral character (Pss. 51:10f.; 143:10). A special kind of power was the power to prophesy, meaning originally simply to act in weird, uncontrollable fashion (1 Sam. 10:10; 19:23f.), but in later, more sophisticated times, implying the ability to know what other men do not know and to enter into the mind of God (Mic. 3:8; Ezek. 8:3). In the beginning, and often later also, the Spirit of God acted unpredictably and only on particular occasions (see the references given above to the Book of Judges; cf. John 3:8), but, especially in later times, it could be understood as a permanent endowment (1 Sam. 16:13; Isa. 11:2). While the conception of the Spirit was usually reserved to explain exceptional powers, it could also be considered, particularly in the Wisdom tradition, as the universal vital impulse that is life itself (Job 27:3; 33:4; Ps. 104:29f.).[5]

The Word

A second conception, not unrelated to the first, is that of "the Word of the Lord." Unlike men of the modern world, for whom a word is a mere passing sound in the air, a transitory utterance of the voice, men of the ancient East conceived of it as an objective entity, which, once spoken, went out on its mission and accomplished the purpose for which it was intended. It is significant that the Hebrew word for "word" (*davar*) is identical with the word for "thing." This conception of the objectivity of spoken words is, of course, part of the ancient view of the objective efficacy of blessings and curses. Isaac having once pronounced a blessing over Jacob, was unable to recover it when he discovered it had been spoken over the wrong person (Gen. 27:33, 35); the psalmist who was cursed by his enemy, knew that the effect of the destructive words could be avoided only by somehow turning them back upon the curser (Ps. 109:18f.).

If even the words of men are objective realities, filled with mysterious potency, how much more powerful must be the words of God! This line of reasoning led quite naturally to the view that the "Word" of Yahweh was another means by which the transcendent God could impose his will upon the world. The prophet Jeremiah, who was in a special sense the prophet of the word, says in Yahweh's name, "Is not my word like fire . . . and like a hammer which breaks the rock in pieces?" (Jer. 23:29). Second Isaiah, in one of the most familiar passages of the Old Testament, states the same truth at greater length:

For as the rain and the snow come down from heaven,
  and return not thither but water the earth,
making it bring forth and sprout,
  giving seed to the sower and bread to the eater,

so shall my word be that goes forth from my mouth;
   it shall not return to me empty,
but it shall accomplish that which I purposed,
   and prosper in the thing for which I sent it.   [Isa. 55:10f.]

The word of which the prophets speak is, of course, the particular word that they speak on God's behalf. But the conception
of the Word of God, though important in the prophetic books
—which, on the whole, prefer the idea of the "Word" to that
of the "Spirit"—is by no means confined to them. The *idea* of
"the Word," though not the phrase, is found in the first chapter
of Genesis, where the whole creative process is described in terms
of "And God said . . ." with the result immediately following. The phrase itself is used of the process in Ps. 33:6, where
it is said,

> By the word of the Lord the heavens were made
>   and all their host by the breath of his mouth.

It is interesting to notice in this reference how "the word" and
"the breath" or Spirit are treated as almost equivalent terms.
   But if creation can be expressed in terms of a mission fulfilled
by the Word of God, so also can God's continuing, providential
care for the things he has created. Ps. 107 speaks of those who
prayed for deliverance from sickness, and how God "sent forth
his word and healed them" (Ps. 107:20). The normal operation
of the world of nature is ascribed by another psalmist to the
activity of God's Word:

> He sends forth his command to the earth;
>   his word runs swiftly.
>
> . . . .
>
> He sends forth his word, and melts them;
>   he makes his wind blow, and the waters flow.
>   [Ps. 147:15–18]

It is of interest to note that in the very next verse (19), the term "word" is used in a more conventional sense as equivalent to mere teaching. The Word of God in the Old Testament is both declarative and active or efficacious, but it is the latter sense that is strange to the Western mind and is our special concern in the present context.[6]

Wisdom

Yet a third medium by which the power of God is extended throughout his world is that of Wisdom, a conception that, by definition, is connected in a special way with the thinking of the wise men. Since they constituted the intellectual class in ancient Israel, the class most nearly approaching that of the philosophers in Western tradition, it will not seem strange if this idea turns out to have a less primitive background and a larger intellectual content than the ideas of Spirit and Word, though, as a matter of fact, the boundary lines among the three concepts are often fluid, especially in the later literature, and occasionally they are treated as equivalent and interchangeable (as when Word and Spirit are made parallel in the quotation from Ps. 33 given above, and when the Spirit and Wisdom are practically identified in the apocryphal book, The Wisdom of Solomon 7:22–25).

The basic, general meaning of "wisdom" (*chokhma*) in Semitic thought is simply that of "skill" in any kind of activity—that of the craftsman, the poet, or the statesman, for example. In Hebrew Wisdom Literature it came to have the special sense of skill in the art of living, a skill that was based upon a true understanding of the nature of the world, the laws of human existence and the ends for which men should strive. Wisdom, understood in this fashion, is of course possible for men only on the assumption that the world itself is orderly, rational and intelligible, or, to put it in other words, that there is a rational and intelligible order which underlies and sustains the whole of visible reality. This rational order of the universe, imposed upon it by the wise mind of God, came also to be called Wisdom. In this way, the concept of Wisdom became, in the thought of the wise men, an objective, quasi-metaphysical reality uniting the mind of the transcendent God with his created world and with the minds of men. The idea of Wisdom, conceived in this cosmic fashion, is practically identical with the idea of the *logos* in Stoic philosophy, and eventually provided an important point of contact for the *rapprochement* between Judaism and Greek thought that was so important a feature of the Hellenistic age.

In its fully developed form, the idea of cosmic Wisdom is expressed most clearly in the Book of Wisdom:

> For wisdom is more mobile than any motion;
> because of her pureness she pervades and penetrates all things.
> For she is a breath of the power of God,
> and a pure emanation of the glory of the Almighty:
> . . . .
> For she is a reflection of eternal light,
> a spotless mirror of the working of God,
> and an image of his goodness.
> Though she is but one, she can do all things,
> and while remaining in herself, she renews all things;
> in every generation she passes into holy souls
> and makes them friends of God and prophets.
> . . . .
> She reaches mightily from one end of the earth to the other,
> and she orders all things well.   [WISDOM 7:24–8:1]

This goes far beyond anything said in the Hebrew Bible, but the roots of the idea are there, particularly in Proverbs, where, as we have seen (p. 102, above) Wisdom is made to say:

> Yahweh created me at the beginning of his work,
> the first of his acts of old.

> Ages ago I was set up,
>> at the first, before the beginning of the earth.
>
> . . . .
>
>> then I was beside him, like a master workman
>>> [or: *mg*, "little child"];
>> and I was daily his delight,
>>> rejoicing before him always,
>> rejoicing in his inhabited world
>>> and delighting in the sons of men.   [Prov. 8:22–31]

In the Proverbs passage, the personification of Wisdom is probably still a mere poetical device (as it obviously is in Prov. 9:1–6), used to make vivid to students the personal challenge of the moral order; but in the Book of Wisdom, where the language is much more consciously philosophical, the author seems to take the image of personality with far greater seriousness. The Spirit of God and the Word of God are also occasionally described in personal terms (on Spirit, see Isa. 63:10; on Word, see Wisdom 18:15), but the use is much less consistent than in the case of Wisdom, and the intention more obviously poetic.[7]

These three Old Testament theologoumena for dealing with God's governance of the world were never systematized, completely rationalized, or clearly defined in relation to each other, but all testify to the uneasiness men of ancient Israel felt about ascribing to Yahweh activity of too crude and anthropomorphic a kind. They are used in a way that shows definite awareness of a philosophical problem and, at least in certain passages, are part of a rudimentary attempt to engage in real philosophical thinking. Their importance for New Testament thought goes almost without saying (Mark 1:10; Acts 2:4; 1 Cor. 1:24; 12:3–13; John 1:1–14; Col. 1:15–17; 2:3).

6

THE BEING OF GOD

I am who I am.

EXODUS 3:14

ISRAEL'S THEOLOGY began, as we have seen, with an
account of what Yahweh had done in the history of
the community; it also included certain convictions
about his continued operation in the present. But this twofold
concern with God's acts by no means exhausts the content of
Old Testament theology or does justice to its range of interests.
Many of the great theological passages of the Bible have nothing
to say about specific actions of God, either in the past or present, but are concerned solely to delineate the principal features
of his being and character. This is notably true of much of the
Psalter. It would be a serious error to suppose that the *only*
distinction between Yahweh's character and that of the pagan
gods lay in the fact that he was a God who made himself known
in history while they were gods who were chiefly manifest in
the world of nature.

Basic as this distinction is, there is also an equally basic distinction between the moral, and even the ontological, character
of the God of Israel and the gods of the surrounding world. The
gods of the pagans are difficult to define ontologically simply because they are so numerous and their nature and functions so
indeterminate. From country to country and period to period

they frequently change in shape, function, importance, and in their relationship to other gods. In Ugarit, for example, El was still regarded as the head of the pantheon, but Ugaritic litera-ture makes it apparent that Baal was gradually taking over his position and power;[1] among the Hittites, it was said that Ku-marbi had deposed Anu, the former chief of the gods, by an unspeakably ferocious attack upon his person;[2] in Mesopotamia, Marduk, a comparatively obscure god, became king of the gods and hero of the creation epic simply because his city, Babylon, had become the chief city of the region;[3] in Egypt, Amon, the god of Thebes, who rose to a pre-eminent position because of the emergence of Thebes as capital of the nation and of a grow-ing empire, was amalgamated with the sun god Re to form a new deity Amon-Re and later assumed the functions and attri-butes of many other gods as well.[4] A modern writer who speaks of "the loves and wars of Baal and Anat" accurately, if unin-tentionally, describes the "theology" of Canaan and the ancient Near East, with its conception of a celestial power-structure always in a state of flux.[5] The relationship of the pagan gods to each other was determined in part by the ever-shifting altera-tions of the natural world, with its uncertain balance of rain and sun, sea and land, desert and sown, growth and decay, life and death; or else it was determined by the relation of cities and states to each other; or, many times, simply by the fickleness of human loyalties and the changing fashions of human thought.

Yahweh stood diametrically opposed to the gods of paganism in respect to the consistency of his character and the constancy of his purpose. "I, Yahweh, do not change" (Mal. 3:6), he says. He was not affected by either changes in the political situation or by the rhythms of nature. He was primarily a God of history, but he controlled it and was not controlled by it. His greatness first became evident in the greatness of Israel in the days of the Davidic empire, but was in no way dependent on it. When the kingdom divided, he did not divide; and when it perished, he

id not perish with it. As a matter of fact the final recognition
f his universal sway was almost exactly coeval with the down-
ll of the Israelite state, as one can see from the teaching of the
reat prophets. It is true that he grew in stature in the course
f time, gained new attributes and increased his domain, but
his development was unilinear and organic, unimpeded by the
eclining fortunes of his people; it was the logical unfolding of
lements that were implicit in his character from the beginning.

Since he was primarily a God of history, it is evident that he
was not affected by changes in the world of nature. His power
was not conceived to be any less when nature was recalcitrant
nd the soil barren than when the rains were plentiful, the
un moderate, and the barns overflowed with corn and wine
nd oil. So far as Israel was concerned, nature's uncertain opera-
ions were an expression of Yahweh's will, not an index of his
itality. For the later Hebrews, at least, the universe was a
mighty organ on which Yahweh could play whatever tune he
wished, and make whatever concords or discords the occasion
alled for.

Yahweh was distinguished from the pagan gods by the fact
that his "being," as the "jealous" and "living" God of Israel,
transcended the restless alternations of nature and secular history, and his moral character was both clearly defined and unchanging. These are the aspects of Israel's "knowledge of God"
that we are about to investigate, and they belong quite as much
to her "theology" as does the record of his mighty acts.

The Sources

The two previous chapters were concerned with
Yahweh's acts in past and present; we now turn to consider his
nature, as Israel gradually came to apprehend it. What kind of
God was this mysterious being whom the tribes of Israel reported they had encountered in the desert, who delivered them

from oppression in Egypt, brought them to the Promised Land, was still "a very present help in trouble" (Ps. 46:1), but also a stern critic of their conduct? There are no convenient formulas such as the various Christian catechisms and confessions of faith to which one can turn for an answer. Obviously Israel had no formal creed in the modern sense of the term.

We have seen that some scholars are in the habit of referring to passages like Deut. 6:21-25, 26:5-10, and Josh. 24:2-13 as "creeds," and for convenience such language may be allowed to stand, but actually they are no such thing. The first of them has the most creedlike form, but in fact it is simply a father's attempt to communicate to his son a bit of summary historical information so that he can understand the background and significance of the Deuteronomic Law—a kind of model Sunday school lesson, while the others are liturgical formulas for particular occasions, one for presenting an offering, the other the pattern of a homily for a national assembly. None of them is repeated or directly echoed elsewhere. The supposition that a simpler, more primitive creed lies back of them is possible, but unprovable, since their similarity arises simply from the fact that they deal with a common history. History is narrative, and historical narrative has a form fixed by the logic of events even for people whose thought is otherwise quite unsystematic. The common source that lies back of these formulas is better described as historical tradition than historical creed, even though we may then go on to say that in early days Israel's historical traditions were the only creed she had.

When we turn to discuss Israel's conception of the being and character of Yahweh, as we now intend to do, we find the sources are much more fluid, since—especially for a prelogical or empirico-logical people like the ancient Hebrews—there was no obvious literary form, like that of historical narrative, into which a series of metaphysical or moral affirmations could be fitted. Nevertheless, there is, as we shall see in the next chapter, one such formula, repeated many times in the Old Testament, which functions much more like a creed than any of the historical summaries.

To discover Israel's theology as it is concerned with God's character rather than with his acts, we must look primarily to her poets and prophets, to those who wrote her hymns and preached her sermons. Out of their remarks, made in many different contexts and for many different occasions, it is not too difficult to reconstruct the basic elements in Israel's understanding of God as he was in his eternal being, his transcendental nature, rather than in his momentary acts. And first, in this chapter, we shall be concerned with what might be called his ontological nature—to make use of an adjective that is entirely foreign to the vocabulary and thought-forms of the Old Testament, but nevertheless useful for our purpose. In the next chapter we shall consider his moral nature, his character in relation to man.

The Existence of God

First, one must note the remarkable fact that the existence of deity is never questioned in the Old Testament. Just how significant this is, is not quite certain, but it is a fact that cannot be overlooked in any discussion of the knowledge of God in the Old Testament. There were no atheists in ancient Israel, not even down to the latest times. It is true that two of the psalms (14 and 53) speak of "the fool who says in his heart, 'there is no God,'" but it would be easy to prove that this does not mean what the bald English words seem to say. What they mean is "God is not here"; the Hebrew construction is identical with that in 1 Sam. 14:17, where the English reads "behold, Jonathan and his armor-bearer *were not there*." When "the fool" said "God is not here," what he meant was simply that God is indifferent to human affairs; he is in control of the cosmos but cannot be expected to intervene in mundane affairs to correct the moral errors of men. This is a kind of deism, such as found developed to a full-fledged philosophy in the Book of Ecclesiastes, but is very far from philosophical atheism. The people of Israel, like the rest of the ancient oriental world, took the existence of God (or the gods) for granted; the only question was, What kind of God is he? Is he powerful, friendly, dependable, or is he weak, querulous, vacillating, or hostile? Is he a god of nature, of some object in nature, of an individual, of the family group, of the tribe, of the nation? When Israel finally came into contact with the Greek world, there began to be suggestions, as in the 13th chapter of the Wisdom of Solomon, that the existence of God—at least of the true God—was subject to demonstration; in the older Israel the nature of God might be subject to discussion, but his existence never.

It would be impossible to deal with the subject of God's existence as understood by Israel without at least treating briefly the suggestion made already in antiquity that the very name of Israel's God, Yahweh, contains an assertion of his existence and therefore intends to say that he is the *sole* existent being, all other beings presumably deriving their being only from him. This view is based upon the fact that the mysterious name of God is, in the Old Testament, interpreted as a form of the Hebrew verb *hayah*. The divine name has the form of the imperfect tense and its meaning is said to be "he is" or "he will be"; it is this theory that underlies the familiar words of Exod. 3:14, where God says of himself (necessarily transposing the verb into the first-person singular), "I am who I am." The Greek version (the Septuagint) renders this *eimi ho ōn*, "I am he who is," thereby giving the name an ontological sense that it has borne ever since and that has been of immense significance in the history of Jewish and Christian thought.

It must be said quite frankly, without attempting to discuss the evidence, that the Hebrew words could never have meant this—at least not until a very late period. The interpretation of the name Yahweh has evidently passed through three periods. In the beginning it was merely a divine proper name—probably borrowed from some other group such as the Kenites[6]—the meaning of which can no longer be discovered.[7] In the second stage, among the nascent theologians of early Israel, it was interpreted as the imperfect tense of the verb *hayah*, but since this verb does not really mean "to be," but "to become," the proper English translation should not be "I am that I am," but "I will become what I will become," meaning that the divine nature is not definable, that Israel's God would disclose himself in the many-sidedness of his being only in the course of time and man's experience with him. Other translations are possible, but this is the most natural. Finally, in the third stage, probably after Israel's first contact with Hellenic ideas, perhaps only at the time of the Greek translation of the Old Testament, the name was interpreted in a metaphysical, but quite un-Hebraic, sense as meaning "He who is," "He who alone possesses the attribute of uncontingent existence."

The significance of the word "Yahweh" for the theology of the Old Testament does not lie in any supposed connection with a verb "to be," but rather in the fact that it provides the God of Israel with a distinctive name (a fact we shall discuss shortly) and, if the interpretation suggested above is correct, asserts that his nature is never entirely comprehensible by men, but is capable of infinite unfoldment as men walk with him in fidelity and obedience. "He will be what he will be," and *exactly* what he will be is something which forever lies beyond the horizons of the future.

The Unity of God

Belief in the unity of God is far more significant in Old Testament theology than belief in God's existence. It has, indeed, often been considered the unique contribution of the Hebrews to the religious thought of mankind. It used to be said that the essence of Old Testament religion could be expressed in the phrase "ethical monotheism," and although this would be regarded as a misleading oversimplification today, it does at least bear witness to the fact that belief in the oneness of God is of central importance.

The doctrine of God's unity does not, of course, take the form of a theoretical affirmation that only one God exists and that he is, incidentally, to be identified with Yahweh, the national God of Israel. Like all the other elements in Israel's knowledge of God, belief in his unity proceeds from her experience with him, not from an intellectual attempt to solve the problem of the unity underlying the multiplicity of phenomena in the physical world.

Basic to Israel's approach to deity was the conviction that, in her early experience, she had come to know him, or rather be known by him, in a specific series of historical events. In the long course of her later experience, there inevitably arose the question of just who he was; whether he was, in fact, merely a tribal god, whose power was limited by the size of the tribe and the land to which he was attached, or whether he might conceivably be the universal God, the only one who *is,* and who is, therefore, in control of all the forces of nature and history. This question became acute in the days of the great world empires—Assyria, Babylonia and Persia, all of whom had gods of their own who seemed, superficially at least, to be far more powerful than Yahweh. In view of Israel's numerical inferiority and the small dimensions of her country, there was a natural temptation to think that Yahweh must be small and insignificant among the gods. But it is further testimony to the uniqueness of Israel, not only in her power to endure but also in her intellectual vigor, that she drew the quite opposite, and seemingly incredible, conclusion that the God Yahweh, whom she had come to know so well in her historical experience, was the only real God at all, that it was he who controlled the destinies of all nations, and that she, his people, must consequently have some kind of universal mission.

It is this stage of her thinking that is expressed in classical form in the grandiose language of Second Isaiah, speaking from the depths of Israel's degradation in the days of the Babylonian exile.

> I am the first and I am the last;
>   besides me there is no god.
>
> . . . .
>
> Is there a God besides me?
>   There is no Rock; I know not any. [Isa. 44:6ff.]
>
> . . . there is no other god besides me,
>   a righteous God and a Savior;
>   there is none besides me.
>   Turn to me and be saved,
>   all the ends of the earth!
>   For I am God and there is no other.
>
> . . . .
>
> To me every knee shall bow,
>   every tongue shall swear.
>   Only in Yahweh, it shall be said of me,
>   are righteousness and strength. [Isa. 45:21–24]

None of Second Isaiah's expressions of belief in absolute mono-theism is more remarkable than one that is explicitly opposed to any kind of dualism, or even the most hesitant suggestion that Yahweh is not in absolute control of every force and event, however perplexing, in the universe:

> I am Yahweh, and there is no other,
>   besides me there is no God

. . . .
I form light and create darkness,
   I make weal and create woe,
I am Yahweh, who do all these things.   [Isa. 45:5ff.]

Such statements as these represent the goal toward which the theological process in ancient Israel had been moving from the beginning, and as such can be regarded as expressing the "doctrine" of the Old Testament. But this is not to say that the people of Israel had always been monotheists in the modern philosophical sense of the word, or had always accepted, even approximately, the sort of views expressed in Second Isaiah. There is much scholarly controversy still upon this point. The records of older days were edited and redacted in later times and one can never be sure how much of the views expressed in them is to be attributed to the original source and how much to the later editor, who naturally saw the attitudes of the ancient world reflected in the mirror of his own. The views of scholars today vary all the way from that which regards Moses, or even Abraham, as a monotheist, to another that sees monotheism as emerging only with Second Isaiah, or, in less theoretical form, with Amos. The truth is probably to be found in a mediating position that sees the germ of monotheism present in early times, with the full flower coming at the end of the Old Testament period.[8]

The nature of that germ, however, needs to be further analyzed. It used to be said that the early Hebrews were "henotheists," this assumption being based upon the theory that all cultures had a tendency to pass through a henotheistic stage, during which they believed in the existence of many gods, but claimed only one for themselves. There are two objections to this interpretation of the development of theology in Israel. The first is that the idea of henotheism is an artificial construction, there being no evidence that cultures do actually and inevitably pass through such a stage. The second is that, even if henotheism existed, it would be far too pallid a word to describe the attitude of Israel toward its God.[9] Even the term "monolatry," the worship of only one God, sometimes suggested as a substitute, is too anemic and theoretical a term to express the vividness of Israel's sense that one God had laid an absolute claim upon her.

Certain facts about Israel's view of Yahweh from the very beginning hint at the uniqueness of her theology, which cannot be simply subsumed under a commonplace anthropological label. There is first the complete absence of mythology in Israelite literature at all stages of its development (using the term "mythology" here in its usual dictionary sense in which "a myth deals with the actions of gods or godlike beings" [Webster], and not in the Platonic sense, popular with some contemporary theologians, of a "reasonable tale" about things too remote in time to be discussed in scientific or philosophical language[10]). The supernatural world of Old Testament man was dominated almost exclusively by the lonely figure of Yahweh, to the exclusion of other gods, demigods, demons or even angels. There are occasionally stories involving "angels" (that is, divine messengers) or spirits, but these figures flit in and out of the picture without names or fixed personalities (except in the very late Book of Daniel); generally speaking they are merely agents or modes of God's own activity and have no independent role to play. The one fragment of real mythology in the Old Testament is in Gen. 6:1-4 where it is related that the "sons of God" fell in love with the daughters of men and married them, but this story is so isolated in the Old Testament that its presence only serves to call attention to the absence of similar stories elsewhere. Stories like that of the flood which can be compared with their pagan originals, where the mythological element is strong, are remarkable for the thoroughgoing way in which the mythology has been purged from them. The same is true of many figures of speech, poetic images and incidental allusions; their obvious mythological background has been so thoroughly blotted out that only poetry remains.[11]

Particularly notable in this connection is the complete absence of the sexual element in the Israelite idea of deity, since the polarity of sex plays so important a role generally in the religious thought of the ancient Near East, and above all among the Canaanites who were the immediate neighbors of the biblical Hebrews. The Bible itself bears abundant witness to the attraction this kind of religion had for many Israelites, who, for quite practical reasons, preferred the worship of the Baalim and the Ashtaroth (see above, p. 110), which was related to the fertility of the soil, to the worship of Yahweh, whose connection seemed to be only with warfare and the affairs of the nation. But authentic Israelite religion was so intolerant of the idea of a sexual element in deity that not only does Yahweh have no consort or family, but the Hebrew language does not even contain a word for "goddess." [12] When, in the prophetic age, the whole realm of agriculture was brought under the control of the God of Israel—as it evidently had not been in the beginning—it was clearly understood that fertility was not connected with the nature of Yahweh, but with his will. Fertility in the natural world was not the result of any sexual mysteries performed in the sphere of divinity, but was purely and simply the free gift of a moral deity who transcended the distinctions of sex.

Among the elements in Israelite religion that emphasized the unity of God from the beginning, along with the absence of mythology and sex, was the intolerance that always characterized it. Whatever one may think of the value of tolerance in the modern world, there can be no doubt that for the biblical world tolerance was a characteristic of paganism. The pagan gods were shifting, protean, ambiguous in nature, and one was easily substituted for another. The real religion of the ancient Near

East was syncretism, and the history of religion among all the oriental cultures was largely the story of the rearrangement of the pantheon from time to time to accommodate new gods. In Egypt, Babylon and Canaan, some gods became otiose and quietly died, while other gods, often as the result of changes in the political structure, climbed the social ladder and sometimes, though originally insignificant, became kings of the gods or at least members of the celestial council.[13]

Syncretism in Israel was regarded as apostasy. From start to finish, Yahweh was the only God, at least in her private pantheon. If other gods existed, Yahweh was nevertheless her Lord, and Israel needed to take no account of them; if he had a celestial council, as I Kings 22:19 and Job 1:6 suggest, it consisted of faceless, nameless beings (the word "satan" in Job is not a proper name)[14] who were entirely under his control. Yahweh had no rivals, and would tolerate none. "You shall have no other gods before me" (Exod. 20:3), i.e. "in my presence." Whatever the date of this commandment, there can be little doubt that it represents the spirit of authentic Yahwism from its first appearance in Israel.

What particularly distinguishes Israel's religion is just this intolerant spirit—a spirit that she has transmitted to her daughter, the Christian Church—and it is this intolerance that gives force and content to the idea of the unity of God in the Old Testament. The conviction that God is one is not the result of Israel's solution of an important intellectual question; it is the result of her ultimate response to the total demand for loyalty that her God laid upon her. She did not dare have other gods in the presence of Yahweh because, as he said, he was a "jealous God" (Exod. 20:5), and his jealousy was like a devouring fire (Deut. 4:24) that destroyed alien gods, their worshipers and the trappings of their worship.

It is interesting that the new Jewish translation of the Torah[15] translates "jealous" by the word "impassioned": "I the Lord your God am an impassioned God." The word "jealous" has an unfortunate sound in English, because it suggests to us a petty, niggling, basically negative, and therefore unattractive, attitude, whereas the Hebrew word is strong, dynamic, more often affirmative than negative. The Jewish translation, while not entirely satisfactory, has the virtue of bringing out this positive quality, for what is most remarkable in the nature of Yahweh, as one meets him in the pages of the Old Testament, is the passionate intensity of his demands. The heart of Israel's creed is not found in the opening words of the Shema (Deut. 6:4ff.), "Hear, O Israel, the Lord our God is one Lord," but rather in the intransigent demand that follows, "and you shalt love the Lord your God with *all* your heart, and with *all* your soul, and with *all* your might."

When Yahweh is called "the living God" (Deut. 5:26; Jer. 10:10), it is with a similar nuance, for "to be alive" in Hebrew is not merely to possess animate existence, but to have force, vigor, abounding vitality. To be "living" is not merely the opposite of being dead, but also the opposite of being weak or sickly.[16] Yahweh is called the "living" God to contrast him with the gods of the heathen, partly no doubt because ancient Israel often confused the actual gods with their lifeless images (Ps. 115:4–7), but also because she was painfully aware that the heathen gods never impinged upon the lives of their worshipers with such relentless, overpowering energy and such inexorable demands for loyalty as Yahweh. Other gods, whether they "existed" or not, seemed literally lifeless in comparison.

Faced with the demands of a God of this kind, who refused to make even the slightest polite concession to syncretism, Israel had ultimately either to exchange him for a more comfortable and civilized deity, or to acknowledge that the God whom she had known so long as her private God was actually the only God there is. It was Israel's final recognition, in the days of Second Isaiah, of this as the only possible view that gave Judeo-Christian-Islamic monotheism to the world.

The Personality of God

The next two items in our discussion of the being of God are what we must call, for want of better terms, the personality and spirituality of God. The term "spirituality" is particularly misleading, but is used here only to indicate that, while men of the Old Testament unashamedly think of God as a person, at the same time they recognize that this manner of conceiving him is due to the limitations of human speech and that the idea of his personality must be hedged about with certain safeguards, that in fact he belongs to an entirely different order of being from man.

That the God of ancient Israel was understood to be personal goes almost without saying. If we define a person as one who is conscious of his own existence, has a will by which he can determine his actions, together with the imagination to foresee their results, and can therefore lay long-distance plans for the future, then there is no doubt that Yahweh was a person. God was certainly not conceived, as so often in modern thought, as an impersonal principle or force, an "absolute" or general ground of being. Yahweh was a personal being with self-consciousness, will, and imagination, and these are characteristics that he maintains to the very end of the Old Testament period; his personality does not tend to fade away into abstractions. In fact his personal nature is as clearly expressed in Second Isaiah, the greatest of Israel's theologians, as anywhere else. His self-consciousness is evident in the frequent self-predications that are so marked a feature of Second Isaiah's style: "I am Yahweh, that is my name; / my glory I give to no other" (Isa. 42:8); "I am Yahweh, who made all things, / who stretched out the heavens alone" (44:24). The force of his will is evident in the urgency with which he gives commands: "Awake, awake" (51:9); "Rouse yourself, rouse yourself" (51:17); "Depart, depart"

(52:11). In such passages as these we see the intensity of the divine nature, which, as we saw before, is the driving force behind Israel's final proclamation that her God was absolutely one and unique; he was an "impassioned" God even in the normal expressions of his will. And this same God had always had in view the ultimate goal toward which he was leading his creation; "I am God, and there is none like me, / declaring the end from the beginning / and from ancient times things not yet done, / saying, 'My counsel shall stand, / and I will accomplish all my purpose' " (46:9f.).

The fact that Israel's God had a personal name shows how realistically his personality was understood. While her theologians later made half-hearted attempts to explain the name "Yahweh" in a philosophical sense, the fact is that a divine name, like a human name, is the principal means by which one person identifies another *person*. In the story of Moses' meeting with God for the first time in the wilderness, Moses said, "If I come to the people of Israel and say to them, 'The God of your fathers has sent me to you,' and they ask me, 'What is his name?' what shall I say to them?" (Exod. 3:13); the point of this questioning is that one cannot identify another person, much less have any kind of relationship with him, unless one knows his name. Israel felt secure in her relationship to God because he had made his name known to her. The point of his having a name was not merely that it served to distinguish him, as in polytheistic systems, from other gods, but that it made Israel's connection with him concrete, intimate, personal. The feeling of ancient man about such things may have been naïve, but it was deeply satisfying in a way in which a more sophisticated feeling could not possibly be. Men of Israel, when they faced the universe with its mystery and terror, felt at home as modern man can hardly do, since the reality they perceived behind it was not some blind, impersonal force, or even some reality that might be coldly spoken of as "deity" or "supreme being," but a person whose Name they knew.

It was this feeling about God that made the anthropomorphisms and anthropopathisms of Scripture seem so natural. Men of ancient Israel could speak quite naturally about their God in early times as having walked in the garden in the cool of the day (Gen. 3:8), as sniffing with delight at the savory odor of a sacrifice (Gen. 8:21), as coming down from heaven to see what men were doing on earth (Gen. 11:5), as wrestling with a man by the riverside (Gen. 32:24, 28). In more cautious later times, they were inclined to speak less pungently, and older texts were changed to modify or eliminate some of the cruder passages, but there was never any systematic attempt to eliminate anthropomorphism. As a matter of fact, even in the latest times it was possible to speak of God in grossly anthropomorphic language. In the grip of deep emotion, a very late psalmist can cry out, "Rouse thyself! Why sleepest thou, O Lord? Awake!" (Ps. 44:23). Second Isaiah, the noblest and profoundest of Israel's thinkers, can say:

> The Lord goes forth like a mighty man,
>   like a man of war he stirs up his fury;
> he cries, he shouts aloud,
>   he shows himself mighty against his foes.   [ISA. 42:13]

In the next verse, Yahweh himself says:

> For a long time I have held my peace,
>   I have kept still and restrained myself;
> now I will cry out like a woman in travail,
>   I will gasp and pant.   [ISA. 42:14]

It is as if the prophet felt it far better to convey by any means the intensity of God's will and the urgency of his purpose than to preserve a sense of his dignity.

The vivid sense of God's personality that is evident in the almost unrestrained use of anthropomorphisms at certain times and in certain writers is also apparent in anthropopathisms—

passages, that is, that represent God not so much as looking and acting like a man, as feeling like a man. All the basic human emotions are attributed to Yahweh. He chose the people of Israel and brought them out of Egypt simply because he "loved" them (Deut. 4:37), while on the contrary he "hates" all those that work iniquity (Ps. 5:5); more strangely, and to our minds without justification, he is said to love Jacob and hate Esau (Mal. 1:2f.). He begs to be let alone while he cherishes and cultivates his anger: ". . . let me alone, that my wrath may burn hot against them" (Exod. 32:10). When Israel's vassals try to free themselves from her control, Yahweh's risibilities are touched and he roars with laughter at their futile strivings:

> He who sits in the heavens laughs;
> the Lord has them in derision.   [Ps. 2:4]

Some of these examples have been chosen less because they are typical than because they show the extremes to which the writers and thinkers of the Old Testament were willing to go in attributing human emotions to God. For the most part the anthropomorphic and anthropopathic expressions are natural and attractive, and even modern man has no difficulty in accepting them as poetry. Taken together, in their exuberant and sometimes undisciplined profusion, they leave no doubt in any reader's mind that the men of Israel believed their God to be a vivid and vehement personality and not a bloodless abstraction.

Although our principal interest here is to expound rather than to defend, one or two explanatory notes should perhaps be added, because to religious thinkers of the modern world anthropomorphism is likely to seem childish and intellectually indefensible. Since all thinking about deity must necessarily be analogical, the real question is from what sphere analogies should be drawn. Are the most adequate analogies those drawn from nature and the objective sciences, which lead one to conceive of deity in terms of natural law, impersonal substance or physical force? Or are the more appropriate analogies those drawn from the world of the human personality, which picture deity in terms of self-conscious mental activity, imagination and will? Since it would be generally agreed that the human personality is the most valuable product of the evolutionary process (granting this may be mere human prejudice!), analogies drawn from human life would seem to be the more adequate. The men of ancient Israel did not, of course, face the choice in these intellectual terms, but one must suppose that if they had, they would have chosen belief in God as person rather than as mere energy or metaphysical substance.

Certain problems arose when Judaism came into contact with Greek philosophy, which tended to think of divinity in impersonal terms, but the problem for the Jews was not whether they should relinquish their belief in a God whom they knew as a person, and simply adopt the Greek view of divinity, but rather how they could harmonize their firm conviction that God is a personal will with their new-found realization that the world is a cosmos ruled by an impersonal natural law. The attempt to reconcile these two apparently antithetic concepts remains to the present day a basic problem of Judeo-Christian philosophy and apologetics, but it has only rarely led to acceptance of the proposition that God is merely order, substance, energy, law rather than will, imagination, self-conscious being, creator, orderer, energizer and lawgiver. For the most part Western religious man has remained firmly in the tradition set by the Old Testament with its many colorful and sometimes offensive anthropomorphisms, a tradition which asserts that one deals with God not as a scientist deals with physical forces, but as a person deals with another person.[17]

A still further contrast needs to be kept in mind when considering the whole question of God's personality in the Old

Testament, and that is the fact that even in the ancient world the gods were often identified with concrete, but impersonal, energies such as the wind and the rain, and the mysterious vitality that manifests itself in the fertility of herd and field, or with tangible objects such as mountains, trees, rocks, the sun, the stars and the sky. This was something quite different from the modern depersonalization of deity and was never incompatible with assigning personal qualities to the deities concerned, but it is notable that the Hebrew conception of God as a distinct and energetic person with a clearly defined "personality" made it impossible ever to confuse Yahweh with any natural object or power; he always stood sharply over against the world of nature as its Creator and Lord. He might be sometimes connected for a time with some particular natural phenomenon such as the storm-wind and the earthquake (as for instance in Ps. 18:7–15), but there was never any question of *identifying* him with the phenomenon. The storm, the earthquake, the wind and the hail, like the armies of the Assyrians, were not part of his nature, but tools that he used.

And finally, another contrast should be noted between Israel's resolutely anthropomorphic conception of God and other views prevalent in the ancient world. Certain of Israel's neighbors, such as the Egyptians, were prone to picture their gods in the form of animals rather than men. Old Testament anthropomorphism does not seem so crude when one sees how it protected Israel from a *therio*morphism that is far cruder and may represent a survival from primitive totemism.[18]

The Spirituality of God

Israel herself was aware, at least in the minds of her great religious teachers, that anthropomorphic expressions about God must not be taken at face value. As we shall see in the next chapter, Yahweh was the "Holy" One of Israel and, in a sense, this is the antithesis of any anthropomorphic conception of him. Even without this word, however, there is plenty of evidence that thinking men in Israel were conscious of the need for exercising a certain reserve about speaking of God in human terms, and knew that anthropomorphic language is in fact merely analogical. There is, for example, the often observed fact that both the Elohistic and Priestly documents in Genesis avoid the use of crudely anthropomorphic expressions such as we have noted above in the work of the Yahwist. The Elohist prefers to represent God as communicating with men by means of dreams and visions rather than directly, thus removing him at least one step from human life, while the Priestly writer prefers to use special, unusual verbs for the activity of God: thus God "creates" rather than "makes" or "forms," and "establishes" covenants rather than "cuts" them.[19] In this way the Priestly writer suggests that God's manner of working is unique and not really comparable to man's work. It is probable that the preference of the Priestly writer for the name "Elohim" rather than "Yahweh" for God is partly motivated by a feeling that the term "Yahweh" should be understood as a mysterious and awe-inspiring communication of the divine essence rather than a mere personal name—a "handle" —for the God of Israel, and therefore should not be used casually and lightly.

Such tendencies, readily found in various parts of the Old Testament, testify to Israel's increasing understanding of God's "spirituality," a word that is useful here simply because no other is available. The modern conception of spirit as the opposite of matter, of spirituality as the life of pure thought in contrast to the life of the body is, of course, one that is totally foreign to the Old Testament world. By speaking of Israel's belief in the spirituality of God we mean principally that she increasingly recognized the poetical and merely analogical nature of anthropomorphic language, since obviously the life of

God must in fact be totally different from the life of man. Nevertheless, a famous passage suggests that Israel herself might have accepted the word "spiritual" as descriptive of the divine nature, granted the Hebrew definition of what "spirit" (*ruach*) means. In Isa. 31:3, the prophet, who has been chiding his people for looking to Egypt for military help against Assyria, observes that

> The Egyptians are men, and not God;
> and their horses are flesh, and not spirit,

clearly implying that flesh is an attribute of man, whereas spirit belongs to the realm of God. Of course, for the ancient Hebrews, spirit, which means merely "wind" or "breath," was no less "material" than anything else and was probably thought of as simply a very fine, invisible form of matter. Nevertheless it is significant that they distinguish between the coarse matter they call flesh and a more refined substance they call spirit, and the latter they regard as belonging distinctively to the realm of divinity.

The remarks we have previously made about the absence of mythology and sex in the God of the Old Testament are also relevant to a discussion of his spirituality. Although crudely anthropomorphic language could be used of him in most respects, there still remained *certain* forms of human relationship and human activity that could not be attributed to him under any circumstances.

The fact that Yahweh is a being unique in kind sets certain obvious limits to anthropomorphism. Human beings, in contrast to him, are social creatures, engaged constantly in social activities. They live in a world of other human beings with whom they are in frequent contact, both by way of attraction and repulsion. To the pagan mind it seems perfectly natural that this should be true of God as well, and hence pagan mythology is full of fascinating—and often horrifying—tales about the loves and wars of the gods. But Yahweh, the God of Israel, lives in lonely majesty; he has no peers. If he has servitors in his heavenly court—angels, spirits, seraphim and cherubim—they are only vague figures moving in the background, without names or personalities; insofar as Yahweh has any "social" life, it is lived in relation only to man, his creature; his heavenly council assembles only to deal with human affairs (I Kings 22:19f.; Job 1:6ff.). The dramatic incidents in which Yahweh is protagonist are those in which men or nations play the opposite role as his friends or enemies. Once there may have been a real mythology in which he was involved; the allusions to the struggle with Rahab or Leviathan (Ps. 89:10; 74:14) and the strange story of the serpent's slandering him in the Garden of Eden (Gen. 3:4f.) seem to indicate there was, but, in the Old Testament as we know it, the former is used only as a poetical image and in the latter story the serpent is not a god, a supernatural figure, but merely an ordinary snake, one of God's creatures that has gone wrong.

For pagans, the sexual element was an inevitable and important concomitant of the supposition that the gods behaved just like men except that they acted on a larger stage. The Canaanite texts from Ugarit tell of the physical love life of El and Baal in explicit language;[20] the sacred marriage of gods and goddesses, or gods and priestesses, was a normal feature of ancient Near Eastern myth and cult.[21] The strict sexual morality of the Hebrews would naturally prevent them from ascribing to Yahweh the irregular amours of a pagan god, but there is never even the whisper of a suggestion in the Old Testament that the likeness between God and men requires that he, like them, should have a consort, children, and family life. Yahweh's only wife is Israel (Hos. 2:2ff.; Jer. 2:2; 31:32); his children are either Israel herself or her citizens or her king (Hos. 11:1; 1:10; 2 Sam. 7:14); and the relationship is not a physical, but an adoptive one, based on choice, affection and willing obedience.

The "spirituality" of Israel's conception of God is also shown by the prohibition of images. The peculiar prejudice against images was, so far as one can see, characteristic of Israel's religion from a very early time. There are, of course, certain passages which seem to show that the prohibition in the days of the judges and the early monarchy was not so absolute as it became in later times, and there can also be no doubt that practices were tolerated in popular religion—in the countryside, among peasants and simple people—that were frowned on in official theology.[22] But such passages are rare and unrepresentative, whereas the bias against portraying Yahweh in visible form seems to be ingrained in the fiber of the religion from the start. It is formulated in a classical statement in the Decalogue (Exod. 20:4ff.; Deut. 5:8ff.), which some, of course, think to be late, but is also found among the undoubtedly ancient ritual laws of Exod. 34 (v. 17). The antipathy to making images of God—or, indeed, of anything else—remains undiminished in Judaism, and its daughter religion, Islam, to the present day. While it is possible to consider various psychological and cultural motives as contributing factors in creating this prejudice, the fact remains that it is an attitude unparalleled among Israel's neighbors, except perhaps during the short-lived Egyptian monotheism of Ikhnaton,[23] and is primarily an expression of a belief that God is so different from man, and so superior to the physical world, that he must never be represented in human form, or by any other physical representation. Anthropomorphic images were limited to literature and language; there they could be instructive and vivifying; in any case, they were always fleeting, changing, only half serious. But anthropomorphism in plastic form was unconditionally forbidden, for there it was fixed, crass, limiting; in the mature thought of Israel the making of an image of God degraded the King of the Universe to a level lower than that of his subjects, the Creator to the status of an object among other objects in his creation.[24]

Another indication of the limits that were placed on the

anthropomorphic conception of God is the use of various theological devices by which Yahweh was kept from coming into too close contact with the world of men. In early times Israel could think of God as appearing to men in human form and speaking with them face to face, as with Abraham just before the destruction of Sodom (Gen. 18:2, 22). But already there had begun to develop a reticence about speaking of Yahweh in this too intimate, too human way. A number of passages in the Pentateuch and Judges speak of a curious figure called the Angel of the Lord, who in each story turns out to be not an "angel" at all, but a special form in which Yahweh himself appears (e.g. Gen. 16:7; 22:11f.; Judg. 6:11, 14; 13:3, 22). The "angel" is a transparent device for avoiding too anthropomorphic a portrayal of the deity's self-manifestation.[25] In the Priestly document the "Glory" of God, the bright glow that surrounded him, serves a similar purpose (e.g., Exod. 40:34; Num. 14:10; Ezek. 8:4), as does "the name" of God in the Deuteronomic literature (Deut. 12:5; 1 Kings 9:3).[26] A less common device is that of the "presence" (literally, "the face"; Heb. *panim*) of God. In Exod. 33:15, Moses prays not that Yahweh himself, but his "presence," will go up with his people out of Egypt; the loaves that are placed regularly before Yahweh in the sanctuary are called the bread of "the Presence" (Exod. 25:30: KJV, "shewbread"); and the author of Ps. 139 asks, "Whither shall I flee from thy presence?" (v. 7).[27] All these surrogates for deity have analogies in paganism, but this proves only that pagans also have sometimes felt the danger of anthropomorphizing deity too literally and have devised specific safeguards against it. The difference is that in Israel this danger was felt more deeply and faced in an incomparably more thoroughgoing fashion.

Finally, there are two attributes of Yahweh in the Old Testament that are entirely incompatible with any serious belief that he was merely like an overgrown man. These are his omniscience and his omnipresence. There are many passages in the

Bible that seem to picture him as limited with respect to both locality and knowledge, such as the one that represents him as "coming down" to find out what was happening at Babel (Gen. 11:7). But for Hebrews of later times, as for us, this was only picturesque language, and the reality was quite otherwise. God does not know as man knows; his knowledge is intimate, unmediated and universal. It is especially wonderful since it can penetrate the depths of the human personality. Just a few passages need be quoted to show how important an element God's omniscience is in Israel's thought:

> . . . render to each whose heart thou knowest, according to all his ways (for thou, thou only, knowest the hearts of all the children of men). . . . [1 KINGS 8:39]
>
> . . . the Lord sees not as man sees; man looks on the outward appearance, but the Lord looks on the heart. [1 SAM. 16:7]
>
> . . . the Lord searches all hearts, and understands every plan and thought. [1 CHRON. 28:9]
>
> Sheol and Abaddon lie open before the Lord,
> how much more the hearts of men! [PROV. 15:11]

The most familiar expression of the thought of divine omniscience is found in the first six verses of Ps. 139, the passage that begins,

> O Lord thou hast searched me and known me!
> Thou knowest when I sit down and when I rise up;
> thou discernest my thoughts from afar [v. 1]

and ends,

> Such knowledge is too wonderful for me;
> it is high, I cannot attain unto it. [v. 6]

The thought of God's universal presence is not expressed so frequently, but the following passages are unambiguous: Ps. 139:7–12 has the marvelous lines,

> If I take the wings of the morning
>   and dwell in the uttermost parts of the sea,
> even there thy hand shall lead me,
>   and thy right hand shall hold me.   [v. 9]

Note also the parallel lines in Amos 9:2f. In Jer. 23:23f. we read:

Am I a God at hand, says the Lord, and not a God afar off? Can a man hide himself in secret places so that I cannot see him? says the Lord. Do I not fill heaven and earth?

And when one understands the meaning of the term "the glory of the Lord" as discussed above, the hymn that Isaiah heard in the temple becomes the most concise and theologically satisfying expression of the doctrine of divine omnipresence: ". . . the whole earth is full of his glory" (Isa. 6:3).

This entire discussion of the "spirituality" of God, which has emphasized the limitations and safeguards attached to the vivid anthropomorphic language of the Old Testament, can be summarized in certain explicit statements: "God is not man that he should lie, or a son of man, that he should repent" (Num. 23:19); ". . . the Glory of Israel will not lie or repent; for he is not a man, that he should repent" (1 Sam. 15:29); ". . . I am God and not man, the Holy One in your midst . . ." (Hos. 11:9). Greatest of all such affirmations is the one in Isa. 55:8f.:

> For my thoughts are not your thoughts,
>   neither are your ways my ways, says the Lord.
> For as the heavens are higher than the earth,

so are my ways higher than your ways,
and my thoughts than your thoughts.

No simple statements of this kind are, of course, ever entirely true and satisfying, either for the high religion of our own day or for the Old Testament. In actual fact the men of ancient Israel were, as we have seen, quite sure, and rightly sure, that in many ways God's ways *were* like their ways and his thoughts like their thoughts. Otherwise, it would be quite impossible to know or serve him. What had to be done then—as now—was to keep the two ideas of God's likeness to men and his utter difference from them in a dynamic tension, where each truth is accepted wholly and simply, but kept in balance. This kind of paradox, of ambivalent thought, is inseparable from every human effort to deal with matters of ultimate concern. In the antiphony of two apparently contradictory statements the essential, indefinable truth often manages to shine forth—sometimes brilliantly and excitingly—like the play of lightning between two opposing cloud masses.

God as both Transcendent and Immanent

The particular paradox of belief in an anthropomorphic deity who is nevertheless utterly different from man is related to other paradoxes, and especially to the familiar one which declares that God is both transcendent and immanent, a paradox of which Israel was also fully aware. She knew, as we have seen, that God is both like man, and yet entirely different from him; she knew as well that God pervades his whole creation and yet is utterly distinct from it, that he is very near at hand to all his worshipers, but is also far away from them, dwelling in a realm of inconceivable splendor. One of her thinkers, a late, anonymous poet and prophet, expressed as well as anyone has ever expressed it the paradox of God's transcend-

ence and immanence. His words provide a fitting conclusion
to our discussion of the "being" of God and a useful transition
to the thought of the next chapter:

> For thus says the high and lofty One,
>> who inhabits eternity, whose name is Holy:
> I dwell in the high and lofty place . . .

at which point one needs to pause briefly to savor the full poig-
nance of the paradoxical conclusion that follows:

> and *also* with him who is of a contrite and humble spirit,
>> to revive the spirit of the humble,
> and to revive the heart of the contrite. [Isa. 57:15]

7
THE CHARACTER OF GOD

I am the Lord who practice steadfast love,
justice, and righteousness.

JEREMIAH 9:24

FOR THE RELIGIONS of primitive man, and even for
many of the higher forms of ancient paganism,
God is pure will, not bound by anything outside
his own nature. What a god wishes to do, he does—just because he feels like doing it, like Browning's god Setebos in
Caliban upon Setebos, who ignores a certain number of march-
ing crabs and then suddenly crushes one for no reason beyond
a momentary whim:

> Loving not, hating not, just choosing so.

In the higher paganism, there is, of course, often some recognition that decent conduct is to be expected even from the gods.
But this attitude, which is rare in the ancient pagan world, came
to be normal in Israel; it constitutes one of the basic distinctions
between the developed religion of Israel and the other religions
of the ancient Near East. Israel's God, as she finally came to
understand him, was of unalterable moral character. He was
good, as men should be good.

There are passages in the Old Testament, it is true, which

suggest that Yahweh can act in purely arbitrary ways and which attribute a certain "demonic" quality to him. There are primitive stories like that of his murderous attack on Moses (Exod. 4:24f.), or his wrestling with Jacob at the river (Gen. 32:24–32), but these are accidental survivals from the dark childhood of the race, preserved usually for some incidental reason that has nothing to do with theology. This kind of primitive thinking could, of course, appear also even during the days of the monarchy, as in the story of Yahweh tempting David to sin (2 Sam. 24:1), or with grim irrationality punishing the prophet from Bethel (1 Kings 13:11–24), or lying to Ahab (1 Kings 22:23). But these examples are taken from popular tales and reflect the unsophisticated folk religion of the countryside and the city streets, not the religion of Israel's prophets and thinkers.

There are even passages in literature as late as Ezekiel, Jeremiah, Second Isaiah and Job that suggest that God sometimes moves in mysterious ways when he performs his wonders, that he habitually conceals his motives from human eyes (Isa. 45:15), that he deals with his creation in the same arbitrary way as a potter does with his clay (Jer. 18:6). But only Ezekiel goes so far as to say that God has ever deliberately misled his people (Ezek. 20:25f.); and even Ezekiel, perverse as his thinking may seem to us, had no doubt that Yahweh's purpose was a moral one. The point of such remarks in the poets and prophets is not that God is really arbitrary, but that his motives are too mysterious and complex for human comprehension; his plans are too grandiose, the sweep of his mind and purpose too vast, to be understood by his creatures.

Power and Morality

Israel's first encounter with Yahweh convinced her of his power; her understanding of his moral nature was a matter of more gradual development. It was stimulated by two factors: in the first place, there were certain elements in the exodus and the Sinai experience that clearly implied that he was good as well as powerful; and, in the second, there was the increasing sensitiveness of Israel's mind and conscience, strengthened by the introduction of the Wisdom movement during the early monarchy, which led her to unfold more and more, in a rational way, the full implications of his goodness.

To a half-civilized people, such as Israel was at the time of the exodus, the most impressive attribute of Yahweh must have been his power, and the early records lay special stress on this. He proved himself more powerful than all the magicians of Egypt, and therefore, presumably, than all their gods. By his power, Israel believed, he brought them through the waters of the sea and destroyed the pursuing host of the Egyptians. One of Israel's oldest hymns, perhaps the oldest of all, strikes this note, and no other:

Sing to Yahweh, for he has triumphed gloriously;
the horse and his rider he has thrown into the sea. [Exod. 15:21]

In similar fashion, the tradition of his self-manifestation at Mt. Sinai puts the stress on his awe-inspiring power:

. . . there were thunders and lightnings, and a thick cloud upon the mountain, and a very loud trumpet blast. . . . Yahweh descended upon it in fire; and the smoke of it went up like the smoke of a kiln, and the whole mountain quaked greatly. [Exod. 19:16–18]

But, though the primary experience was one of power, it was accompanied by other experiences that revealed Yahweh's moral character as well. For one thing, the very fact that he had taken pity on an insignificant group of people in Egypt and used his power for their benefit was evidence that he was a generous benefactor, a saviour, a guide and a strengthener. These were the attributes that were to be increasingly emphasized with the passage of the years; the beneficence that prompted his action on Israel's behalf came to seem even more wonderful than the sheer power that enabled him to carry it through.

Furthermore, an integral element in the earliest account of the exodus (according to a majority of scholars) was his establishment of some kind of covenant with Israel, based upon obedience to his law. Israel's existence was, therefore, not dependent on the whims of an arbitrary, and possibly fickle, deity, but on her own continuing fidelity to the requirements of a law, primarily moral in content, in which her God had set forth his unchanging will. Just how much of the law now found in the Pentateuch actually goes back to these early times is a difficult question to answer, but there is no reason for doubting that the conception of Israel as a community based upon divine law was, in nuclear form at least, present from the very beginning.[1] This means, of course, that from her first appearance in history Israel had a genuine sense of the morality of deity; since her God demanded morality from his people, he must be himself a moral God.

If Israel's grasp upon the moral character of her God was based first of all upon her experience of him as saviour and lawgiver, the eventual unfolding of all the implications of his morality was certainly a matter more of logical thinking than of sudden inspiration. Israel was quite as capable as any other people of subjecting life and theology to rational criticism, and with the rise of the monarchy, and the introduction of Wisdom into the main stream of the nation's life, the rational approach to moral, intellectual—and theological—problems grew in importance. She began more and more to engage in theological ratiocination by means of analogy: to think, for example, that, if God is moral, as one knows he is, he cannot destroy human life without reason, because this is something a good *man* would not do; one cannot suppose that God is morally inferior to the best of his creatures. The classical expression of this way of reasoning about the morality of deity is found in Gen. 18:25, where Abraham is represented as presenting to Yahweh a rational argument that he should not destroy the innocent citizens of Sodom along with the guilty. "Far be that from thee!" he says. "Shall not the Judge of all the earth do right?" To destroy the innocent is a dreadful crime in an earthly judge (Exod. 23:6ff.; Deut. 27:25); the man of sensitive conscience finds it impossible to believe that God would take advantage of his power to do something forbidden to men. So "the Judge of all the earth" quite rightly and naturally comes to be clothed with the virtues that men demand of human judges; the Creator comes to be conceived of as exhibiting in a pre-eminent degree the moral qualities that seem desirable in the creature (2 Chron. 19:6f.).

The later refinement of God's moral character as seen by the men of the Bible, the softening and lightening of the divine countenance, is largely the result of the Wisdom strain in Israel's theology; as her own conscience became more sensitive and delicate, under the tutelage of the wise men, her understanding of the nature of deity became more sensitive and delicate also. The most moving expression of the gentle side of deity—the one that begins "The Lord [is] a God merciful and gracious, slow to anger . . ." (Exod. 34:6 etc.), which contains no reference at all to Israel's experience with God in history—is undoubtedly a pronouncement of the Wisdom school of theology. It is significant that this passage is treated more like a modern "creed"—that is, a formula to be learned, recited and quoted—than any other in the Old Testament.[2]

Holiness

In the rest of this chapter we shall turn our attention to some of the major descriptive adjectives that are used in the Old Testament to characterize God's moral nature. The first of these—the word "holy"—is particularly interesting since, in Hebrew thought, it has both a metaphysical and a moral sense and is therefore especially suited to provide a transition from the thought of the last chapter to the thought of this one.

The adjective "holy" (Heb.: *qadosh;* the noun is *qódesh*) was not, in all probability, applied first of all to deity, but rather to things that belonged to him. It is not a peculiarly biblical word, but is part of the common vocabulary of the ancient Semitic Orient. It seems likely that the basic meaning is related to that of a whole family of similar-sounding verbal roots which have some such sense as "cut," "cut off," "cut away," [3] the basic idea of "making holy" being that of cutting something, or some person, away from its parent stock or natural environment so as to introduce it permanently into the new and totally different environment of things that "belong to God." Certain places, for example, are called holy, because, in some special way, God is there. Moses is told, "Put off your shoes from your feet, for the place on which you are standing is holy ground" (Exod. 3:5) and, therefore, should not be contaminated with the residual profanity (*chol* [4]) that clings to shoes which have been used for ordinary purposes. "The Lord is in his *holy* temple," says the prophet (quoting a liturgical formula), "let all the earth keep silence before him" (Hab. 2:20).

Clothing and other objects that are set apart for use in the holy place are also holy. ". . . they made finely wrought garments, for ministering in the holy place; they made the holy garments for Aaron" (Exod. 39:1). Times, too, are holy when they are set apart for the honoring of deity. "Remember the sabbath day, to keep it holy" (Exod. 20:8). And, finally, people who are set aside for the service of God are also called holy. "Let no one enter the house of Yahweh except the priests and ministering Levites; they may enter, for they are holy . . ."

(2 Chron. 23:6). The most shocking, but in some ways most instructive, use of the adjective "holy" is in connection with the prostitutes who were attached to the shrines of the fertility cult in Canaanite, and sometimes in popular Israelite, religion, as, for example, in Hos. 4:14, where the prophet speaks of the men who "themselves go aside with harlots, and sacrifice with cult prostitutes" (lit. *"holy* women").[5]

Nothing could make it clearer that, in origin, the idea of holiness is a purely metaphysical one, without moral content. That which is holy is that which is reserved for the exclusive service of deity. But, in addition to this passive, negative connotation of the adjective there is also an associated positive one. That which is holy, set apart for God, has about it the aura of power that surrounds deity itself. From this point of view, holiness is a kind of material effluvium, like an electric current, that flows out from the holy place or thing and endangers the life of those who come near it unprotected. This was why Jacob "was afraid" when he awoke at Beth-el, and said, "How awesome is this place! This is none other than the house of God, and this is the gate of heaven" (Gen. 28:17). The classic illustration of this destructive aspect of holiness is the terrifying experience of Uzzah, who was struck dead when he attempted to steady the holy ark during the solemn procession when it was brought from Kirjath-Jearim to Jerusalem (2 Sam. 6:6f.). Uzzah's intentions were excellent, his conscience was entirely clean, but for unconsecrated hands to touch a holy object like the ark was like touching a live electric wire without rubber gloves. In neither of these stories does the word "holy" actually occur, but it is unquestionably the power of holiness that is the frightening and potentially fatal element in both of them. Because the holiness of a holy thing or holy place can destroy a man, it inspires terror and awe in the hearts of those who, unprepared, suddenly confront it as Jacob did.

But, if the term "holy" is applied first of all to places, things, times and persons connected with the deity, it comes, second-arily and by way of association, to be applied also to God him-self, and, as first applied, has the same purely metaphysical, nonmoral sense it had when used of the objects and persons connected with his worship. It is clear enough that the word "holy" cannot have a moral sense when applied to a place, a time or a thing, and it is obvious that, when originally applied to deity, it did not have a moral sense either. To say that Yahweh was "holy" did not, in the first instance, mean that he was "good," but only that he was remote from the sphere of the merely human, and exuded a dreadful and even deadly energy.

Another story of the ark, in which the word "holy" actually does occur, is the best illustration of this. The incident belongs to the same context as the one related above, but is prior to it. The men of Bethshemesh, it is said, came to look into the ark when it was brought back from the land of the Philistines, and seventy of them were struck dead for their impudence.[6] "Then the men of Bethshemesh said, 'Who is able to stand before Yahweh, this *holy* God?' " (1 Sam. 6:20). It is plain enough that what they are commenting on is not the fine moral character of Yahweh, but his awe-inspiring, destructive potency. The citizens of Bethshemesh had dared to trespass on the realm of the holy and were destroyed, like Uzzah in the later story. But what is significant in this incident is that it is not the ark which is called holy, but Yahweh himself; the destructive energy that is holiness does not burst out like a flame from some conse-crated object, but from the deity. Whenever the word "holy" is used of God in the Old Testament it always has these two basic connotations: of *remoteness,* the impassable gulf that separates men and created things from their Lord and Creator; and of awe-inspiring *power,* a power that would instantly consume those who approach it too closely.

But in the course of time, the word acquired another meaning also, and in the latest parts of the Bible, as in modern thought, this latest sense is primary—the sense of *transcendent moral goodness*. Just how this came about is not certain, but the first clear evidence for it is in the Book of Isaiah, and for this reason it is often said that Isaiah is the prophet responsible for the "moralizing" of the concept of holiness. This may be true, but cannot be proved. What is certain is that "the holy one of Israel" is one of Isaiah's favorite names for Yahweh, and that, when he uses it, it frequently has the overtone of "goodness" attached to it. This is clearest in the story of his inaugural vision in the temple (Isa. 6:1–7). There he heard the choir of seraphim singing the antiphonal hymn "Holy, holy, holy, is the Lord of hosts." The phenomena that accompanied the hymn were typical expressions of the metaphysical holiness of deity: ". . . the foundations of the thresholds shook . . . and the house was filled with smoke." But Isaiah's quite characteristic reaction of fear in the presence of majestic and overwhelming holiness—"Woe is me! For I am lost . . . for my eyes have seen the King, the Lord of hosts"—was not the product of metaphysical sensitivity, but of moral anxiety: "I am a man of unclean lips, and I dwell in the midst of a people of unclean lips." What removed this anxiety from him was the assurance that "your guilt is taken away, and your sin forgiven" (v. 7). The rest of Isaiah's career provides abundant evidence that ethical integrity, not mere ritual purity, is the proper preparation for approaching "the holy one of Israel" (Isa. 1:4, 10–20; 30:9–14).

The ethical character of holiness in the later thought of Israel is underlined most sharply in the so-called Holiness Code of Lev. 17–26, a special document of the Pentateuch now included within the Priestly Document, the motto and governing principle of which is "You shall be holy, for I the Lord your God am holy" (Lev. 19:2). The meaning of "holy" in this context, as applied to the people, is quite different from the sense it has in earlier passages which speak of Israel's "holiness." Israel had always been called, in some sense, a holy nation. Exod. 19:6, for example, says that she is called to be "a kingdom of priests and a holy nation," meaning that she is to be holy in the sense in which priests are holy—that is, a nation set aside for the service of Yahweh. This interpretation is reinforced by the previous verse (5), which anticipates the use of the word "holy" by declaring that Israel is to be God's "own possession." The same meaning is found in Jer. 2:3, where it is said that Israel, in the days of the wilderness wanderings, "was holy to the Lord" and therefore under his special protection; if any attacked her, "evil came upon them." In both these instances, as in many others, the word "holy" is obviously used in a nonmoral sense: like the word "saint" in the New Testament, which is precisely parallel to it, it refers to the objective status of the elect community, without any necessary inference that it is morally better than other communities that are not "holy." But in some passages, and especially in the Holiness Code, holiness is less an objective state than an ideal to be attained. To put it in other words, the community and its members, who are objectively holy because of their special relationship to God, are called upon to realize the true nature of holiness by exhibiting a quality of moral life superior to that of other nations.

It is true that many of the provisions of the Holiness Code have to do with purely ceremonial matters, where the concern is with keeping Israel ritually pure, and therefore objectively distinct from her neighbors. But the distinctive element in this particular code is its strong emphasis upon a high standard of ethical conduct and social justice. It is significant that the chapter in which the motto "You shall be holy, for I the Lord your God am holy" appears is precisely the chapter which contains the most advanced ethical thought of the Old Testament outside the Wisdom Literature.[7] It includes the noble summarizing precept, "You shall not hate your brother in your heart . . .

but you shall love your neighbor as yourself" (Lev. 19:17f.; cf. 34). Our concern here is, of course, not with the ethical teaching as such, but only with the way in which it is connected with the holiness of God. After almost every provision of the chapter comes the statement, "I am the Lord," with the implication that it is God's holiness (his ethical character) that demands holiness (ethical character) in his servants.

In this way the word "holy" has become almost an epitome of the whole character of the God of Israel. On the one hand, in its original metaphysical sense, it speaks of his inexpressible remoteness from everything created, his absolute otherness to everything that is, and of his ineffable power, manifest in the violent forces of nature, that summons all the earth to kneel before him in reverent awe. But, on the other hand, it speaks with equal clarity of the moral purity of his being, which excludes the ugly, the cruel, the irresponsible and the arbitrary, and makes him "of purer eyes than to behold evil" (Hab. 1:13). When the several "Isaiahs" who produced the Book of Isaiah speak so regularly of Yahweh as the "Holy One" (Isa. 40:25)— "the Holy One of Israel" (Isa. 1:4; 41:14), the one "whose name is Holy" who dwells "in the high and holy place" (Isa. 57:15)— it is in both these senses, the metaphysical and the moral, that they use the term, but the major stress has come to be on the latter.[8]

Righteousness

A second primary attribute of God's moral character is his "righteousness" or "justice." Unlike the word "holy," which belonged to the religious or sacral sphere from the beginning and had to have a moral meaning infused into it, the Hebrew words translated by "righteousness" or "justice" are words that belong originally to secular, human life and are only secondarily and analogically applied to the deity.

Yahweh is the ruler or "judge" of his people, so it is natural that the terms which describe his activity from this point of view should be derived from the practice of government and jurisprudence; they are, in other words, "forensic" terms. To get their full meaning it is important to see this, since the English word "justice" has a forensic meaning like the Hebrew, but the word "righteousness," used to translate exactly the same Hebrew word, ordinarily has only a general moral sense. In English the word "righteousness" is vague, moralistic and abstract, whereas in Hebrew the image it conjures up is precise, juridical and concrete.

The Hebrew root of which we are speaking (*tsadaq*) is sometimes defined as meaning "to be in conformity with a norm." This definition is not entirely satisfactory, but will do for the ordinary secular sense of that verb. It will perhaps be clearer if we translate it in English by the phrase "to be right" rather than "to be righteous." "To be righteous" in English has a distinctly moralistic sound, often with unfortunate overtones of priggishness. But the Hebrew verb, with all its related nouns and adjectives, has only the meaning of "being right," viz., "being what one ought to be."

So, for example, Hebrew speaks idiomatically about "scales of righteousness" (*mozney tsédeq*), meaning scales constructed fairly and honestly, not overweighted on one side or the other. The English versions, of course, translate the phrase less cumbrously: in Lev. 19:36, part of the great ethical chapter mentioned above, we read that one significant manifestation of Israel's "holiness" is that she shall have "just balances" (*mozney tsedeq*), "just weights" (*'avney tsedeq*), etc. By analogy with these examples any reader can correct the familiar mistranslation in Ps. 23:3, which should not read that Yahweh leads one in "paths of righteousness," but in "right paths" (see RSV margin), for the reference is not to moral guidance, but to the fact that a good shepherd will always lead his sheep on the *right* path, the one that leads to food and security—to the pasture of the fold—

and not to dangerous cliffs or the haunts of savage animals. So also, the precisely parallel phrase in Ps. 51:19 means "right sacrifices"—that is, the *normal*, prescribed sacrifices—as the RSV translates it, and not "sacrifices of righteousness" as in the KJV. In every instance "rightness," though awkward and unidiomatic in English, gives a more accurate sense than the somewhat woolly word "righteousness."

When transferred to the realm of human character, the concept of "rightness" does not lose this simple, basic sense of conformity to a norm, but naturally its meaning becomes a bit more complex, so that it might better be defined as "fidelity in the discharge of obligations" or "the fulfillment of responsibilities inherent in a relationship." It is in this sense that it is particularly applicable to judges and rulers. Nothing is so reprehensible in a judge or king than a lack of concern for "rightness" (what is right), or, as we would more naturally say in English, for "justice." Deuteronomy prescribes the character and conduct of judges:

You shall appoint judges and officers in all your towns which the Lord your God gives you, according to your tribes; and they shall judge the people with righteous judgment. You shall not pervert justice; you shall not show partiality; and you shall not take a bribe, for a bribe blinds the eyes of the wise and subverts the cause of the righteous. Justice, and only justice [*tsedeq, tsedeq*] you shall follow, that you may live and inherit the land which the Lord your God gives you. [DEUT. 16:18ff.]

In Ps. 72, the people pray that the king may conduct his government in accordance with principles of "rightness":

> Give the king thy justice, O God,
>   and thy righteousness to the royal son!
> May he judge thy people with righteousness
>   and thy poor with justice!
>
>   . . . .

> May he defend the cause of the poor of the people,
>   give deliverance to the needy,
>   and crush the oppressor! [Ps. 72:1-4]

It is this kind of "rightness" also that is to characterize the ideal king of the future—the "messiah"—as he is described in the Book of Isaiah:

> He shall not judge by what his eyes see,
>   or decide by what his ears hear;
> but with righteousness he shall judge the poor,
>   and decide with equity for the meek of the earth
> . . . .
> Righteousness shall be the girdle of his waist,
>   and faithfulness the girdle of his loins. [Isa. 11:3-5]

It is, of course, true that the words "righteous" and "righteousness" are also used frequently in the Old Testament in a purely moral sense, particularly in the Wisdom Literature, where they refer primarily to "right," or "approved," conduct. They are also used, in forensic contexts, in the sense of "innocent," and "innocence" as the quality that belongs to the unjustly accused, and the reader of the English Bible needs to be regularly on the lookout for passages in which, even in the RSV, one would get a better sense by translating "righteous" as "innocent." [9] It is obvious, however, that, when the term is applied to God, it refers to his character as judge and ruler. When one speaks of the "righteousness of God" one does not mean his blameless moral character in a general sense or (ordinarily) his innocence as the accused party in a lawsuit (though it does have this sense in Jer. 12:1), but, rather, the integrity of his character as a judge, and as sovereign ruler of both his people and the universe.

The kind of reasoning that led men to attribute righteousness to him is best illustrated in the story told in Gen. 18 to which we have already referred. It is precisely applicable here even though the word "righteousness" (*tsedeq* or *tsedaqah*) does not occur in it. When Abraham asks the question, "Shall not the Judge of all the earth do right (*mishpat*)?" the only possible answer is a ringing affirmative. If human judges are required to be "just" and "righteous," it is unthinkable that the Judge of all should be any less so.

So "righteousness" became one of the fixed attributes of Yahweh. An ancient poet says:

> . . . I will proclaim the name [i.e., the character] of Yahweh.
> . . . .
> The Rock, his work is perfect;
>   for all his ways are justice [*mishpat*].
> A God of faithfulness and without iniquity,
>   just [*tsaddiq*] and right [*yashar*] is he. [DEUT. 32:3f.]

A psalmist declares:

> . . . Yahweh sits enthroned for ever
>   he has established his throne for judgment
> and he judges the world with righteousness,
>   he judges the peoples with equity. [Ps. 9:7f.]

And another combines the purely physical or metaphysical attributes with the moral and proclaims that

> Clouds and thick darkness are round about him;
>   righteousness and justice are the foundation of his throne.
> [Ps. 97:2]

The attribute of righteousness has yet a further meaning that we have not touched on thus far and is not implied at all in the English use of the term. This too arises from the idea of the righteousness that belongs to a judge. But, whereas in English the term "judge" is used in a relatively passive sense to describe someone who has the authority merely to discriminate between the innocent and the guilty (the "righteous" and the "wicked") the Hebrew term *shofet,* translated "judge," has a much more active sense. It means one who is passionately committed to the cause of the innocent; paradoxically, a judge in Israel seems not to be one who has a judicial *temperament.* It is for this reason that the heroes of early days such as Gideon and Jephthah were called "judges." In the Book of Judges the verb "to judge" means "to vindicate" or "to liberate" as well as to rule The judge was a man of action, whose primary function was not the quiet adjudication of difficult legal questions, but the positive assertion of the rights of the innocent—"the righteousness of the righteous." To judge someone very often meant not "to pass judgment" upon him, but rather "to vindicate" him against his adversaries and oppressors. So, for example, in Ps. 10:18, where the KJV translates literally and meaninglessl "to *judge*" the fatherless and the oppressed, the RSV gives the precise meaning when it reads "to *do justice to* the fatherless and the oppressed." These "righteous acts" of the righteous judge can be called collectively his "righteousness" or, in Hebrew (though impossibly in English) "his righteous*nesses.*"

In many ways, it is this positive, dynamic aspect that is most important in the idea of the righteousness of God. Because he is the Judge of all the earth, Israel knows that he is "righteous," not so much in the sense that he makes correct judicial decisions in accordance with accepted legal norms, as that he is actively, passionately, and unappeasably involved in the struggle for the right. It was noted above that the statement that Yahweh is a jealous God could properly be translated that he is a "passionate" God, and it is of the greatest importance to see that his "passionateness" is a basic ingredient in his righteousness. It was because Israel believed in a God who was ardently committed to maintaining the rights of the righteous that the psalmist could advise the worshiper not to put his trust in earthly rulers,

> in a son of man in whom there is no help,

but rather in "the God of Jacob"

> who made heaven and earth,
> the sea and all that is in them;
> who keeps faith forever;
> who executes justice [*mishpat*] for the oppressed;
> who gives food to the hungry.
> [who] sets the prisoners free.   [Ps. 146:3–7]

The fact that the righteousness of God in the Old Testament has this active, dynamic sense explains the frequent, though to our Western minds curious, use of the term "righteousness" (*tsedeq* or *tsedaqah*) as equivalent to "vindication" or "victory." It appears in this sense both in early and late passages. Thus we read in the Song of Deborah that in the time of the judges men met at the watering places to "repeat the triumphs [*tsidqot:* literally, the 'righteousnesses'] of Yahweh, the triumphs of his peasantry in Israel" (Judg. 5:11). This use of the term is especially characteristic of Second and Third Isaiah. In Isa. 46:13, where the KJV reads, "I bring near my righteousness; it shall not be far off, and my salvation shall not tarry," the RSV translates correctly, as the parallelism dictates, "I bring near my *deliverance;* . . ." And again, in the magnificent poem of Isa. 63:1, where the KJV represents the divine victor as declaring, "I that speak in righteousness, mighty to save," the RSV gives what is undoubtedly the correct sense by reading, "It is I, *announcing vindication,* mighty to save."

When deprived of these dynamic associations—which lead, as the last quotation shows, from the idea of Yahweh as judge or ruler to that of a warrior fighting on behalf of the right—

the idea of the divine righteousness loses most of its force and is reduced to a bloodless, generalizing, moral abstraction. But when the concept is filled with its proper biblical content, one begins to understand the enthusiasm it evoked in the Israelite worshiper and how natural it was for him to connect it with the thought of God's power, and with the strong, towering things of his creation, as in Ps. 36:6:

Thy righteousness is like the great mountains [KJV; RSV literally, "mountains of God"]
    thy judgments are like the great deep;
    man and beast thou savest, O Lord,

or Ps. 71:16, 19:

    With the mighty deeds of the Lord God I will come,
      I will praise thy righteousness, thine alone.
    . . . .
    Thy power and thy righteousness, O God,
      reach the high heavens.

God's righteousness, in Old Testament thought, does not denote primarily the moral excellence of his character, but his power and willingness to save.

Faithfulness and Truth

A third note of the divine character is specified by the words variously translated "faithfulness" and "truth." What is meant is that Yahweh can be depended upon, he does not change from day to day, there is no uncertainty about his character. The thought can be expressed in various ways, but the words most commonly used for this purpose are derived from a Hebrew root, *'aman,* which means "to be firm or steadfast." As anyone can see, this is the word that underlies the familiar liturgical response, "amen," familiar in all the languages of the Judeo-Christian world. Various forms of this root occur in combinations where the meaning is something like "sure" or "steadfast." So in Isa. 22:23: "I will fasten him like a peg in a *sure* [*ne'eman*] place." Isa. 33:16: "his bread will be given him, his water will be *sure.*" 2 Sam. 7:16: "your house and your kingdom shall be made *sure* forever." Job 39:24: the war horse "cannot *stand still* [*ya'amin*] at the sound of the trumpet." Exod. 17:12: Moses' "hands were steady [*'emunah*] until the going down of the sun."

Like the ethical teachers of other times and other parts of the world, the moralists of ancient Israel regarded the virtue denoted by this root and its derivatives as basic to most of the others. Where men are shifty, evasive, whimsical, and fickle, social and business life are almost impossible; society thrives only where it can be assumed that most men are true to their word, steadfast, reliable, unchanging as respects their character within and their obligations without. If one has a mission to be entrusted to another person, it is an enormous relief to know that that person is reliable:

> Like the cold of snow in the time of harvest
> is a faithful [*ne'eman*] messenger to those who send him,
> he refreshes the spirit of his masters.   [PROV. 25:13]

It seemed worthy of special remark, and implicit praise, that it had not been necessary to audit the business records of the contractors who repaired the temple in the reigns of Jehoash and Josiah because "they deal faithfully" (*be'emunah;* RSV "honestly"; 2 Kings 12:15, Heb. 16; 22:7). Nehemiah explains that the men whom he appointed as overseers of the temple storehouse were chosen because they had the reputation of being faithful (*ne'emanim;* Neh. 13:13). Among those whom the Old Testament characterizes specifically as faithful are Abraham

(Neh. 9:8), Moses (Num. 12:7 KJV), David (1 Sam. 22:14), Zadok the priest (1 Sam. 2:35), and the future Messiah (Isa. 11:5). As a human quality faithfulness inspires universal respect and wins the approval of God:

> Lying lips are an abomination to Yahweh,
> > but those who act faithfully [*'osey 'emunah*] are his delight.
> > > [PROV. 12:22]

To minds that are ethically sensitive it is inconceivable that a quality so universally admired in men should not be found in the Godhead also. The people of ancient Israel had no doubt that their God was altogether reliable. What could especially be relied on was his good will toward the afflicted and his desire to help. So it was natural to speak of his faithfulness almost in the same breath with his righteousness as, for example, one of the psalmists does when he comes to offer thanks for deliverance from trouble:

> I have not hid thy saving help [literally, "righteousness"] within my heart.
> > I have spoken of thy *faithfulness* and thy salvation;
> I have not concealed thy steadfast love and thy *faithfulness*
> > from the great congregation.
> Do not thou, O Lord, withhold thy mercy from me,
> let thy steadfast love and thy *faithfulness*
> > ever preserve me!   [Ps. 40:10f., HEB. 11f.]

The expression of the faithfulness of God in the Hebrew version of this psalm is slightly less monotonous than in the English, since the Hebrew has two words for the concept, whereas the English has only one. Both are derived from the root *'aman* and have approximately the same meaning, but they are different in form. In the first instance above, the word is *'emunah*, which is the one most commonly used, but in the last two instances, the Hebrew word underlying the English is *'emét* (the *n* of *'amen* having been assimilated into the following *t*). In older English versions like the KJV the word was rendered, even in contexts like this, as "truth." Elsewhere, the RSV also frequently gives it the sense of "truth," because in numerous other instances this is exactly what it means; as, for example, in 1 Kings 22:16, where Ahab says to Micaiah ben Imlah, "How many times shall I adjure you that you speak to me nothing but the truth in the name of the Lord?"

The difficulty we have in translating the word into English arises from the different way in which the Hebrew mind understood the notion of "the true." For us, truth is an intellectual concept: it means the correspondence between an idea held in the mind and some objective fact. If the idea exactly corresponds to the fact, we say the idea is true. But the Hebrew conception of truth seems to have an almost moral quality. There is no thought of a comparison between "ideas" in the mind and "facts" outside of it. False ideas are simply those that are undependable; they are crooked, uncertain. True ideas are those which do not waver when put to the test; truth is that which stands like a rock in all circumstances. So it is natural that the concept "truth" should be expressed by a word derived from *'aman,* to be firm or steadfast.[10]

It can be seen from this that the phrases "God of truth" or "the truth of God" mean no more than *"faithful* God" or "God's *faithfulness."* To translate the word in this context as "truth" is, indeed, quite misleading, since the English word introduces an intellectual element that is wholly foreign to the Hebrew. "God of truth" means to the English reader that God is the source of true ideas, while "truth of God" is likely to be misunderstood as meaning "true ideas that derive from God." There is no suggestion of such a thought in the Hebrew, and the translation "truth" is justified only if it is immediately redefined for these contexts as "faithfulness, fidelity, reliability."

God's faithfulness has two aspects, a general and a specific one. God is praised, in the first place because he is dependable in the sense in which a human being may be dependable, as a matter of principle, in all situations and under pressures of any kind. This is presumably the kind of faithfulness referred to by the psalmist in the extract given above. But there is another kind of faithfulness that is often singled out as giving to Israel a special sense of confidence, viz., God's special faithfulness with respect to his obligations under the covenant. There is no sharp distinction between these conceptions, and in most cases it is impossible to tell whether the writer of a hymn or prayer is thinking chiefly of faithfulness as a general quality that might inspire anyone to approach the throne of deity for help, or whether he is thinking particularly of those promises that are specifically given under a covenant, which the God of Israel may be confidently expected to fulfill. A clear example of the latter, specific sense can be found in Ps. 89, a royal lament which has more to say about God's faithfulness than any other psalm. It explicitly bases the appeal for God to help his king upon the covenant once made with David:

> I will sing of thy steadfast love, O Lord, for ever;
>> with my mouth I will proclaim
>> thy faithfulness to all generations.
> For thy steadfast love was established for ever,
>> thy faithfulness is firm as the heavens.
> Thou hast said, "I have made a covenant with my chosen one,
>> I have sworn to David . . ."   [Ps. 89:1–3]

and then comes the complaint,

> Lord where is thy steadfast love of old,
>> which by thy faithfulness thou didst swear to David?   [v. 49]

Although the king was in danger because of defeat in battle (vv. 43f.), and it seemed that Yahweh had forsaken him, the psalmist knows that the God who promised David an everlasting throne will not reject a plea based on his faithfulness—not just because he is generally dependable as a good and righteous Creator, but specifically because of his well-known fidelity to particular obligations—here, the covenant with Israel's king.

Yahweh's faithfulness to his covenant with Israel as a whole was no less certain than his covenant with David. It is expressed in classical form in the Deuteronomic version of Israel's little liturgical "credo":

> Know therefore that Yahweh your God is God, the faithful
> [*hanne'eman*]
> God who keeps covenant and steadfast love with those who
> love him and keep his commandments to a thousand generations.
>
> [Deut. 7:9]

In times of national distress it was the assurance of Yahweh's faithfulness to his promises that kept Israel faithful to him. It was because this was a fixed element in the theology of Israel that the prophet of the Babylonian exile could confidently say:

> Thus says the Lord,
>   the Redeemer of Israel and his Holy One,
> to one deeply despised, abhorred by the nations,
>   the servant of rulers:
> "Kings shall see and arise;
>   princes, and they shall prostrate themselves;
> because of the Lord who is faithful [*ne'eman*]
>   the Holy One of Israel, who has chosen you."   [Isa. 49:7]

Love and Compassion

The last attribute of Israel's God to be considered here is that of his love. Other qualities, like justice and power, have been emphasized so frequently in discussions of the God of the Old Testament, especially those which are primarily concerned with contrasting the Old Testament and the New, that it requires a conscious effort of reorientation to realize that love is quite as fundamental a quality. It may seem that a disproportionate amount of attention is devoted in the Old Testament to the theme of Yahweh's wrath and his intention to punish. But this is because so much of the Old Testament consists either of laws, where the imposition of sanctions is necessarily an important element, or of prophetic oracles and historical treatises (the "Deuteronomistic" histories) based upon them, where the major concern is with Israel's breach of the covenant and the inevitable reaction of her covenant Partner. Very little of the Old Testament is taken up with general statements about the character of God, and, for the most part, these are found only in liturgical contexts and in late prophets like the Second Isaiah who were probably influenced by liturgical style. But where such statements occur, it is significant that what they tend to stress is not the wrath of God against sinners,[11] but his love for the righteous, and his desire to help them.

The basic article of Israel's faith, as we have seen, was that of her election, i.e. the belief that Yahweh had chosen her to be his own. It is an inevitable corollary of this doctrine that Yahweh is a God of love—in the restricted sense, at least, that he was a God who loved *her*. This is not to say that Israel had always been aware of this corollary, or had always defined her election in terms of his love; it may well be that she originally was inclined to look upon it as pure mystery, the result—gratefully received—of an arbitrary act of divine free will or inexplicable impulse. But, in the long run, she could hardly fail to note the analogy between this kind of divine action and the equally arbitrary, or at least unpredictable impulses which lead a man to choose one woman for his wife rather than another, or one man rather than another to be his friend. And so, by the time of Hosea, and perhaps much earlier, it seemed natural to describe God's choice of Israel, and the settled relationship that followed, in terms of the love that underlies the marriage bond.

Thus Hosea pictures Israel's breach of the covenant in his time as comparable to a wife's infidelity to her husband and dramatizes Yahweh's final rejection of her in terms of a formula of divorce. Yahweh speaks to the citizens of the elect community as though they were the children of the marriage between himself and Israel and says, "Plead with your mother, plead—for she is not my wife [i.e., any longer—this is the divorce formula], and I am not her husband . . ." (Hos. 2:2, Heb. 4). Jeremiah, speaking in the mood of Hosea, pictures the honeymoon between Yahweh and Israel in the old days, "I remember the devotion of your youth, your love as a bride, how you followed me in the wilderness, in a land not sown" (Jer. 2:2). Ezekiel, too, inhibited though he was in the expression of tender emotion, was familiar with the delights of marital love (Ezek. 24:16, 18), and describes the covenant relationship in terms of marriage (16:8). But the clearest expression of the nature of Yahweh's basic relationship to Israel is to be found in the carefully formulated theological statement of Deut. 7:6–8:

. . . the Lord your God has chosen you to be a people for his own possession, out of all the peoples that are on the face of the earth. It was not because you were more in number than any other people that the Lord set his love upon you and chose you, for you were the fewest of all peoples; but it is because the Lord loves you . . . that the Lord has brought you out with a mighty hand, and redeemed you from the house of bondage. . . .

A good many years ago N. H. Snaith, in a valuable little book,[12] made the distinction between two kinds of love that are both important in Old Testament thought. The first is what he calls Election Love, which is represented by the Hebrew noun *'ahavah* and its cognates. This is the kind of love of which we have just been speaking, the kind of love that finds expression in the free personal choice, sometimes inexplicable because purely emotional, that leads one to select this person rather than that for wife or friend. But there is another kind of love also, represented by the Hebrew word *chésed,* which he calls Covenant Love.[13] While this, too, has warm, emotional overtones, it has stern duty as its essence. This is the kind of love that provides the continuing foundation for a relation that has once been established by election love. Whereas—all too obviously in human beings—election love is unpredictable and unstable because based on emotional preference alone, covenant love is shot through with a sense of loyalty and obligation, and for this reason is entirely dependable, unsusceptible to whim and caprice. Election love establishes a marriage, but only covenant love can sustain it.

There is no precise English equivalent for the Hebrew word *chésed,* which expresses this idea, but the RSV tried to bring out its presence by translating it wherever possible by the phrase "*steadfast* love," thus emphasizing both the emotional aspect of the conception and its strong moral underpinnings. For obvious reasons, it is a favorite word of Hosea, but is frequent throughout the Old Testament in theological as well as secular contexts, to denote the affective bond and sense of mutual obligation that should bind together the partners in any kind of voluntarily undertaken relationship. It is of course often used for the attitude that Israel should exhibit toward God, as in the famous passage from Hosea, "I desire steadfast love and not sacrifice" (Hos. 6:6).

But we are interested in it here because of the many places in which this kind of love is attributed to God. It is naturally used in the context of Yahweh's covenant with David:

> Great triumphs he gives to his king,
>> and shows *steadfast love* to his anointed,
>>> to David and his descendants forever.   [Ps. 18:50]

But the more basic covenant is that with the nation as a whole, and the word is used repeatedly in this connection also. Its importance in the liturgy is shown by Ps. 136, which relates the whole story of God's dealings with his people in their formative days and includes in every verse the refrain:

for his steadfast love endures for ever.

By a striking *tour de force,* the Second Isaiah extends the promises of the Davidic covenant to the whole nation: "I will make with *you* an everlasting covenant, my steadfast, sure love for David" (Isa. 55:3), where the Hebrew word for love (*chasdey*) is actually in the plural (KJV, "sure mercies") because the Hebrew mind did not see love merely as an abstract emotion, but as issuing in a series of concrete actions on behalf of the beloved.

Since the theology of Israel is so largely expressed in liturgical forms, it is not surprising that the word occurs with greatest frequency in the psalms, and in hymns and prayers elsewhere. When Nehemiah prayed, it was natural for him to begin, "O Lord God of heaven, the great and terrible God who keeps covenant and steadfast love with those who love him and keep his commandments . . ." (Neh. 1:5; cf. 9:32, a prayer of Ezra). The sense of being surrounded by God's steadfast love was probably the predominant mood of worship in the temple: "We have thought on thy steadfast love, O God, in the midst of thy temple" (Ps. 48:9), for, as Israel knew from her past experience

· The Lord has made known his victory,
    he has revealed his vindication [literally, "righteousness"]
        in the sight of the nations.
He has remembered his steadfast love and faithfulness
    to the house of Israel. [Ps. 98:2f.]

Thus far, we have spoken only of God's love for Israel (and David), but the concept of his steadfast love was just as meaning-

ful for individual members of the community as for Israel as
a whole. Just two examples out of many will suffice to illustrate
the fact. The author of Ps. 26 prays for help in his trouble:

> Vindicate me, O Lord,
>   for I have walked in my integrity,
>   and I have trusted in the Lord without wavering.
>
> . . . .
> For thy steadfast love is before my eyes.   [vv. 1–3]

And the author of Ps. 86 gives thanks to God:

> For great is thy steadfast love toward me;
>   thou hast delivered my soul from the depths of Sheol.   [v. 13]

It must be confessed that in instances like the last two it is
often impossible to distinguish the meaning of *chésed* as strictly
"steadfast love" (i.e., the kind of love that is obligatory in the
framework of a covenant) from just lovingkindness in general.
There is no question that in later times the word, like so many
words in every language, gradually lost its specific meaning—
and its connection with covenant—and came to be equivalent
to ordinary good will and benevolence. In many of the passages
in the psalms where the individual appeals to God on the
strength of his *chésed*, it is quite probable that the petitioner is
simply thinking of the character of God as being loving or
kindly rather than making any conscious connection with the
promises of the covenant.

This is a natural development in the realm of religious
thought as well as in linguistic usage, for, with the broadening
and deepening of Israel's spiritual consciousness, it was inevitable that the thought of a God who loves should be seen
in a larger context than merely that of his relationship with
Israel. The influence of the wise men—Israel's teachers, philosophers and intellectual leaders—was undoubtedly important in

this connection, since by definition their thought did not move in the area of covenantal concerns, but rather in that of universal relationships and universal truths.[14] So, if love was a desirable quality in man, as it certainly was according to their view (Lev. 19:17f., 34; Prov. 10:12; 15:17), it must be a quality of God also.

If, in Israel, the sense of God's love had its *origin* in the doctrine of election and the covenant, the sense of his universal benevolence is connected with the doctrine of creation. Thus we read in one of the late Wisdom books:

> He who lives for ever created the whole universe
>
> . . . .
> Who can measure his majestic power?
>   And who can fully recount his mercies?
>
> . . . .
> What is man, and of what use is he?
>   What is his good and what is his evil?
>
> . . . .
> Like a drop of water from the sea and a grain of sand
>   so are a few years in the day of eternity.
> Therefore the Lord is patient with them
>   and pours out his mercy upon them.
> He sees and recognizes that their end will be evil;
>   therefore he grants them forgiveness in abundance.
> The compassion of man is for his neighbor,
>   but the compassion of the Lord is for all living beings.
>
> [SIRACH 18:1–13]

While the words used here are patience, mercy, forgiveness, and compassion, they add up to love, for as Paul says in 1 Cor. 13:4–7 it is precisely by such qualities that love is recognized. Furthermore, one can see from the last verse, that Ben-Sira has in mind the commandment of Lev. 19:18, to "love your neighbor," and deliberately extends its scope to the entire family of man.

The author of the Wisdom of Solomon expresses a similar thought,

> . . . thou art merciful to all, for thou canst do all things,
>   and thou dost overlook men's sins, that they may repent.
> For thou lovest all things that exist,
>   and hast loathing for none of the things which thou hast made,
>   for thou wouldst not have made anything if thou hadst hated it.
>
> . . . .
>
> Thou sparest all things, for they are thine, O Lord who lovest the
>   living.   [WISDOM 11:23–26]

In another place he describes God's Wisdom as "beneficent" and "loving toward man" or "humane" (*euergetikon, philanthropon;* 7:23).

For various reasons, nothing precisely like this is to be found in the canonical Wisdom Literature of the Old Testament, but the feeling for God's universal love that finds such clear expression in the Wisdom Literature of the Apocrypha is only what one would expect by extrapolating from the tendencies of the older wise men, and there is no reason to suppose that the wise men who wrote our Book of Proverbs would have felt in the least uncomfortable with what Ben-Sira and the Book of Wisdom have to say about the universal reach of God's mercy and lovingkindness. It is also not at all impossible that the wise men may have influenced the prophets and were in some measure responsible for the sense of Yahweh's universal beneficence that frequently breaks through in the prophetic books (e.g. Amos 9:7; Isa. 2:2–5; 19:23–25; 42:1–4; see above p. 95).

It is significant, again, that Israel's understanding of God's love, like all the rest of her theology, began with historical experience and not with general abstractions. She did not begin with a vague sense of God as universal father and men as universal brothers, but with a keen sense that God had shown his love to *her* in a particular and unique way, a love that created a new relationship in strange, inexplicable fashion, and sustained it with unwavering fidelity. The love of God thus had for Israel an immediate reality that is far removed from mere theological speculation. Inevitably, however, with the progress of her thought and the refinement of her conscience in later days, her profoundest spirits came to understand that the love of the Creator of all things cannot be limited to any part of his creation, but must be shed impartially on all. Many passages which speak of the "steadfast love" of God must certainly be interpreted in this, and not in the narrower, fashion.

So Ps. 103, though it pays formal tribute to the doctrine of Israel's special election in v. 7 ("He made known his ways to Moses, and his acts to the children of Israel") and v. 18 ("his covenant . . . his commandments"), really moves in a much larger framework where

> The Lord has established his throne in the heavens,
> and his kingdom rules over all [v. 19]

and where, as in Sirach 18:8–10, God's affectionate concern for men is determined by their helplessness and the inherent pathos of their situation as created, and therefore transient, beings:

> As a father pities his children,
> so the Lord pities those who fear him.
> For he knows our frame;
> he remembers that we are dust.
> As for man his days are like grass;
> he flourishes like a flower of the field;
> for the wind passes over it, and it is gone,
> and its place knows it no more.
> But the steadfast love of the Lord is from everlasting
> to everlasting
> upon those who fear him. . . . [vv. 13–17]

It is the same kind of love that is attributed to God in the formal summary of God's qualities that appears so frequently in the Old Testament and has the best claim to be considered the real creed of ancient Judaism, at least in its later development:

The Lord [is] a God merciful and gracious, slow to anger, and abounding in steadfast love and faithfulness, keeping steadfast love for thousands, forgiving iniquity and transgression and sin. . . . [EXOD. 34:6]

However true it may be that the creed upon which Israel's existence as a people was founded is one which simply recited the mighty acts of God in the past, it is equally true that the creed by which men lived their daily lives was one like this, which was less immediately concerned with what God has done than with what he is and will always continue to be. Without its basis in the national experiences of God's love, such a creed would have been empty theorizing, but without this creed and many other expressions of conviction about the divine *nature*, the mere summary of what God had done for Israel in the past would have been only history and archaeology, with no power to affect the ordinary man in his ordinary life.

8

DIGRESSION:
THE NAMES OF GOD

Holy and terrible is his name!

PSALM 111:9

NAMES WERE far more important for men of the ancient Near East than they are for modern man, since the very existence of a thing was thought to be tied up with the fact that it had a name. The theological importance of the name is shown by the opening lines of the Babylonian creation epic,

When on high the heaven had not been named,
Firm ground below had not been called by name,
. . . .
When no gods whatever had been brought into being,
Uncalled by name, their destinies undetermined—
Then it was the gods were formed within them [i.e., in the primeval waters].
Lahmu and Lahamu were brought forth, by name they were called.[1]

In the Hebrew creation story also, the giving of a name is, in several instances, explicitly connected with the creative act (Gen. 1:5, 8, 10; 2:19). A name is a part of the essence of a person, place or thing, and can therefore frequently be taken as

an expression of character. The puns that are so common especially in the prophetic books (though usually invisible to the
English reader) are not merely rhetorical fancies, but are at
least half-serious attempts to explain the true nature or destiny
of a thing by disclosing the real meaning of its name. So Babylon, said Old Testament man, was not really "the gate of god"
(*bab-el*), but the city of "confusion" (connecting the word with
the Hebrew root *balal,* "to mix up"; Gen. 11:9); and Nabal, the
husband of Abigail, really was a fool, for that is what the Hebrew word *nabal* (*naval*) means (1 Sam. 25:25).[2]

Because of this ancient, and semimagical, understanding of the
importance of names, the idea of the divine name plays a
significant role in Old Testament thought. One who knows a
divine name is able to invoke the presence and obtain the help
of the god who bears it. If a god does not wish to be put in the
power of a man, he may simply refuse to communicate his name,
as the river god (who was not originally Yahweh) refused to tell
his name to Jacob (Gen. 32:29). Since one can have no abiding
relationship to a god whose name is unknown, Moses insisted
upon learning the name of the god who revealed himself at the
burning bush. When he returns to Egypt and tells of his meeting with a god, he knows the first question the people will ask
is, "What is his name?" (Exod. 3:13). One way the ancient Hebrews had of expressing practical atheism—denying that there
is a God who has any relationship to man—was simply to ask
the skeptical question, "What is his name?"—the implication
being that no one knows it, and his existence can therefore be
ignored (Prov. 30:4).

God himself can speak of his name in such a way as to indicate that it is in some way identical with his being. When Ezekiel
represents Yahweh as doing great deeds "for the sake of his
name" (Ezek. 20:9, 22, etc.), he does not mean that God acts
merely to save his reputation, but in order to demonstrate his
power and show what kind of God he is. Such is the meaning

also in the Twenty-third Psalm: "he leads me in the right paths, for his name's sake" (v. 3), in other words, he leads me because it is in accordance with his nature to do so. We have already seen how the Deuteronomic literature avoids speaking of God dwelling in his temple, and prefers to say that he causes his name to dwell there (1 Kings 8:16). This is because the name is identical in essence with the person; the name of God is a surrogate for God himself; where his name is pronounced, there is he.[3]

Yahweh

The distinctive name of the God of Israel is, as we have previously noticed, the mysterious word that we render in English as Jehovah or Yahweh. The former pronunciation is certainly wrong; the latter is only a reasonable scholarly guess. Actually, all that has been preserved of the name is its consonantal structure, YHWH.[4] Because of the atmosphere of awe that came to surround it, another word was always substituted, in later times, when it occurred in prayers and Scripture reading, and eventually the true pronunciation was forgotten. In the days of the second temple it was pronounced only once a year by the high priest when, on the Day of Atonement, he entered the most holy place. With the destruction of the temple in A.D. 70, even the priests forgot the form of the name. The feeling that led to this development is already foreshadowed in the Decalogue, which contains a prohibition against taking God's name "in vain," meaning originally using it in curses and magical formulas (Exod. 20:7). Later it came to seem wise, in order to avoid possible profanation of this kind, not to use the name in any ordinary, secular context, and finally it seemed best not to use it at all, even in public worship. But reverence for the mysterious, unpronounceable name of the deity, which invoked his actual presence, and for the consonants that spelled it out, continued to be a vital factor in the devotional life of Israel and remains so to the present day.

Since the full spelling of the name, and its pronunciation, are still uncertain, it is futile to speculate on what it originally meant. The Hebrews in the time of the monarchy liked to derive the name, as we have seen (pp. 131f.), from the verb "to be" or rather "to become" and perhaps thought of it as expressing the certainty of God's future presence with them, and the inexhaustible possibilities of his nature as it unfolded during the course of their history. "He will be what he will be," or as he himself would say, "I will be what I will be" (Exod. 3:14, RSV margin). In the beginning, Israel's possession of the name was primarily a sign of the reassuring intimacy that existed between her and her God; it was like being on a "first-name basis" with a person whom one respects and whose character one trusts. But later, with the growth of speculative tendencies and the development of a more formal type of reverence, it came to function rather as a concentrated expression and symbol of the mysterious essence of Yahweh's character.

Adonay

The word which was ordinarily substituted, in reading and speaking, for the sacred, unpronounceable tetra-grammaton YHWH was the artificial name Adonay, formed from the common noun *'adon* meaning "lord." The common noun can be used of either man or God, as when Joseph says to his brethren, "God . . . has made me a father to Pharaoh, and lord (*'adon*) of all his house" (Gen. 45:8), or when the psalmist says of Yahweh that he is "the *Lord* of all the earth" (Ps. 97:5). The form *'adonay* is simply the plural of this word with the possessive suffix of the first-person singular, meaning literally "my lords" (and is so translated in Gen. 19:2). By artificially lengthening the final vowel (*'adonāy*) the form has

been converted into a kind of proper name, with the suffix sometimes translated and sometimes treated as a purely formal element, the plural being regarded as a plural of majesty or abstraction. In this form, it is then simply translated in the Greek
and English versions as "my Lord" (e.g., Exod. 4:10) or "the
Lord" (e.g., Ps. 37:13). Eventually it became the practice to
substitute this word for the awesome, never-to-be-pronounced
divine name YHWH wherever this appears. In the Greek version of the Old Testament (the Septuagint) the phrase "the
Lord" (*ho kurios*) is the regular rendering of both YHWH and
Adonay, and the same practice is followed in such familiar
English translations as the KJV and RSV.[5]

Unfortunately, when God is spoken of as "the Lord," the
phrase, though accurate, is a cold and colorless one, even as
compared with the Hebrew Adonay, which still conveys something of the warmth and mystery of a proper name. Although
the practice can hardly be avoided, one needs to remember
that by translating YHWH or Adonay as "the Lord" one introduces into many passages of the Old Testament a note of
abstraction, formality and remoteness that is entirely foreign
to the original text.

The Lord: Adon, Baal

Nevertheless, the concept of Yahweh as *'adon* or
Lord is of fundamental importance for Old Testament thought.
It is certainly more characteristic of the way in which Israel
thought about her God than terms denoting physical or blood
relationship such as "father" or "brother," although these terms
are also sometimes used, as in the proper names Abijah and
Ahijah, meaning respectively "YHWH is my father" and
"YHWH is my brother" (1 Kings 14:1; 11:29).[6] Whatever else
Yahweh was in ancient Israel, he was the sovereign Lord of the
community and its members, and had the right, as such, to ex-

pect obedience from them. All other accounts of the character of Israel's God and his relationship to his people must be evaluated in the light of this basic and invariable fact.[7]

It is still disputed among scholars whether at any time Yahweh was also called *ba'al*. The Hebrew term is identical in meaning with the word *'adon,* even though it is most familiar to English readers as the name of a particular pagan god. The common, nonreligious meaning of the word is found, for example in Isa. 16:8 ("the lords of the nations"); elsewhere, it is given a more specific secular sense by being translated "master," "owner," or "husband" (e.g., Isa. 1:3; Exod. 21:28f.; 21:22). These meanings are entirely appropriate for describing Yahweh's relationship to Israel, and certain proper names compounded with *ba'al* (e.g., Eshbaal, 1 Chron. 9:39; and Bealiah, 1 Chron. 12:5, Heb. 6) seem to show that, at least in the early days of the monarchy, Yahweh was indeed addressed with the title "baal" as well as "adon." Although the meaning of the two terms is identical, the name "baal" was ultimately dropped in connection with Yahweh because of its associations with the fertility cult and the Canaanite high god whose name was Baal. Hos. 2:16 (Heb. 18), ". . . you will call me 'my husband' [*'ishi*], and no longer will you call me, 'My Baal,' " seems to reflect this change in sentiment (in Hebrew, both terms mean simply "my husband" and would be equally appropriate except for the pagan connotations of the latter).

'Elohim, 'Eloah

Along with Yahweh, the most common name of the God of Israel is simply "God," in Hebrew *'elohim*. This word is plural in form (meaning literally "gods"), the plural being probably a kind of plural of abstraction, having almost the sense of the English word "deity," except that it has greater warmth and color. However the usage arose, the plural was probably believed in later times to indicate that Yahweh contained within himself the totality of divine attributes; it could become, therefore, a suitable vehicle for expressing genuine monotheism.[8] Certain portions of Scripture—the P document of the Pentateuch and the "Elohistic" portion of the Psalter[9]— show a decided preference for this rather than Yahweh as the name of Israel's God, partly no doubt through a reverential desire to avoid pronouncing the mysterious proper name, but partly also, perhaps, from a certain sense—shared of course by the modern mind—that it is more fitting to speak of God in the abstract than to give him a proper name, as the pagans do.

Occasionally, also, as notably in the Book of Job, the singular of this word, *'eloah,* is used. But this usage is late, and probably artificial.[1]

'El

Still another word is used for Yahweh, the simple monosyllable *'el,* which is usually indistinguishable from *'elohim* in the English versions, since both are translated "God," as, for example, in Ps. 55:19 (Heb. 20), "God will give ear, and humble them . . . because they keep no law, and do not fear God," where at its first occurrence the word "God" represents the Hebrew *'el,* but at the second, *'elohim.* This is enough to show that the ordinary dictionary meaning of the two terms is identical, even though the connotations may be slightly different. Both mean simply "god," but *'elohim* (when used in a singular sense) is distinctively Hebrew and therefore can be used as a synonym for YHWH, whereas *'el* is a common Semitic word and can be used either for Yahweh or for a god of the heathen (the contrast is something like that in English between the capitalized "God" and the lower-case "god").

Among the Canaanites, the word *'el* was used not only as a common noun, but as a proper name to designate the chief god of the pantheon.[11] When Israel settled in Canaan, she rejected all attempts to identify Yahweh with the younger god *ba'al,* but apparently felt differently about *'el,* with whom, because he was after all the chief god, Yahweh could be identified without offense. Yahweh evidently took over some of the attributes of *'el,* particularly in connection with creation. For this reason, the name *'el,* when used of Yahweh, conveys special nuances to the student of the history of religion. These overtones should be apparent even to the ordinary reader of the Old Testament if he considers how often Yahweh is identified with what are obviously older gods and numina who bear names compounded with *'el,* such as El-Elyon ("God Most High," Gen. 14:18),[12] El-Roi ("God of Seeing," Gen. 16:13f.), El-Olam ("the Everlasting God," Gen. 21:33), El-Bethel (Gen. 35:7), and, most important of all, El-Shaddai ("God Almighty," Exod. 6:3), meaning perhaps "the mountain god." (Shaddai by itself, "the Almighty," is a favorite name for God in Job: Job 5:17 etc.)[13] The original meaning of the word *'el* is still disputed by scholars, but the most probable explanation seems to be that which derives it from a verbal root meaning "to be strong." [14] Whether or not *'el* and *'elohim* are in any way related words is another question to which scholars are as yet unable to give a definitive answer. In actual usage, *'el* is often merely a useful synonym for *'elohim,* but—insofar as any difference can be detected—*'elohim* is a more "correct," more philosophical and theological word, while *'el* has about it a certain poetic liveliness, a touch of mythological vigor, inherited from its originally pagan associations.

Yahweh of Hosts; King

A compound name for Israel's God that appears very frequently from the time of Samuel on (1 Sam. 4:4; Ps. 24:10; Isa. 1:9, etc.), is "Yahweh of hosts" (*yhwh tseba'ot*), but

the real meaning of this is also uncertain. The word *tsaba'* (pronounced *tsava'*), translated "host" in English, is simply the normal Hebrew word for "army," but what armies (*tseba'ot*) are
meant? The human armies of Israel, or the heavenly armies of
angels, or the celestial bodies? Or is the word to be understood
in a merely adjectival sense ("the militant Yahweh")? [15] Whatever it may have meant in the beginning, it seems to have been
later understood to refer to the heavenly armies or "forces"
that were at God's disposal; and, finally (as in the Septuagint),
it was taken to be an expression of God's omnipotence, Yahweh
being in control of all the "forces" or "powers" of the world.[16]

An epithet that is frequently associated with Yahweh, especially in the later literature and above all in apocalyptic, is that
of "King" (*mélek*). The reticence about using the term in the
earlier period is possibly due to its association with Canaanite
ideas, and specifically with the cult of Molech (1 Kings 11:7)—
a distorted form of the word for king.[17] It does, however, occur in some psalms that are almost certainly early (Ps. 24:7–10;
Ps. 29:10), so it presumably had a place in the vocabulary of the
Jerusalem temple (it also occurs significantly in Isaiah's temple
vision: Isa. 6:5), but the earliest idea of Yahweh's kingship was
probably that of sovereignty over other gods rather than over
Israel. The idea of God's kingship on earth, and especially the
hope of the eschatological establishment of his "kingdom,"
which we shall consider in the next chapter, was in large part
a product of the downfall of the Davidic monarchy. It became
one of the dominant ideas in postexilic thought (1 Chron.
28:5; 29:11; Ps. 145:12f.; Dan. 4:3; Zech. 14:16).[18]

There is obviously no theological system implicit in the
various names for God in the Old Testament. The nomen-
clature consists partly of quite natural survivals from the ancient
Semitic world (*El, Adon, Melek*), and, in part, of new forms
of old names which have been given new semantic reference
(*Yahweh, Elohim, Adonay*). The most one can say about them

theologically is that they give expression, in the cult and in ordinary life, to some of the well-known emphases of Old Testament theology—the mystery of God's nature (Yahweh, and El in various combinations), the power of God (El, Yahweh of hosts), and the sovereignty of God (Adon, Adonay, Melek).

9

GOD IN THE FUTURE

. . . he comes to judge the earth.

PSALM 96:13

IT IS UNLIKELY that early Israel had any genuine eschatology—any theory, that is, about the ultimate goal of human and cosmic history. Some scholars have attempted to show that she did have eschatological interests and took over from other nations of the ancient Orient a definite framework of eschatological ideas, but the evidence for this view is decidedly meager.[1] One has to base it on inferences from later works rather than on any clear statements in the early sources. Scholars today are generally inclined to think that eschatology in Israel was a comparatively late development.

This is not to deny, of course, that ancient Israelite literature attributes a kind of eschatological attitude to the ancestors of the nation, and thus provides a certain pattern for the genuine eschatology of later times. The patriarchs, and the Israelites of the exodus period, are represented as living in expectation of the gift of the Promised Land, which for them would be a goal lying at the end of a particular series of historical experiences. So also there is more than one passage in early Hebrew poetry that can be interpreted as referring to the future coming of

197

David, the ideal, victorious ruler. A famous passage in Genesis, the so-called Blessing of Jacob, says:

> The scepter shall not depart from Judah,
>   nor the ruler's staff from between his feet,
> until he comes to whom it belongs,
>   and to him shall be the obedience of the peoples.
>   [GEN. 49:10][2]

And the oracles of Balaam speak of

> a star [that] shall come forth out of Jacob,
>   and a scepter [that] shall rise out of Israel

to "crush the forehead of Moab, and break down all the sons of Sheth" (Num. 24:17). But the most natural interpretation of all these passages is that they are retrospective, and the "prophecies" *post eventum*. The poems in their present form, at least, were written after David had become king, and the passages that speak of the future gift of the land were actually composed long after Israel had taken possession of it. If one can use the term "eschatological" about them at all, it is only in the sense of a "realized eschatology." The future to which the ancestors were believed to have looked forward had already arrived and Israel was enjoying the benefits of it. This is the point of view of a prosperous and contented people who lived in the heyday of the Hebrew kingdoms before the rise of the great universal empires.

One might also say that there is a germinal eschatology in the J document, expressed in the five-times repeated promise:

I will make of you a great nation and I will bless you, and make your name great, so that you will be a blessing. I will bless those who bless you, and him who curses you I will curse; and by you all the families of the earth will bless themselves.   [GEN. 12:2f.]

This formula may not have been created by the Yahwist, but his almost obsessive repetition of it (Gen. 18:18, 22:18, 26:4, 28:14) shows how important it seemed to him. Anyone who writes on the philosophy of history must have some conception of the goal toward which history is moving, and the Yahwist, who appears the first to have attempted such a philosophy, was no exception. His chief concern was to show how all of history in the past, from the creation of man to Israel's occupation of Canaan, had been under the control of Yahweh, the God of Israel; but he could hardly avoid giving some thought to the ultimate purpose of it all. The answer seems to have come to him in the form of the folk motto quoted above.

Apparently he never got beyond the general, rather vague, belief that God's future action would so increase the prosperity of Israel that she would become the most "blessed" of nations and a source of envy to others. In later times, the words about the other families of the earth "blessing themselves" by Israel would be interpreted to mean that they would somehow share in her blessing, and some scholars have argued that such was also the Yahwist's understanding.[3] This is not impossible, but, if it was, it seems strange that he does not expand the thought or hint at it in other passages. Actually, the Yahwist has no detailed program for the future; for him it is merely the sphere in which God will increasingly manifest his benevolence, certainly toward Israel and, just possibly, toward other nations as well. In the Yahwist's vision the future is without contours, a vast, sunlit plain, with no roads and no commanding features visible on the horizon. Probably this was the common view in Israel before the rise of classical prophecy in the eighth century. It was undoubtedly shared by the priesthood and the wise men, since neither the Priestly Document of the Pentateuch, nor the Chronicler—the priestly historian—nor the Book of Proverbs shows any concern with eschatology, in the technical sense, as we see it emerging in the prophetic literature.

The Eschatology of Judgment

It is only with the classical prophets that genuine eschatological thinking begins. They were the first to be concerned primarily with the future rather than the past, the first to realize that the character of God as it had been revealed through Israel's historical experience demanded that he act in some definitive way in the future. The earlier prophets saw this action as taking place only in the very near future, and as resulting from his reaction to the deplorable moral condition of his people. Some scholars would insist that this is still not really eschatological thinking, and would reserve that term for the later prophets and apocalyptic writers who viewed history in more doctrinaire fashion and saw it moving inexorably toward a predetermined conclusion. The distinction is a real one and needs to be kept in mind, but, for the sake of simplicity, we shall use the term "eschatological" here for any kind of thinking that includes an emphasis upon God's definitive action in the future. It is in this sense that we can speak of eschatologically oriented thought as beginning with the great prophets of the eighth century. It was they who first directed the gaze of Israel away from the past and what God *had* done, and toward the future and what he was yet *going* to do.

Certainly their view of the future was eschatological for Israel, since they foresaw the imminent end (the *eschaton*) of Israel, at least in the form in which men had known her in the past. The earliest eschatology was an eschatology of judgment. It appears suddenly and fully formed in the preaching of Amos. The character of Amos' message was unmistakable, and quite without parallel in the previous experience of the nation. Like Moab in the days of King Mesha, Israel had known defeat in battle, caused by God's anger,[4] but never before had she, or any other nation, been threatened with total extinction

by the national God. The main function of a God, men believed, was to protect his people against their enemies; he might
be angry sometimes, but his anger was part of a family quarrel
that could always be settled.

Now Amos declares that a final breach has taken place in
the relationship. It is true that a very few passages in his book
suggest the rupture could be healed if only Israel would re-
spond to the prophet's call to repentance (Amos 5:4, 6, 14f.).
No doubt these are to be taken seriously, but Amos did not
expect his message to be favorably received. Like Jeremiah at
a much later date, he was sure that the leopard could not change
his spots nor the Ethiopian change his skin (Jer. 13:23). The
result of Israel's contumacious spirit, which she had manifested
now for centuries, could only be a disaster, limited for the moment to the northern kingdom, of almost inconceivable pro-
portions.

> Fallen, no more to rise,
>   is the virgin Israel;
> forsaken on her land,
>   with none to raise her up.   [AMOS 5:2]

In the past, God had attempted to turn Israel from her evil
path by sending punishment after punishment (4:6–11), but
to no effect. Now the end was at hand, and the prophet's message was, "Prepare to meet your God!" (4:12).[5]

One passage in Amos has often been taken as evidence for
the existence of a preprophetic eschatology. This is 5:18, in
which the prophet announces, "Woe!" upon those "who desire
the day of the Lord." "The day of the Lord" was evidently
a popular idea which might, conceivably, have had an eschatological reference. The phrase has frequently been interpreted
as referring to a definite occasion when Yahweh would triumph
over all opposition and allow Israel to enter into full possession

of her promised blessings. This is not an impossible interpretation, but other interpretations are equally possible. Mowinckel
thinks the reference is to an annual event in the cultus,[6]
while von Rad sees in it a survival from the days of the "Holy
War," [7] a technical term for Yahweh's victory in battle. While
there may have been some kind of eschatology before the time
of the prophets, this slight and ambiguous phrase is quite
insufficient to prove the fact, much less to give us any information about its nature. More important is what Amos does with
it. In a brilliant paradox, he simply turns it upside down and
fills it with new content. Whatever its original meaning may
have been, it is obvious that "the day of the Lord" had always
seemed something bright and desirable. But Amos declares:

> It is darkness, and not light;
>> as if a man fled from a lion,
>> and a bear met him;
> or went into the house and leaned with his hand against
>>   the wall,
>> and a serpent bit him.
> Is not the day of the Lord darkness, and not light,
>> and gloom with no brightness in it?   [AMOS 5:18ff.]

The eschatology of doom could hardly be expressed in more
uncompromising fashion.

The message of Hosea, in spite of his emphasis upon Yahweh's love, was quite as uncompromising and his images of
doom quite as appalling.

> So I will be to them like a lion,
>> like a leopard will I lurk beside the way.
> I will fall upon them like a bear robbed of her cubs,
>> I will tear open their breast,
> and there will I devour them like a lion,
>> as a wild beast would rend them.   [HOSEA 13:7f.]

Because of the infidelity of Israel, the wife, Yahweh has turned from playing the role of a loving husband to become like a savage animal.

These unprecedented words of Amos and Hosea, which were spoken publicly during the regular exercises of the cult, must have created consternation in the minds of their audiences. The reaction of Amaziah the priest of Bethel is sufficient evidence of that (Amos 7:10–13), if any evidence were needed beyond the bitter words themselves. The religious life of Israel up to this time had centered, as we have seen, in the cult with its continual reaffirmation of Israel's election, its comforting repetition of the story of the mighty saving acts of God toward the nation in the past, its proclamation of the laws by keeping which God's favor was assured, and its imposing sacramental rites in which it seemed evident to all that God was presently active in the midst of his chosen people. Now an Amos or a Hosea, both speaking in the name of Yahweh, dared to say that the age of divine favor was past, that God had decided to pass a sentence of condemnation upon his people, that the heavenly bridegroom was determined to divorce his faithless bride.

We naturally ask the question: Why did this violent mutation of thought arise suddenly at this particular period in Israel's history? The answer is by no means easy. It is tempting to rationalize the phenomenon by saying that an Amos and a Hosea were simply men of great intelligence and political sensitivity who perceived the moral bankruptcy of the nation and could feel the acids of dissolution at work. The fact is, however, that moral conditions were probably no worse in the middle of the eighth century than they had been previously. The age of Solomon or of the dynasty of Omri had presented a far more radical challenge to the morals and customs of the past than did the age of Jereboam II, and yet these periods produced no threats of a final break between Yahweh and his people. And it is a further fact that the destruction of the kingdom of Israel was in no sense the result of ethical failure and loss of morale. Israel was destroyed by a vastly superior military machine after courageous resistance.[8] It must be recognized that Amos and Hosea and the later prophets were preachers and zealots, whose strictures on their own age must not be taken as accurate sociological analyses based on calm appraisal of the existing situation. The abuses they were attacking were those endemic to civilized human society at all periods. This is, of course, the reason the prophets continue to be studied.

What is unique and original about these men is that they actually saw the moral disease in the society of their own day—the indifference of the rich toward the poor, the universal and undisguised pursuit of purely selfish ends, the general toleration of moral laxity, the love for luxury as an end in itself, the total disregard of the more serious ethical demands of the divine law accompanied by a frivolous concern with its ritual and ceremonial requirements. These things they saw and loathed, and they could not but believe that Yahweh loathed them also. And if Yahweh loathed these things wherever he found them, as the opening paragraphs of Amos' book forcefully declare, it seemed obvious that he must find them even more detestable in Israel, the people whom he had chosen for his own. Since, as an Amos might have said, God's "noble experiment" had obviously failed, and Israel was neither better than other nations nor showed any signs of moral improvement from one generation to the next, it seemed to the prophet—as he felt it must to Yahweh—that the time had arrived for calling the experiment to a halt. Most zealous moralists in every stage of human history and in every country have made similar negative judgments about society in their own day, though they have not usually been able to support their censures, as the prophets did, by appeal to the doctrine of election and the curses attached to disobeying the law that accompanied it.

What is unique about the prophets is not the unparalleled corruption of the times in which they lived, but the unparalleled ethical sensitivity which caused them to react so violently to a fairly normal society. What was new was not the social structure, but the new mind that judged it.

To explain the emergence of this new mind is probably beyond the capacity of the historian. Ultimately such questions are insoluble. As with the emergence of the new Greek mind in the age of Pericles, some of the contributing factors are evident, but similar factors have often been present elsewhere without producing a Sophocles, a Herodotus, or a Socrates, an Amos, a Hosea, or an Isaiah. We can see in Israel certain factors that contributed to the rise of classical prophecy: increased prosperity and the growing refinement of life, which always lead to growth of intellectual activity; a broader familiarity with the moralistic Wisdom teaching that had formerly been confined largely to the court; and, above all, the rising power of the first great universal empire, Assyria, with the widening of intellectual horizons that necessarily went with it, together with the specific threat it brought to the continued existence of Israel. All these things contributed to create the peculiar situation that produced classical Hebrew prophecy, but none of them—nor all of them put together—really explain it. The existence of the great Hebrew prophets is simply a datum of Old Testament theology, and can no more really be explained than the existence of Israel herself.

After the fall of the kingdom of Israel, which must have seemed in direct fulfillment of the predictions of Amos and Hosea, a line of similar teachers, who had already begun their work in Judah, continued for nearly a hundred and fifty years to prophesy that the fate of the southern kingdom would be the same, and such it eventually proved to be. It is unnecessary to review here the teaching of Micah, Isaiah, Jeremiah, and Ezekiel, because, despite many differences of nuance, in essence it was the same as that of Amos and Hosea. The fulcrum of all their thought was that Yahweh is a God of such moral integrity that he can no longer tolerate the lack of integrity of his people. The doom of Israel is, therefore, the one certain fact about the future. This grim eschatology of condemnation is the first stage in an evolving knowledge of God's action in time to come.

Whether or not the eighth-century prophets looked beyond the doom to a restoration and to new gifts of grace for a morally rehabilitated people in the future is a question that need not concern us here. There are passages in all the prophetic books that speak of a future hope, and there is a tendency in present-day criticism to attribute at least some of these to the prophet himself rather than to a postexilic redactor. But, however one explains them, they are relatively few in any case, and there can be no doubt that the main thrust of prophetic teaching before the exile was on the coming of the dreadful day of judgment rather than upon some glorious future that might hopefully lie beyond it. The idea of future blessing for Israel belonged, as we have seen, to the vague hopes of older, more optimistic times. The concept of an imminent and terrifying judgment was the particular contribution and principal burden of the eighth- and seventh-century prophets.

With the passage of time, the day of doom was more and more detached from the specific realities of history and became simply a fixture in Israel's view of the future. In the elaborate eschatologies of later times, the first act continued to be a day of judgment in which God would pass a sentence of final condemnation on the powers of evil. This stage had not yet been reached at the time of the prophet Zephaniah, who was active in the latter half of the seventh century, but it was he who provided the classic picture of the day of Yahweh, whatever may have been the sense in which he understood it:

The great day of the Lord is near,
  near and hastening fast:

  . . . .

A day of wrath is that day,
  a day of distress and anguish,
a day of ruin and devastation,
  a day of darkness and gloom,
a day of clouds and thick darkness,
  a day of trumpet blast and battle cry
against the fortified cities
  and against the lofty battlements.   [ZEPH. 1:14–16]

The Eschatology of Hope

If, in the nature of the case, it was the pre-exilic
prophets who introduced into Israel a belief in the coming day
of judgment, it was the prophets of the exile and postexilic
periods who completed the eschatological scheme by insisting
that the day of judgment was only the first act in the drama
of the future, that God's ultimate purpose was not to condemn,
but to redeem. For the vivid descriptions of the coming doom
that made up the bulk of the proclamations of the older
prophets, they provided equally vivid pictures of a time of
unimaginable blessings that was yet to come.

This change of emphasis begins with the two Judean prophets, Jeremiah and Ezekiel, whose careers overlapped the beginning of the Babylonian exile. Like the prophets of the eighth
century, and unlike the later apocalyptic writers, the thought
of these two men was tied to the realities of the historical
situation. For them belief in the coming of a day of judgment
had not been a theoretical, dogmatic belief connected with
the end of history, but an event in the immediate future that
must inevitably result from the moral and religious conditions
of their time. Both of them lived to see their worst forebodings

realized in the capture of Jerusalem by Nebuchadrezzar and the transplanting of the best part of the population to distant Babylonia (2 Kings 25:1–21; Jer. 39; Ezek. 33:21). So, for both these men, the expected doom had come; for the moment, at least, there was nothing more to be said in this area, and their intellectual and creative energies could be directed along other, more positive, lines. If the older prophets had used all their imaginative skill to terrify their auditors by depicting the terrors of the coming day of judgment, the younger prophets proved themselves no less skillful in stirring the emotions of those who listened to them by describing the beauty and happiness of that day when God would restore his people to their land and once more show his favor upon them:

> Thus says the Lord:
> Behold I will restore the fortunes of the tents of Jacob,
>   and have compassion on his dwellings;
> the city shall be rebuilt upon its mound,
>   and the palace shall stand where it used to be.
> Out of them shall come songs of thanksgiving,
>   and the voices of those who make merry.
> I will multiply them, and they shall not be few;
>   I shall make them honored, and they shall not be small.
>   [JER. 30:18f.]

As one would expect, the voice of Jeremiah is a sober one. His picture of the future lies entirely within the lines of historical possibility, with only a few poetic touches to heighten the emotional tone. Speaking to a broken, prostrate nation, his only desire was to assure them that God's final word was not condemnation but restoration:

> I have loved you [God says] with an everlasting love;
>   Therefore I have continued my faithfulness to you.
> Again I will build you, and you shall be built,
>   O virgin Israel!   [JER. 31:3f.]

As the older prophets' certainty about God's holiness and righteousness had made them feel that judgment was bound to come,
so the later prophets were driven by an equally strong conviction that his faithfulness and love would find a way to bring
triumph out of disaster.

Ezekiel's description of the blessed future is far closer to
genuine eschatology than Jeremiah's, though it must be said
that a good many modern commentators have thought the more
extravagant elements in his picture may have been added by
overenthusiastic disciples of the prophet at a later time. His
vision of the valley of dead bones is not, of course, an account
of the physical resurrection of the dead, but only an extremely
vivid parable of the resurrection of Israel as a nation (Ezek.
37:1–14). He foresees the reunion of the peoples of the southern
and the northern kingdoms (37:15ff.), with kings of the Davidic
dynasty once more ruling over them (37:24f.; 34:23f.). Up to this
point he continues to speak in terms that belong to the realm
of actual, at least possible, history. But then the book goes
on in chapters 38–39 to depict the arrival and subsequent
annihilation of the dreadful armies of Gog of Magog, and, in
chapters 47–48, which describe the miraculous reconstruction
of the physical aspect of the Holy Land, it is evident that we
are moving out of the sphere of history into that of a theoretical
and dogmatic eschatology.

It is with Second Isaiah, at the end of the Babylonian exile,
and his disciples whom we lump together for convenience under
the name of Third Isaiah, that the prophetic imagination
achieved the most sublime heights in picturing the blessed
world of the future. The poetic touch is so strong that it is
often hard to tell whether the prophet is really speaking in
graphic metaphors about ordinary historical events—the conquests of Cyrus and the return of the Jews from Babylon—or
whether his dreams are wholly eschatological, uncontaminated
by any reference to prosaic happenings in the world of his

own time. Most commentators, probably correctly, believe the former to be true—that the prophet was actually talking about the Persian conquest and the consequent rebuilding of Jerusalem—but at least two modern writers have been so much impressed by the disparity between the prophet's high-flown poetry and the matter-of-fact events it is supposed to refer to that they have insisted the language can only be understood as picturing the end of history, not just the end of Babylon.[9] In any case, it is significant how easy it has been for later generations, especially in the Christian Church, to interpret Second Isaiah's poems in a purely eschatological sense—so much so, indeed, that it requires a wrench of the imagination for most of us to realize that, in their original setting, the words probably have a definite, limited historical reference.

Such words as the following suggest to our minds far greater events and broader vistas than simply the return of the Jews to Jerusalem in 538 B.C. They are filled with a sense of the grandeur of Israel's God, of his undying love for his people, of his saving purpose that runs through the whole of history, and the ultimate establishment of his kingdom:

> How beautiful upon the mountains are
> > the feet of him who brings good tidings,
> who publishes peace, who brings good tidings of good,
> > who publishes salvation,
> > who says to Zion, "Your God reigns."
> Hark, your watchmen lift up their voice,
> > together they sing for joy;
> for eye to eye they see
> > the return of the Lord to Zion.
> Break forth together into singing,
> > you waste places of Jerusalem;
> for the Lord has comforted his people,
> > he has redeemed Jerusalem.
> The Lord has bared his holy arm
> > before the eyes of all the nations;

and all the ends of the world shall see
    the salvation of our God. [ISA. 52:7–10]

For a brief moment I forsook you,
    but with great compassion I will gather you.
In overflowing wrath for a moment
    I hid my face from you,
    but with everlasting love I will have compassion on you,
says the Lord, your Redeemer. [ISA. 54:7f.]

Second Isaiah illustrates better than any other prophet how easy it was for Israel's thinking in the long run to pass from the historical to the eschatological. This is the way in which Israel's theology always developed. It was never entirely *a priori;* its characteristic movement was not from general theory to particular application; but from particular experience to universal truth—in this instance, from a confrontation with God in the actualities of past and present history to an understanding of the far-off goal and purpose toward which history was tending.

Eschatology comes late in Israel's history because the historical experience that made it credible and necessary had to come first. Israel had first to gain an adequate understanding of how God acted in the past and in the present before she could begin to see how this same God would act in the future. And she had, furthermore, to have the experience of rejection and reconciliation, of exile and return, in the actual events of the eighth, seventh, and sixth centuries, before she could see that her God would always be standing before her at history's end in his twofold character as Judge and Redeemer. It was not the ideal dreamings of impractical visionaries which created the eschatology of Israel, but the hard facts of historical experience in those three centuries and in the sometimes even harder times that were still to follow. From the bitterness of the exile she learned that God would come to be her Judge, for that was the way he *had* come; from her ancient experience of the exodus, now reinforced by her deliverance from exile, she was sure that ultimately he would come to be her Saviour.

Apocalyptic Eschatology

Thus far we have been discussing the eschatology of the great, classical prophets, and have noted that, in the main, it is not eschatology in the strictest sense of the word, since the prophets were concerned quite realistically with events in their own times rather than with what was going to happen at the end of history. But we have also noticed how, almost imperceptibly, especially in Second Isaiah, this kind of historically rooted eschatology tends to merge into a genuine theoretical eschatology, how the immediate future so easily becomes a paradigm of the remote future, and how the gaze of the prophet is so easily lifted up from considering the events that lie immediately before him to a consideration of the whole meaning of future history.

The tendency toward theoretical eschatology grows stronger as time passes. The simple pattern of judgment, redemption, and final rule of God, which emerged from the teaching of the great prophets, had to be filled in with more concrete details and there arose a more intellectual attitude toward the problem that made eschatological speculation almost an end in itself. One needs to say "almost," for it is certainly true that, in the Old Testament, even the most elaborate eschatological passages had the practical purpose of encouraging the faithful to persist in their faith, and dissuading the faint-hearted from succumbing to temptation. Nevertheless, the involved schemes these passages contain must have been created by men of thought rather than action, men who had an intellectual, speculative interest in lifting the veil from the future. The schemes are too elaborate for the use to which they are put.

While traces of this kind of theoretical speculation about the future can be found in some of the prophets, the phenomenon itself appears full-blown only in the apocalyptic writers, and it is to them we must now turn our attention. Most of the apocalyptic writers come after the Old Testament period, but the canonical Old Testament contains one complete apocalypse, the Book of Daniel, one inchoate apocalypse, Isaiah 24–27, and three chapters in Zechariah (12–14) that have a strong apocalyptic flavor.[10]

There is a definite line of connection between older prophecy and later apocalyptic, but the differences are quite as marked as the similarities and one cannot assume that prophecy simply evolved without assistance into apocalyptic. Apocalyptic probably represents the confluence of several tendencies, perhaps some of them foreign,[11] with prophecy only one among them. One important and clearly identifiable strain is that of the wise men. In the first chapter of the book named for him, Daniel is introduced to the reader as one among several who was "skilful in all wisdom, endowed with knowledge, understanding learning, and competent . . . to teach . . . the letters and language of the Chaldeans" (Dan. 1:4). In other words, he is a "wise man," and we can expect him to speak in an intellectual manner quite different from the fervid emotionalism of the prophets. And this is just the way he is represented as speaking in the apocalyptic parts of the book (chaps. 7–12). While the author of Daniel undoubtedly wished to evoke a moral response from those whom he addressed—desired that they should make what the modern evangelist would call a "decision for God"—he did it less by way of confronting the readers' consciences with ethical imperatives or summonses to repent, than by presenting to their minds a key by means of which the future—and therefore the present—could be understood. If one will only *understand,* he seems to say in almost Pauline language, that "the sufferings of this present time are not worth comparing with the glory that is to be revealed" (Rom. 8:18), then one will have no difficulty in remaining faithful to God and the practices of true religion, however difficult the circumstances may become.

It is in this appeal to the intellect and the understanding that the mark of the wise men can unmistakably be seen. It is, of course, a new role for them to play, one which seems very different from the one they play in Proverbs, but it would be a mistake to limit the concerns of the wise men too narrowly. They were not mere teachers of morality and the good life, statesmen and counselors, but the intelligentsia of the nation, taking all knowledge as their field. They were the scientists of ancient Israel and its historians (being the only ones professionally equipped to write); it was they who presumably collected, edited, and sometimes annotated the oracles of the prophets; they no doubt wrote many of the psalms (and not only those that have identifiable Wisdom elements in them), and collected all the psalms into the single book we call the Psalter;[12] so it is not surprising that they were also interested in the future and in trying to unveil its mysteries. If this seems to us a strange field for the intellectual and the scientist, it is well to remember that, even in the Western world, only in recent times could any sharp line be drawn between the chemist and the alchemist, or the astronomer and the astrologer. The kind of wise man who, like Solomon, was interested in all the mysteries of nature "from the cedar that is in Lebanon to the hyssop that grows out of the wall" (1 Kings 4:33) would, in the long run, be interested also in the mysteries of time, from the beginning of things in creation (Prov. 8:22–31; Job 38:4–11) to the things that lie behind the veil of the future.[13]

This is not to say, of course, that apocalyptic is simply to be classed with Wisdom Literature, but only that in apocalyptic the influence of a certain type of wise man is quite as apparent as the influence of the prophet.

In the nature of things the science of the future cannot have the consistency and precision of a science of the past. Since its sources are ultimately to be found in dreams and visions rather than in historical records, it tends to have the wild variety of dreams and to proliferate in fantasies as one dream is imposed upon another. All apocalyptic has this fantastic character, in which one series of nightmarelike images follows another without any evident unity of design or logical dramatic development. Yet, underneath the shifting imagery that is only the decoration of the basic theme, one can see that the apocalyptic drama has a certain broad unity, and that it moves forward in three great acts, which are simply taken over from the developed eschatology of the prophets. It begins in *history,* moves forward to *judgment,* and ends with the *triumph* of God and his righteous people.

This pattern is clearly seen in Daniel 7, the most important apocalyptic chapter in the Old Testament, most important both for what it contains and for its subsequent influence. Here, the first eight verses deal with actual history. They picture in fantastic fashion the rise of the four world empires—Babylon, Media, Persia, and Greece—under whose rule the recent history of Israel had run its course. The last, and worst, period was the one in which the apocalypse was written, the time of Antiochus Epiphanes, the "little horn" with "eyes like the eyes of a man, and a mouth speaking great things" (Dan. 7:8).[14] At this point, act one ends and act two—the judgment—begins, for

> thrones were placed
> and one that was ancient of days took his seat;
> . . . .
> the court sat in judgment,
> and the books were opened. [DAN. 7:9-10]

When the judgment has taken place and the beasts are condemned, the third act, the triumph, arrives. ". . . dominion and glory and kingdom" are at last given to the "one like a son of man," who, in fact, is the symbol for "the people of the saints of the Most High," whose "kingdom shall be an everlasting kingdom, and all kingdoms shall serve and obey them" (Dan. 7:13f., 27).[15]

Exactly the same pattern, though with entirely different details, is evident in the "Isaiah" apocalypse (Isa. 24–27).[16] Again there is a beginning in some kind of actual history, although here the starting point is mentioned only in passing and in such general terms that there is no general agreement as to what historical occasion the author had in mind. Some great city that had threatened others has been captured and destroyed,

> The city of chaos is broken down,
>> every house is shut up so that none can enter
>> . . . .
> Desolation is left in the city,
>> the gates are battered into ruins.   [Isa. 24:10ff.]

According to the author's understanding, this event in actual history,[17] described in such allusive fashion, was only to be the preface to a universal judgment:

> On that day the Lord will punish the host of heaven, in heaven,
>> and the kings of the earth, on the earth.
> They will be gathered together as prisoners in a pit;
> they will be shut up in a prison,
>> and after many days they will be punished.   [Isa. 24:21f.]

After that comes the last act, when

> . . . the moon will be confounded, and the sun ashamed;
>> for the Lord of hosts will reign on Mount Zion and in Jerusalem
> and before his elders he will manifest his glory.
>> [Isa. 24:23; cf. 25:6–8; 27:6, 12f.]

It is in this form that the eschatology of ancient Israel was finally crystallized. The future is no longer thought of as simply a continuation of present history, in which Israel would move forward vaguely into an era of ever greater and greater prosperity and blessing. Rather, it was seen that somewhere "time must have a stop." In apocalyptic thought history itself has no meaning; meaning lies outside of history. Therefore, the time is coming when the treadmill of historical events with its dreary procession of hideous beasts and chaotic cities will arrive at its preordained terminus. God will condemn and destroy the evil forces that now control it, and after that will establish his righteous rule for ever and ever.

The thought of God coming as Judge was not one which inspired terror in the Israelite mind, for, as we have seen, a judge is a "vindicator (see above, pp. 170f.). A judge may, incidentally, have to condemn the wicked, but his primary function is not so much "to terminate the evil" as "to diadem the right." So the eschatology of later Israel, with all its pictures of the grim things that were to happen at the last day, was not gloomy and terrifying in the sense of the medieval *Dies irae* or Michael Wigglesworth's *Day of Doom*; the terrors were only for the rulers of the world and their unrighteous sycophants. The emphasis of Amos had shifted once again; the "day of the Lord" had come once more to seem a "day of light." The condemnation of the wicked would be a part of it, but beyond the condemnation was the day of victory for God's faithful people, a people who were not merely, as in Amos' day, the smug, self-satisfied members of an elect and prosperous community, but, rather, a people who had learned, through the tuition of the prophets, to conform themselves to God's Law and live in humble submission to his will. For a people like this, in the discouraging days after the Babylonian exile, when they were impoverished, humiliated, governed by aliens who cared nothing for them or their queer religion, the day of the Lord's judgment could only be an event to be anticipated with joy and longing. It is, of course, this joyful eschatology that we hear in a psalm which, at whatever period it may have been written, summarizes in classical fashion the essential content and spirit of developed Old Testament eschatology:

> Let the heavens be glad, and let the earth rejoice;
>   let the sea roar, and all that fills it;
>   let the field exult, and everything in it!
> Then shall all the trees of the wood sing for joy
>   before the Lord, for he comes,
>   for he comes to judge the earth.
> He will judge the world with righteousness,
>   and the peoples with his truth.   [Ps. 96:11ff.]

Special Features in Developed Eschatology

This threefold pattern of the end of history, the condemnation of the wicked, and the establishment of God's righteous rule, provides the basic framework for all eschatological thinking in later Israel. But within that larger pattern, there are many details that appear in one or another of the prophets or apocalyptic writers which are also part of the common stock of later eschatology. Among these are such ideas as the physical resurrection of the dead, the creating of a new heaven and earth, the gathering of all nations into communion with the God of Israel, the establishment of a new covenant, the outpouring of the spirit of God upon God's people, and the reign of the messianic prince.

The most novel and startling of these ideas, that of *the resurrection of the dead,* is found only in Daniel and, possibly, in the "Isaiah" apocalypse. Daniel is, of course, quite explicit:

And many of those who sleep in the dust of the earth shall awake, some to everlasting life, and some to shame and everlasting contempt. [DAN. 12:2]

Isa. 26:19, "Thy dead shall live, their bodies shall rise," is part of a very difficult and corrupt passage, whose precise meaning is uncertain, but the translation given in the English versions is probably correct. This belief was not universally accepted in Israel even in New Testament times, as we know from the contrast made there between the opinions of the Sadducees and the Pharisees, the Pharisees accepting the doctrine while the Sadducees rejected it. The same difference of opinion is also to be observed in the Apocrypha, where the Second Book of Maccabees relates the history of Maccabean times with several allusions to the resurrection (2 Macc. 7:9; 12:43ff.; 14:46), while First Maccabees, which tells much the same story, is completely silent on the subject. The idea of the resurrection of the dead is so remarkable a reversal of the ancient Hebrew view of the afterlife that it is not hard to understand why it caught on so slowly. Nevertheless, while the stimulus to believe it may derive immediately from foreign sources, there is nothing in the doctrine that was in conflict with Hebrew thought and much that was certainly consonant with it.[18]

It is significant that when Israel finally came to consider some form of belief in a blessed life after death, the form that was accepted did not depend on any theory as to the "immortal" nature of the human soul, but was based entirely on the thought of God's righteousness and omnipotence. The resurrection of the dead was not an item in Israel's doctrine of man; it was a product, rather, of her understanding of God. The final conquest of death in Israelite thinking did not result from any revision in her basic view of human nature, but from her increasing certainty in regard to the power and goodness of her God.

The idea of the resurrection of men is a late and rare bloom in the garden of Old Testament thought. The idea of *a renovation of the physical world,* on the other hand, is relatively common in the later prophets. Sometimes the notion is expressed only in terms of changes in the land of Israel, as when the tem-

ple hill is pictured as elevated above the highest mountains
(Isa. 2:2; Mic. 4:1), or Ezekiel depicts a river flowing from the
temple to sweeten the bitter waters of the Dead Sea and make
its barren shores productive (Ezek. 47:1–12), or when the latest
annotator of the Book of Amos describes how the grapes will
be ready for treading almost as soon as the seed is dropped in
the ground, and how the springs in the hills will flow with wine
instead of water (Amos 9:13). But in Third Isaiah we hear of
a complete renewal of the cosmos, an act of re-creation parallel
to the first creation (although, significantly, the prophet's cosmic vision is still dominated by concern for the New Jerusalem,
the capital of Israel):

For behold, I create new heavens and a new earth;
and the former things shall not be remembered
    or come into mind.
But be glad and rejoice forever in that which I create;
for behold, I create Jerusalem a rejoicing,
    and her people a joy.

. . . .

No more shall there be in it an infant that lives but a few days,
    or an old man who does not fill out his days

. . . .

The wolf and the lamb shall feed together,
    the lion shall eat straw like the ox;

. . . .

They shall not hurt or destroy
in all my holy mountain,
                        says the Lord.   [ISA. 65:17–25; cf. 66:22]

The scope of the vision shows that we are getting close to the
age of the apocalyptic writers, for whom the ideas of cosmic
convulsion and universal renovation are part of the regular
stock in trade.[19]

The idea of the restoration of universal harmony appears even

more frequently with respect to the world of man than it does in
the cosmos, for it is a common idea that in the ideal age of the
future *the Gentile nations will be brought under the dominion
of Israel's God* and become his faithful servants. In the familiar
passage from Isaiah and Micah referred to above, the miraculous
elevation of the temple hill to become the highest place of the
earth is to be only a symbol of its pre-eminent spiritual importance, for:

> . . . all the nations shall flow to it,
>   and many peoples shall come, and say:
>   "Come, let us go up to the mountain of the Lord,
>   to the house of the God of Jacob;
> that he may teach us his ways
>   and that we may walk in his paths."
> [Isa. 2:2f.; cf. Mic. 4:1ff.]

Sometimes this future ingathering of the nations is described
in terms of a narrow nationalism that sees them only as future
servants of Israel, as in a famous passage from Second Isaiah:

> And nations shall come to your light,
>   and kings to the brightness of your rising.
>   .   .   .   .
> Foreigners shall build up your walls,
>   and their kings shall minister to you.
>   .   .   .   .
> The sons of those who oppressed you
>   shall come bending low to you;
> and all who despised you
>   shall bow down at your feet.   [Isa. 60:3, 10, 14]

The apparent harshness of such a picture undoubtedly reflects
the harshness of the postexilic age and its still embittered recol-
lections of the fall of Jerusalem and the ignominy of the Babylonian exile. Israel's seers were quite capable of looking at the

Gentiles in a kindlier spirit and seeing them as objects of God's care simply for their own sake, as in the apocalyptic vision of Isa. 25:6f.:

On this mountain the Lord of hosts will make for all peoples a feast of fat things. . . . And he will destroy on this mountain the covering that is cast over all peoples, the veil that is spread over all nations [the veil, that is, that prevents all men from seeing Yahweh as their Lord]. He will swallow up death for ever, and the Lord will wipe away tears from all faces. . . .

It is true the passage then goes on to speak more particularly of the taking away of "the reproach" of the people of Israel, but this is only in order that Israel may be the equal of the others and share in a feast that God has prepared for all the nations, not that she may triumph over them.

The noblest expression of this idea is the one found in a late passage of the Book of Isaiah, where Israel is pictured as a partner with Egypt and Assyria, using her strategic position on the highroad between these great empires of the pagan world to bring to both of them the universal blessing that was the original object of her election (Gen. 12:3). All three nations are called God's people, and Israel is not the first, but the third:

In that day Israel will be the third with Egypt and Assyria, a blessing in the midst of the earth, whom the Lord of hosts has blessed, saying, "Blessed be Egypt my people, and Assyria the work of my hands, and Israel my heritage." [Isa. 19:23ff.]

One of the prophetic books, Jeremiah, speaks of Yahweh's future relationship to his people as a *new covenant* (Jer. 31:31). One might think it strange that this conception, which seems natural and even inevitable to modern students of the Bible, should appear explicitly only in this one passage. It is a fact, however, that the word "covenant" (*berit*: see above, pp. 47ff.), did not come so easily to the lips of Old Testament man as it does to many contemporary exponents of biblical theology. The idea of a special relationship between Yahweh and Israel is omnipresent in the Old Testament, but the word "covenant" is only one of the ways in which this could be expressed. Indeed, as we have seen, the word seems to have been deliberately avoided in some circles (such as the eighth-century prophets), perhaps because its connotations seemed too juridical. But, since the Hebrew word can also be used to denote friendly, personal relationships of a quite nonjuridical kind, it was always at least a possible designation for Yahweh's unique relationship to Israel. It became highly popular in the Deuteronomic age, when it came—quite unashamedly—to imply a kind of legal arrangement like a contract or a treaty.

Jeremiah, who lived in the age of Deuteronomy, probably used the word because it was current coin in his time, but the way in which he uses it shows that he does not understand it in a legal sense. Many scholars have felt that Jeremiah was in rebellion against the legalism of the Deuteronomic movement, and his conception of the new covenant may reflect this attitude. When he says that God will establish a new covenant, he does not mean that God is going to offer his people a new contract with revised terms and a more sensible set of rules. He thinks of it in terms of a miraculous transformation of the character of man that will make any kind of external compact entirely unnecessary. In the glorious coming age the eternal law of God will be written in the hearts of his people (Jer. 31:33); it will be so deeply engraved in their natures that they will obey it automatically as the birds obey the laws of migration (Jer. 8:7). Because "they all shall know me, from the least of them to the greatest," professional teachers of covenant law will not be needed (Jer. 31:34). Jeremiah uses the term "covenant" in its broadest sense, to designate not an arrangement, but a relationship. For him, the establishment of a new covenant is merely a convenient name for the creation of a new type of man.

Ezekiel, Jeremiah's younger contemporary, also speaks of a

future "covenant" (Ezek. 37:26), but the term is used without any suggestion of mutual agreement, or even of imposed law; it is used very loosely as equivalent to a promise of blessing.[20] In another passage—where the word "covenant" does not occur—Ezekiel (or possibly one of his later disciples) speaks in terms very similar to those of the new covenant in Jeremiah:

A new heart I will give you, and a new spirit I will put within you; and I will take out of your flesh the heart of stone and give you a heart of flesh. And I will put my spirit within you, and cause you to walk in my statutes and be careful to observe my ordinances. [EZEK. 36:26f.]

As in Jeremiah, the future age is to be marked by so fundamental a transformation of human nature as to make external arrangements unnecessary. God will so alter the constitution of man that obedience to God's commands will be automatic, and the tensions that arise from the innately rebellious and self-seeking tendencies of man as we know him will be done away.

The idea of *an eschatological outpouring of God's spirit,* such as this passage refers to, is also found elsewhere, and becomes another important element in the eschatological hope. "The spirit of God" in Old Testament thought is simply the power of God that enables men to do what otherwise they could not do.[21] The future age, therefore, will be an age when man's spiritual and moral capacities will be vastly enhanced. God's spirit, which in times past had been available only to a few—to those specially favored men who became judges, prophets, wise men—will be available to all. The most notable of these promises of the eschatological bestowal of the spirit is in Joel, where the reason for giving it is to make all men prophets:

And it shall come to pass afterward,
    that I will pour out my spirit on all flesh;

> your sons and your daughters shall prophesy,
> your old men shall dream dreams,
> and your young men shall see visions.
>> [JOEL 2:28, HEB. 3:1]²²

In Isa. 32:15 and 44:3 the outpouring of the spirit is not limited to any special purpose, but is simply a part, and a cause, of the general prosperity and well-being of the nation.

A number of portrayals of the future age have *the restoration of the Davidic dynasty* as one of the central features. So, for example, in the Book of Ezekiel, God says, "And I will set up over them one shepherd, my servant David, and he shall feed them . . . my servant David shall be prince among them" (Ezek. 34:23f.). And the Book of Jeremiah speaks of God's intention of redeeming the explicit promises made in his covenant with David (where the word "covenant" is definitely of a contractual character). Yahweh will "cause a righteous branch to spring forth for David; and he shall execute justice and righteousness in the land" (Jer. 33:15–22). Because of the importance of the covenant with David and the central role played by the Davidic dynasty in the long history of Judah, this idea of the righteous king of David's line who was going to become Israel's ruler in the coming age—the "Messiah" of later Jewish thought—is historically of greater importance than some of the ideas previously mentioned, although it is by no means an invariable element in Israel's eschatology. There is no suggestion of it, for instance, in either of the two Old Testament apocalypses, Daniel and Isa. 24–27, and references to it in other Old Testament literature are less frequent than one is likely to suppose from the prominence given it later in Christian, and some postbiblical Jewish, circles.

There is, as a matter of fact, only one absolutely consistent element in the eschatology of Israel, and that is the conviction that God would one day act to establish his perfect sovereignty, which would never again be open to challenge by hostile powers. This conviction appears in characteristic form in Second Isaiah:

> Listen to me, my people,
>   and give ear to me, my nation;
> for a law will go forth from me,
>   and my justice for a light to the peoples.
> My deliverance draws near speedily,
>   my salvation has gone forth,
>   and my arms will rule the peoples;
> the coastlands wait for me,
>   and for my arm they hope.
> Lift up your eyes to the heavens,
>   and look at the earth beneath;
> for the heavens will vanish like smoke,
>   the earth will wear out like a garment,
>   and they that dwell in it will die like gnats;
> but my salvation will be forever,
>   and my deliverance will never be ended.
>   [ISA. 51:4ff.]

The prophet is thinking of the end of the Babylonian exile, but there can be no doubt that he saw, in these events of his own day, the beginning of that final age in which God would rule without opposition and his people find at last the perfect blessedness for which God had chosen them. Most of the prophets and apocalyptic writers who followed him also saw the age to come as beginning to arrive in the history of their own times.

The name that was finally given to the culminating fact of this new age was *the kingdom of God*, the word kingdom (*malkut*) being used in the sense of "sovereignty" or "rule." Although the phrase "kingdom of God" never occurs in the Old Testament with this meaning, the idea of God's coming sovereignty is implicit in the whole of Israelite eschatology.[23] God's ultimate purpose, in the developed thought of Israel, is never just to correct certain particular wrongs, but to vindicate before the world his claim to be its sole, unchallenged ruler. This can of course be expressed in many ways, but the image of Yahweh as the universal King came in the long run to seem the most adequate. In the time of the tribal confederacy, Yahweh was probably rarely spoken of as "king," but with the rise of the monarchy and Israel's increasing contact with the civilization of Canaan, where the idea of a particular god as "king" over the other gods was commonplace, it came to seem more and more natural to speak of Yahweh in these terms, as in Psalm 95:

> For Yahweh is a great God,
>> and a great king above all gods. [v. 3]

Even under the monarchy this way of speaking of the God of Israel was relatively uncommon, but once the monarchy had fallen and there were no more any earthly kings to reverence, the idea of the kingship—or "kingdom"—of Yahweh really came into its own. In the end it came to sum up everything that was hoped for through God's action in the future—the resurrection, the new creation and new covenant, the outpouring of the spirit, the universal fellowship of nations, the rule of the new David in Israel, and a host of other features too numerous to be discussed. This whole complex of ideas, some of them central and indispensable, some merely peripheral and occasional, was called vividly to mind, in later Israel, by the summary declaration, "The Lord reigns" (Ps. 93:1; 96:10, etc.; Isa. 52:7), or by the summary phrase "the kingdom of God," which meets us so frequently in the pages of the New Testament.

The idea finds perfect expression in an otherwise rather repellent chapter of Zechariah, where a late, apocalytic writer describes a great eschatological battle that the enemies of Yahweh and his people will one day wage against Jerusalem. After the city has been taken and the inhabitants have suffered indescribable horrors, the enemy army will be defeated, for

. . . Yahweh your God will come, and all the holy ones with him . . . and Yahweh will become king over all the earth; on that day Yahweh will be one [that is, there will be no other god] and his name one. . . . Then every one that survives of all the nations that have come against Jerusalem shall go up year after year to worship the King, Yahweh of hosts, and to keep the feast of booths [the feast, that is, which celebrates his sovereignty].   [ZECH. 14:5, 9, 16][24]

More appealing, however, to modern readers is another late passage which promises that

> Your eyes will see the king in his beauty;
> . . . .
> Your eyes will see Jerusalem,
>   a quiet habitation, an immovable tent,
> whose stakes will never be plucked up,
>   nor will any of its cords be broken.
> But there the Lord in majesty will be for us
>   a place of broad rivers and streams,
> where no galley with oars can go,
>   nor stately ship can pass.
> For the Lord is our judge, the Lord is our ruler,
>   the Lord is our king; he will save us.
>   [ISA. 33:17, 20–22]

10

ANCIENT ISRAEL
AND THE MODERN WEST

O that today you would
hearken to his voice!

PSALM 95:7

DESPITE THE FACT that the purpose of this book is mainly descriptive, its aim being simply to delineate as accurately as possible the main features of ancient Israel's understanding of God, it would hardly be possible to end the discussion without at least raising some question as to the value and contemporary validity of the ideas with which we have been concerned. Is the religion of ancient Israel just a chapter in a universal "history of religions," to be studied only as a curious historical phenomenon? Or does it contain, along with much that is time-conditioned and outmoded, some conceptions, perspectives, insights—whatever one chooses to call them—that belong among the permanent achievements of human thought, certain truths that are easily lost and of which men need to be reminded in every new generation?

The question is rhetorical and the answer must be an affirmative one if the foregoing pages have managed to convey anything of the vital spirit of ancient Israel's knowledge of God. The intent of this final chapter is to summarize the main points and to indicate briefly, without extended argumentation, their importance for the modern theological enterprise. Simply as a matter of method, we shall not be concerned here with whether or not the Old Testament is the Word of God, and therefore contains an indispensable revelation of deity, or with the authority claimed for it as the divinely given substructure for New Testament thought. These are profoundly important questions, but the discussion of them would take us far beyond the boundaries envisaged for this book. Our sole concern here is with what the men of ancient Israel actually believed about God and what contribution they may possibly have made toward the permanent enrichment of human thought on theological matters.

God in History

The first, and most distinctive emphasis in ancient Israel's religion was upon the fact that God has acted, and continues to act, in history: that, out of the multitude of human families upon earth he chose one for his own; delivered it from the slavery in which he found it; provided wise rules to guide it in most of the perplexing situations that life presents; gave to it a land, a capital, and a king; and continued to shape its destinies through the vicissitudes of later times. All this was done in the world of actual, recognizable human affairs, and on the scale of normal, secular time, not in a mythological world lying before and beyond the world of daily life, or in some superhuman, mythological time. Every event in Israel's sacred history was theoretically datable, and many scholars have devoted their energies to trying to fix the dates more precisely.

This belief that God is to be met first of all in the world of history is Israel's most remarkable contribution to theology. Other nations have of course often seen God at work in historical events, in particular in the victories and defeats of their armies; but these were always special, discrete incidents, without connection with other events that preceded and followed them. Only in Israel was God's historical action seen as part of a historical nexus that began at a certain point in the past, continued in a series of events that logically culminated in the present situation, and was presumably directed toward some ultimate goal in the future (though, as we have seen, this last point emerged only gradually and by way of extrapolating from past experience). It was this central emphasis on God's historical activity that caused the science of history to develop first of all in ancient Israel, several centuries before the time of Herodotus and Thucydides. History was important to Israel because history was the sphere of revelation, the place where God was chiefly at work.[1]

The alternatives to revelation in history are revelation in nature and in thought. For most of the ancient Near East, nature was the characteristic sphere of the divine, and the gods were personifications of natural forces; the task of religion was to adjust man's life to the laws and rhythms of the natural world. For Greece, at least in the classical age, the approach to the eternal world was through the realm of thought; reality could be known only through the examination of ideas in the mind of man. But for ancient Israel, God showed himself primarily through the forces that operate in human society, through the processes that bring about the rise and fall of nations.

All three of these modes of approach to deity are valid options and it would be ridiculous to claim that they are mutually exclusive. Modern religious man certainly endeavors to find all that he can of deity through each one of them. And it was so in ancient Israel also. The preceding discussion should have been sufficient to show that, while Israel knew God first, and most of all, through the world of history, she also recognized, especially in later times, that he had not left himself without witnesses in nature and in human thought. The great nature poems of the Old Testament, which picture the physical world as shining with the reflected glory of God and immediately responsive to his presence (Pss. 8; 19:1–6; 104; Job 38–39; Judg. 5:4; Hab. 3:3–11), show that Israel found the same God there as in her own past history; and the inclusion of the Wisdom Literature in the Bible is evidence that the attempt to understand God through reflection on life and the human condition was not considered incompatible with her basic approach to God through historical events.

The permanent contribution of Israel lies in her emphasis upon the *priority* of the historical approach, for it was the God who was known in history who was later found in other spheres, and not *vice versa*. Since the knowledge of God grew out of concrete events in actual, recorded history, events in which genuine human beings were involved, the God of Israel always had a relevance to particular human situations, a concern for the moral and social order, a continuing involvement in the historical process, that he could not have had if he had been merely a God of nature or philosophy. The gods of nature are, on the whole, inhuman and amoral, while the gods of philosophers tend to be impersonal, and socially irrelevant, abstractions. It is only a God who comes to men *through* their historical situation who can continue to speak to them *in* their historical situation. Because Yahweh was believed to have spoken at the Red Sea and at Sinai, men of ancient Israel could believe that he was still speaking to them as they faced the armies of the Assyrians and heard of the conquests of Cyrus.

If we are to believe in God at all, this is really the only kind who is worth believing in. The God of philosophy serves a useful function in helping to fill up the blank spaces in human thought; belief in the God of nature gives us, like Wordsworth, a satisfying sense of the numinous when we contemplate nature's wonders; but only a God whom men first met in the disasters and triumphs of human history is able to speak to men in the depths of their being when they too are involved in the clash of historical forces. This is the God of ancient Israel.

God's Personality

We have noted that anthropomorphism is, for good or ill, an inescapable characteristic of Old Testament thought about God. For many today, as in times past, this seems a crude and unsophisticated way of thinking which must be summarily discarded, the supposition being that God needs to be distinguished from man as sharply as possible. But, if God exists at all, we have no language adequate to describe him, and must avail ourselves of the language of analogy—of metaphor and symbol. Granted that all metaphors are inadequate and misleading, the only question is which are the least inadequate and misleading. We are not concerned to argue here whether God exists or not, but only to try to see, if he does exist, how we should talk about him. Are we likely to be any closer to the truth, for example, if we describe God as "the ground of our being"—that is, speaking literally, the foundation, the base, the earth floor, on which we stand—than if we speak of him as "our Father and our King"? There seems, intrinsically, no reason to suppose that language that likens him to some sort of impersonal object, force or principle is really more acceptable than language that compares him, even crudely, to a human being.

All the language that can be brought to bear is necessary, of course; God *is* the Prime Mover, the Absolute, Supreme Reality, Unconditioned Being, the Ground of all Being, a Power not ourselves that makes for righteousness, and so forth. But all impersonal reality is in some sense less than man, for man has shown himself increasingly able to manipulate the impersonal forces of the universe—like light, gravity, electricity, atomic energy—to his own advantage. If God is to be in any way greater than we are and not subject to human manipulation, he must be seen as one who has in a pre-eminent degree all the special qualities that distinguish man from the lower creation: his dignity, self-consciousness and self-control, his creativity and freedom. The only language that can describe him as such is language derived from human life, language that takes seriously the biblical doctrine that man is created in the divine image and therefore sees in every man a kind of window through which shines something of the being and character of God.

This idea may, of course, be wholly erroneous, but it will prove difficult to construct a satisfying religion for the Western world that is based on any other. The nontheistic religions of the Far East are the product of a very different kind of culture from our own, and are based upon a different set of values: in many instances upon a negative and pessimistic view of life and human individuality. Whatever may be the validity of such views, they are hardly compatible with the typical outlook of the West, particularly in a period when its material horizons are widening with such incredible speed. The religions that belong to this basically optimistic, forward-looking, aggressive culture of the West—Judaism, Christianity and Islam—whether one regards them as being its cause or only one of its products, are all based upon the biblical view of God as willing, freely acting, creative, personal Being. It seems unlikely that any other conception of God will ever be really meaningful to Western man.

The conception of God as personal enhances the dignity of the human personality; God's freedom can be seen as justifying man's struggle to be truly free; God's creativity is a constant stimulus to creativity in man. The activity of God has its counterpart—for good or bad—in the activism of Western society. All these are important values for our culture which, historically, have been bound up with the biblical view of God. It is

not likely that they can be sustained in their pristine purity
if severed from it. Whether man was made in God's image or
not, it is undeniable that he tends to conform his own character
to that of the God he worships. The character of Western man
has been shaped by the character of the biblical God; it seems
likely that in the future he will either continue to worship God
in this form or else in no form at all.

God's Jealousy

Personality was not, of course, a quality unique to
the God of ancient Israel; the gods of the heathen—Amon-Re,
Marduk, Anath and Baal—were personal also. What was unique
was the fiery intensity of Yahweh's personality, the uncompromising rigor of his demands, the fierce urgency of his love, that
aspect of his nature which leads the Bible to call him the "living"
God—that is the "lively," the "vital" God—and the "jealous"
or impassioned God, the quality that led ultimately to the absolute monotheism of Second Isaiah and the denial even of existence to other gods. The passionate intensity of Yahweh's
nature is reflected, above all, in the passion and intensity of the
Hebrew prophets, but also in the intense vitality of the whole
race that worshiped him. It is at least arguable that this intensity of the God whom it worshiped is the true explanation
of the mystery of Israel of which we spoke in the first chapter
of this book. It seems likely that faith in the "living," "jealous"
God is in fact the animating spark that produced in "Israel,"
under all its changing forms and in the face of all opposition,
the remarkable vitality that characterizes her even to the present
moment. If it is true, as suggested above, that man is molded
in the image of the God whom he worships, then it is only
natural that such a God should produce a race of men capable
of passionate commitment to the ends they believe in. The
devotion, zeal and heroism of long generations of prophets,

martyrs and saints are a visible reflection, an inevitable concomitant, of the "jealousy" of the God whom they served. The
vitality of Western society will be seriously diminished if it
loses faith in this kind of God; the result can only be an increase in world-weariness, indifference, moral neutrality, a de-
cline in personal integrity and psychic force.

God's Righteousness

Nevertheless, however high an importance one may
attach to the ideas of personality and passion as essential ingredients in the character of the God of Israel, they would have
only a dubious social value if they were not coupled with an
equal insistence upon his righteousness. When the notion of
God's intensely demanding personality is not connected with
convictions about his justice and love, devotion to him most
naturally takes the form of bigotry and fanaticism. Unfortunately, neither the history of the old Israel nor of the new has
been free from this deplorable spirit. The evident relish with
which some of the Old Testament writers describe the slaughter
of Canaanites and other foreigners, the sword-point conversions
to Judaism in the days of John Hyrcanus and Aristobulus (perhaps reflected in the Book of Esther), the iniquities of the Wars
of Religion, the brutality of a Torquemada, and the pogroms
that have sometimes disgraced the name of Christians are all
evidence of the perils of worshiping a God of pure personal
force whose character and demands are regarded as beyond
good and evil, who is impervious to criticism based on ordinary
human standards of justice and decency. It was against just such
a God that Abraham, in the familiar story, protested when he
said, "Shall not the judge of all the earth do right?" Although
the pages of the Old Testament are frequently disfigured by
cruel actions and barbarous sentiments, the meaning of the
Old Testament is not to be found in them. Its meaning for the

future of man is to be found, rather, in those passages, also very numerous, in which it is declared that the Judge of all the earth can only do that which is right, and that God's understanding of right can never be inferior to what man conceives to be right, and that, furthermore, his principal demand upon his people is not that they should conform to a system of ritual *tabus*, but that they should exhibit in their personal and national life a passion for justice similar to his own.

Psychologically speaking, it was presumably necessary that Israel should learn of Yahweh's unity and "jealousy" before she learned fully of his justice. In human society, a source of power must first be discovered in unregulated form before it can be directed to useful purposes; electricity was first discovered as a form of wild energy before its social utility was realized. The analogy is by no means perfect and one would not wish to suggest that the energy of God is merely useful, or that it can be consciously directed to merely human ends. But it is true that knowledge of the existence of power is usually antecedent to a knowledge of how it should be used. So, at any rate, it was in Israel. She knew the power, the energy, the intensity, the jealousy, the vitality of her God before she became aware of the ends to which that power was directed. Some of her people never advanced beyond this primitive stage. But in the long run the best of her thinkers knew that their God was not a capricious, demonic being, but a God of unchangeable "truth," always faithful and consistent, and they knew that he was a God of "righteousness," that is, one whose behavior, however inexplicable it might seem at times, was always consonant with man's highest understanding of the right.

It is the combination of these two qualities, the jealousy and the righteousness of God, that has given to the religion of ancient Israel and its daughter religions—Judaism, Christianity and Islam—their tremendous moral force. When the balance has been shifted too far toward emphasis upon God's jealousy, fanaticism has been the result; when his righteousness has been stressed too much at the expense of his power and vitality, the result has been a kind of sickly moralism; but when the two elements have been held in their true biblical balance, the belief that there is in God a perfect fusion of irresistible power and absolute righteousness has been the source of such incomparable moral energy as is manifested in the Hebrew prophets, in Jesus of Nazareth, in Paul of Tarsus, and in countless others who have walked the same way, careless of their own comfort, concerned for the poor, the weak and the disadvantaged, seeking for nothing except to establish on earth the righteous rule of the righteous God. These were men who had a true understanding of the "theology" of the Old Testament.

The knowledge that Yahweh, "the Lord," the "jealous" God, was also the righteous God was the true glory of ancient Israel, as one of her prophets said:

. . . let him who glories glory in this, that he understands and knows me, that I am the Lord who practice steadfast love, justice and righteousness in the earth; for in these things I delight, says the Lord. [JER. 9:24]

God's Love

If to some the word "justice" has too formal and juridical a sound, it should be remembered that God's concern for justice is an expression of his concern for people, that is of his love for them. One would not wish to pretend that the idea of God's love is as central in the Old Testament as it is in the New, but it would be a gross misapprehension to suppose that it is not there at all. We have seen in a previous chapter that, even though one cannot say that the God of ancient Israel *is* love (1 John 4:8), one can certainly say that he *does* love. It is true that most of the passages that express the thought of his love have to do only with Israel (Deut. 7:8; Jer. 31:3; Hos. 11:1, etc.), but such books as Ruth and Jonah, as well as many passages in the prophets (see above, pp. 220f.) show how the theology of the Old Testament at its best sees his concern, and therefore his love, as extending to all his creatures. Passages from the Wisdom tradition, such as the following, can hardly be interpreted in a narrow, nationalistic fashion:

> The steadfast love of the Lord never ceases,
>   his mercies never come to an end;
> they are new every morning. . . .
>   . . . .
> The Lord is good to those who wait for him,
>   to the soul that seeks him.
>
>   . . . .
> . . . though he cause grief, he will have compassion
>   according to the abundance of his steadfast love;
> for he does not willingly afflict
>   or grieve the sons of men.   [LAM. 3:22–33]

The emphasis upon the kindness and love of God is, for the most part, a later element in Old Testament thought, but it was an important one and was destined to be of incalculable significance in the subsequent history of Israel and the world. It is the final, crowning touch on the portrait of the God of ancient Israel which this book has been attempting to paint. The continuing influence of the doctrine of Yahweh's love, kindness and compassion is seen in the Islamic formula, "In the name of God the compassionate, the merciful" and in the Christian insistence that God so loved the world that he gave his only son (John 3:16).

Eschatology

The last element in Israel's understanding of God that we shall include in this summary brings us back from the consideration of his nature to a reminder that he is a God who acts. If Israel's theology begins with that assertion that God *did* act in the past, it ends with the promise that he *will* act in the future.

As we saw in the preceding chapters, eschatology seems to have been another late development in Israel's thought, but it grew inevitably out of her knowledge of God's actions in her own history and the abiding conclusions she had drawn from these actions as to his moral nature. One could be sure that the God who had acted for the salvation of his people in the past would also act finally and definitively for their salvation in the future. Several important collections of literary material in the Old Testament have this idea as their dominant theme (Isa. 24–27; Jer. 30–33; Ezek. 37–48; Joel 2:28–3:21 [Heb. 3:1–4:21]; Zech. 12–14; and, above all, Dan. 7–12). One pregnant phrase, "the kingdom [or, rule] of God," came to be used as a summary expression of all that Israel hoped for.

This meant that the thought of Israel was, in its later phases at least, optimistic and forward-looking. Even in earlier times it was optimistic and world-accepting, but this was based upon her faith in God's saving work in the past and in the assurance she felt of his continued working in her midst. When, toward the beginning of the Babylonian exile, the world grew dark around her and she ceased to enjoy the material prosperity that had always been a kind of sacramental token of God's care, she preserved her optimism by transferring all her hopes to the more distant future. When the time came, she was ready to welcome the conquests of Cyrus as the beginning of a new exodus and the breaking in of the kingdom of her God. In this, too, she was largely disappointed, but her disappointment was unable to destroy her confident expectation of good things yet to come. This spiritual resilience in the face of repeated defeat and humiliation is the most amazing example of Israel's capacity to adapt her faith in God to new conditions. Even if one regards her hope for the future as a somewhat pathetic instance of corporate self-deception, of the human capacity for dreaming and wish-fulfillment, it is nevertheless a most remarkable one, since it was destined to persist in all the forms that Israel would take in years to come. It continues to be a vital element in the thought of orthodox Judaism and orthodox Christianity to the present day; in more liberal forms of both it continues in transmuted form as the hope for a better world which will be animated by a spirit of brotherhood and organized according to principles of justice; in an even more radical transmutation it is the animating principle of Marxism, which, having repudiated the theological substructure of the eschatological hope, nevertheless holds firmly to the conviction that all creation and all society are moving irreversibly in the direction of the perfect state. Wherever in the Western world men take for granted the idea that the future is bound to be better than the past, they are being influenced at least unconsciously by the eschatological hope of ancient Israel, and to that extent are still worshipers of Israel's God.

This is the God for whose people the future is always full of new, previously unrealized possibilities for good, who bids them

> Remember not the former things,
>   nor consider the things of old.
> Behold I am doing a new thing;
>   now it springs forth, do you not perceive it?
>   [ISA. 43:18f.]

This eager hopefulness about the future, this assurance that "the best is yet to be," is one of Israel's most important legacies to the Western world, a mood which, either in the form of religious millennialism or secular optimism, continues to be a distinguishing element in our culture.

"This is my God, and I will praise him," said the ancient Hebrew as he considered the miracle of his people's deliverance at the Sea (Exod. 15:2). The purpose of this book has not been so much to praise him as to describe him, to see his face and character as the men of ancient Israel saw them. It has not been our purpose to ask whether such a God exists or not, whether Israel's faith has ontological validity or whether her God is merely a projection of her own character, ideals and aspirations. Even if the God of Israel is only a creation of the human mind, only a gigantic reflection of the ideal Israelite or the Israelite father-figure thrown upon the screen of the cosmos and eternity,[2] he is still worth knowing, for he ranks among the greatest imaginative creations of our race and, after all these centuries, continues to live in the minds and lives of millions of men, whether he reigns in the heavens or not.

But every man who knows about the God of the Bible must sometime inevitably face the question of whether or not he truly exists; he must decide whether or not the God whom Israel thought she knew is an authentic reflection of Ultimate Reality, however partial and inadequate that reflection may be. Those who have long ago made this decision for themselves and daily join with the men of ancient Israel in saying, "This is *my* God, and I will praise him" can only hope that others who have come to "know" this God as an important factor in the intellectual history of the Western world will also come to know him in the Hebrew sense, which means, as we saw in an early chapter, to apprehend him in heart as well as in mind, and to submit to his claims in love, trust and obedience.

NOTES

Abbreviations

ANET: Ancient Near Eastern Texts Relating to the Old Testament, ed. by J. B.
Pritchard (Princeton, 1950; rev. ed. 1955)
ASTI: Annual of the Swedish Theological Institute
BA: Biblical Archaeologist
BJRL: Bulletin of the John Rylands Library
BZ: Biblische Zeitschrift
CBQ: Catholic Biblical Quarterly
HTR: Harvard Theological Review
HUCA: Hebrew Union College Annual
ICC: International Critical Commentary
Int: Interpretation
JBL: Journal of Biblical Literature
JNES: Journal of Near Eastern Studies
JSS: Journal of Semitic Studies
JTS: Journal of Theological Studies
RB: Revue biblique
RSPT: Revue des sciences philosophique et theologiques
SBT: Studies in Biblical Theology
TLZ: Theologische Literaturzeitung
VT: Vetus Testamentum (Suppls.: Supplements to)
ZAW: Zeitschrift für die alttestamentliche Wissenschaft (Beih.: Beihefte zur)
ZTK: Zeitschrift für Theologie und Kirche

Further discussion of the major topics treated in the text of this book and in
the following notes will be found in the standard works on Old Testament
theology by Erichrodt, Köhler, Procksch, Jacob, Vriezen, von Rad, Baab, Knight,
Heinisch, and van Imschoot (consult the indices), as well as in the standard
Bible dictionaries (Hastings, Interpreter's), and the biblical word-books edited
by Kittel, Richardson, and von Allmen. References to such works are not normally included in the following notes, but are simply presupposed. Readers

mally included in the following notes, but are simply presupposed. Readers in search of additional information on the subjects discussed will find these books invaluable.

Preface

1. In my introductory study *Preface to Old Testament Theology* (New Haven, 1950; rev. ed., New York, 1963), I attempted a definition of Old Testament theology as an academic discipline (rev. ed., pp. 122f.), and argued that the three traditional divisions of dogmatic theology—doctrines of God, man, and salvation—provide the most satisfactory framework for the discussion and treatment of the subject (rev. ed., pp. 119f.). The present work is mainly concerned with the first division, the doctrine of God, but also includes some matters (especially in chapters 3, 4 and 9) that could with equal propriety be treated as part of the Old Testament view of salvation. The term "doctrine" is used, of course, only in the etymological sense of "teaching," not in the ecclesiastical sense of "approved dogma."

2. Since a nearly complete bibliography of works in the field of Old Testament theology will be found in the revised edition of my *Preface* (pp. 126–144), it seemed unnecessary to include one in the present volume.

3. *Op. cit.*, p. 122.

4. The principal work is Walther Eichrodt, *Theologie des Alten Testaments:* Vol. 1, *Gott und Volk* (Leipzig, 1933); Vol. 2, *Gott und Welt* (1935); Vol. 3, *Gott und Mensch* (1939); Eng. tr. in two vols. by J. A. Baker, *Theology of the Old Testament* (Philadelphia, 1961, 1967). Other articles and monographs are listed in the bibliography mentioned in note 2 above; particularly relevant to the subject of the present book is Eichrodt's pamphlet *Das Gottesbild des Alten Testaments* (Stuttgart, 1956).

5. The principal work is Gerhard von Rad, *Old Testament Theology* (tr. by D. M. G. Stalker): Vol. 1, *The Theology of Israel's Historical Traditions* (New York, 1962); Vol. 2, *The Theology of Israel's Prophetic Traditions* (1965). Other articles and monographs are listed in the bibliography mentioned in note 2, above.

6. The word "covenant," as a description of Yahweh's relationship to Israel, occurs only in Hos. 6:7 and 8:1, and not at all in Amos, Micah or Isaiah of Jerusalem. Some older commentators deny the relevance of the references in Hosea; W. R. Harper, for example, says that 6:7 does not refer to the covenant with Israel and the reference in 8:1 is "clearly a later addition" (*Amos and Hosea, ICC*; New York, 1905, *ad loc.*).

7. Von Rad's view that Old Testament theology is simply a résumé of God's saving acts in history was first introduced to English-speaking readers by G. E. Wright in *God Who Acts: The Theology of Recital (SBT* 8; Chicago, 1952), a book that continues to be influential in the field and well deserves to be. Wright himself acknowledges that Old Testament theology must also deal with other matters, but considers them of secondary importance (pp. 57f., 85).

8. *The Holy Scriptures: A Survey* (New York, 1949); *The Design of the Scriptures: A First Reader in Biblical Theology* (New York, 1961); *The King and His Cross* (New York, 1965).

Chapter 1: *The Mystery of Israel*

1. If, as some argue, the name Yahweh originally meant something like "creator" (see below, ch. 6, note 7), this fact might be taken to indicate that the idea of creation had more theological importance for earliest Israel than we have made allowance for. But the stubborn silence of Israel's early confessions of faith still remains to be explained, as does the fact that the name Yahweh is never understood in this sense in extant Hebrew literature. Special stress is laid on the latter point by H. Kosmala in a brief article on "The Name of God (YHWH and HU')" in *ASTI* 2 (1963), pp. 103–106.

2. Commentators are generally agreed that the two descriptions (vv. 4–8 and v. 9) refer to the same group. See, e.g., G. B. Caird, *A Commentary on the Revelation of St. John the Divine* (London, 1966), *ad loc.* The idea of the Christian Church as the "new Israel" is integral to the thought of Revelation, which denies to the older Israel any title even to the ethnic name of "Jew" (Rev. 2:9; 3:9), an extreme position not met with elsewhere.

3. H. W. Robinson, *The Christian Doctrine of Man* (Edinburgh, 1911), pp. 27–30; "The Hebrew Conception of Corporate Personality" in *Wesen und Werden des Alten Testaments*, Bei.ZAW 66 (Berlin, 1936), pp. 49–62, reprinted in a pamphlet entitled *Corporate Personality in Ancient Israel* (Philadelphia, 1964), pp. 1–20; included in the pamphlet is also his essay "The Group and the Individual in Israel" (1937), pp. 21–35.

4. G. A. Danell, *Studies in the Name of Israel in the Old Testament* (Uppsala, 1946), discusses, among other things, the etymology of the name, pp. 15–28.

5. John Bright, *A History of Israel* (Philadelphia, 1959); see especially pp. 120–127, 145f.

6. M. Noth, *History of Israel*, tr. by S. Godman (New York, 1958; 2nd ed. rev. by P. Ackroyd, 1960), Part I, chs. 1–2. A more basic work is his *Überlieferungsgeschichte des Pentateuch* (Stuttgart, 1948).

7. The most important of von Rad's studies is *Das formgeschichtliche Problem des Hexateuch* (1938), included as the title article in *The Problem of the Hexateuch and Other Essays*, tr. by E. W. Trueman Dicken (New York, 1966). Mention might also be made of the intriguing, but unproved and probably unprovable, theory of G. E. Mendenhall that the original Israel was a small group of escaped slaves from Egypt, who, by rallying about them a large body of disaffected Canaanite peasants (*habiru*), succeeded in overthrowing the local lords of Canaan and thus became masters of the land ("The Hebrew Conquest of Palestine," *BA* 25 [1962], pp. 66–87). According to this view, the historical Israel was as much Canaanite as "Israelite," and, though its origins were religious, its development was due as much to political as to strictly religious factors.

8. The contention of von Rad and Noth that the Sinai tradition was originally independent of the exodus and settlement traditions and was only added to them at a relatively late stage has probably been more widely rejected than accepted. W. Beyerlin, *Origins and History of the Oldest Sinaitic Traditions*, tr. by S. Rudman (Oxford, 1965), pp. 169f., argues against it on form-critical grounds; Beyerlin believes the form of the covenant, based on ancient forms of

suzerainty treaties, requires both the recitation of the suzerain's acts of benevolence (exodus tradition) and the imposition of the treaty stipulations (Sinai tradition). (See below, ch. 3, note 3, on the "suzerainty treaty" hypothesis.) G. Fohrer, *Überlieferung und Geschichte des Exodus, Beih. ZAW* 91 (Berlin, 1964), on purely literary-critical grounds, also rejects any attempt to separate the exodus and Sinai traditions (p. 35), as does H. Seebass, *Der Erzvater Israel, Beih. ZAW* 98 (Berlin, 1966) on grounds inherent in the history of the traditions (pp. 61–73).

9. The idea that Israel was originally a confederation of tribes analogous to the Greek amphictyonies was first developed in detail by M. Noth in *Das System der zwölf Stämme Israels* (Stuttgart, 1930); see also his *History of Israel,* Part I, ch. 2. W. F. Albright, in *The Biblical Period from Abraham to Ezra* (New York, 1949; Torchbook ed., 1963), pp. 36f., notes succinctly both the similarities, and one major difference—as he conceives it—between the Israelite "amphictyony" and those of Greece and Italy.

10. Although many scholars now accept the amphictyony theory as almost axiomatic, others, such as H. H. Rowley (*Interpreter's Dictionary of the Bible,* Vol. E-J. Nashville, 1962; pp. 753f.) and G. Fohrer ("Altes Testament—'Amphiktyonie' und 'Bund'?" *TLZ* 91 (1966), cols. 801–816, 893–904), continue to regard it as doubtful, if not positively implausible. H. Orlinsky has presented a strong case against it in his article "The Tribal System of Israel and Related Groups" in *Studies and Essays in Honor of Abraham A. Neuman* (Leiden, 1962), pp. 374–387; see also his *Ancient Israel* (Ithaca, 1954), pp. 58ff. While I marvel at the precision and dogmatic certainty with which some scholars venture to reconstruct the organization and institutions of this obscure period, and feel strongly the force of Orlinsky's arguments, I also find it difficult, in my own mind, to account for the origin of Israel, and her continuing self-consciousness, without assuming the existence of some kind of central organization and common cult, although I hesitate to use the foreign word "amphictyony" in this connection. It cannot be emphasized too strongly that any attempt to define the nature of Israel's premonarchical institutions and forms of worship is entirely hypothetical.

11. The theory that Israel's central cultic act was a regular "renewal of the covenant" was propounded by S. Mowinckel, *Le Décalogue* (Paris, 1927), pp. 119–129, although only in connection with the Jerusalem temple; A. Alt advocated the view that it took place at seven-year intervals rather than annually ("The Origins of Israelite Law," 1934; included in A. Alt, *Essays on Old Testament History and Religion,* tr. by R. A. Wilson, Oxford, 1966; pp. 128f.); G. von Rad locates the original covenant festival at the sanctuary of Shechem in the tribal period (*The Problem of the Hexateuch and Other Essays,* pp. 33–39). M. Noth accepts von Rad's view, while noting some of the basic objections to it (*Überlieferungsgeschichte des Pentateuch,* p. 64). See also M. Newman, *The People of the Covenant* (New York, 1962), p. 112, with the references given in fn. 27 on that page. The details of the observance are worked out imaginatively by A. Weiser, in the introduction to his commentary on *The Psalms,* tr. by H. Hartwell (Philadelphia, 1962), pp. 28–35. For criticism of Weiser's theory, see J. K. Kuntz, *The Self-revelation of God* (Philadelphia, 1967), pp. 171f., 223f., with the footnote references. K. Baltzer denies that there was any regular covenant-renewal festival before the exile; previous to this, he believes, it would have been performed only in times of national crisis (*Das Bundesformular,*

Neukirchen, 1960, pp. 68, 91). It must be affirmed with some emphasis that what evidence there is for such a festival in ancient Israel is merely inferential, and is patient of other interpretations. The first unambiguous evidence for a regular covenant-renewal ceremony is postbiblical, and comes from the Dead Sea Scroll community (The Rule, I:16–II:23; A. Dupont-Sommer, *The Essene Writings from Qumran*, tr. by G. Vermes, New York, 1962, pp. 74–76) and from Jubilees 6:17.

12. A sober discussion of the nature of sacral kingship in Israel will be found in C. R. North, "The Religious Aspects of Hebrew Kingship," *ZAW* nf9 (1932), pp. 8–38. A more extreme view is set forth in S. Mowinckel, *He That Cometh*, tr. by G. W. Anderson (New York, 1954), ch. 3, "The Ideal of Kingship in Ancient Israel." See also A. R. Johnson, *Sacral Kingship in Ancient Israel* (Cardiff, 1955). The extravagances of the British and Scandinavian "ritual-pattern" school in this area (e.g., S. H. Hooke, ed., *Myth and Ritual*, Oxford, 1933; *id.*, *The Labyrinth*, London, 1935), as well as some of Mowinckel's more debatable ideas, are criticized at great length by J. de Fraine, *L'aspect religieux de la royauté israelite* (Rome, 1954) and K.-H. Bernhardt, *Das Problem der altorientalischen Königsideologie im Alten Testament*, Suppls. *VT* 8 (Leiden, 1961).

13. Both Jews and Gentiles are divided as to the significance of the establishment of the Israeli state, and opinions range from those which regard it as an event of messianic importance to those which think of Israel simply as a fortunate refuge for a persecuted people. The American Council for Judaism, the principal Jewish "anti-Zionist" organization, while sympathetic to Israel as an interesting and valuable political experiment, refuses to attribute to it any religious value, and rejects entirely the idea that Jews constitute a race or nation rather than a purely religious community. There are also extreme orthodox Jews in Israel itself who repudiate the Jewish state on the ground that it was founded by human effort rather than by the Messiah.

Chapter 2: *The Nature of Israel's Knowledge*

1. Interesting studies of the psychology and logic of ancient Israel will be found in J. Pedersen's *Israel: Its Life and Culture*, Vols. I–II (Oxford, 1926), pp. 99–181 ("The Soul"); T. Boman, *Hebrew Thought Compared with Greek*, tr. by J. Moreau (Philadelphia, 1960); C. Tresmontant, *A Study of Hebrew Thought*, tr. by M. F. Gibson (New York, 1960). All these works, though containing useful information, must be used with circumspection; the type of approach they represent has been severely criticized in J. Barr's, *The Semantics of Biblical Language* (Oxford, 1961), and—briefly but emphatically—by W. F. Albright in his *New Horizons in Biblical Research* (New York, 1966), pp. 18f. For a more objective approach to the nature of the Hebrew psyche, see A. R. Johnson, *The Vitality of the Individual in the Thought of Ancient Israel* (Cardiff, 1949) and G. Pidoux, *L'homme dans l'Ancien Testament* (Paris, 1953). The psychic functions of the different organs of the body are described in the articles on "Heart," "Kidneys," etc., in the various dictionaries (e.g., *The Interpreter's Dictionary of the Bible*; see above, ch. 1,

note 10) and theological word-books of the Bible (e.g., G. Kittel, *Theological Dictionary of the New Testament*, tr. by G. W. Bromiley; Grand Rapids, 1964; the words are listed in Greek); see also the bibliographies appended to the articles.

2. "Wer 'Theologie' in die Sprache des Alten Testaments übersetzen wollte, muste *da°at °elohim* sagen" ("One who wishes to translate 'theology' into Old Testament language must say *da°at °elohim*"), says H. W. Wolff in the article " 'Wissen um Gott' bei Hosea als Urform von Theologie" in his *Gesammelte Studien zum Alten Testament* (Munich, 1964), pp. 182–205. He stresses the intellectual content of the idea.

3. It has been suggested that the Hebrew verb *yada°*, when used with this particular nuance, is probably related to the Arabic root *wada°a*, with the sense "care for, keep in mind," rather than to the ordinary Hebrew root that means "to know" (D. W. Thomas, "The Root *yada°* in Hebrew," *JTS* 35, 1934; pp. 298–306). The new Jewish Publication Society version proposes to translate the word in these instances by something like "care for," "be mindful of." The theory of originally distinct verbal roots is not really necessary, since the same semantic range can be found in words for "knowing" in other languages. In English, for example, the noun "ignorance" (from the Latin *ignorare*, "not to know") means "want of knowledge," whereas the verb "to ignore"—from the same root—which once (like the French *ignorer*) meant "to be ignorant of, or not acquainted with" has come to mean "to *refuse* to take notice of," "to disregard *willfully*," thus providing, in a kind of mirror image, the same range of meaning as the Hebrew *yada°*. Similarly, the English word "mind," in its nominal and several verbal meanings, illustrates the ease with which a purely intellectual concept can be extended to include both the emotional and the volitional ("to have in mind," "to mind if something happens," "to mind one's mother," "to mind the baby"!). In any event, the Hebrew verb undoubtedly embraces all three meanings, and all are relevant to an understanding of "the knowledge of God."

Chapter 3: *God in the Past*

1. The most important discussion of the ancestral gods of Israel is that of A. Alt, "The God of the Fathers" (1929; included in his *Essays on Old Testament History and Religion*, pp. 1–77); see also F. M. Cross, Jr., in the article referred to below in ch. 6, note 7, who argues that the patriarchal god was the Canaanite El.

2. See G. von Rad, *Das Gottesvolk im Deuteronomium* (Stuttgart, 1929), p. 28.

3. For the text of a typical Hittite suzerainty treaty, see *ANET*, pp. 203–205 (tr. by A. Goetze). The view that these treaties, taken to be representative of international treaties of the period, provide the original model for Yahweh's covenant with Israel was first set forth at length by G. E. Mendenhall in a monograph entitled *Law and Covenant in the Ancient Near East* (Pittsburgh, 1955). The same view was developed independently by K. Baltzer in *Das Bundesformular* (see above, ch. 1, note 11), and expounded in detail by W. Beyerlin, in the volume mentioned above in chap. 1, note 8. A more critical position is taken by D. J. McCarthy in his exhaustive study *Treaty and Cove-*

nant: A Study in Form in the Ancient Oriental Documents and in the Old Testament (Rome, 1963), who finds significant parallels chiefly in the Deuteronomic conception of the covenant (7th century), and believes the original Sinai covenant was, in contrast, personal, "familial" and ritual, in form, not political (pp. 163, 166f., 173–177). The relevance of the Hittite treaties is denied by J. Barr in *Hastings Dictionary of the Bible* (New York, 1962) p. 184a; by E. Gerstenberger (in the work cited below in ch. 7, note 1, pp. 99–110); criticized by C. F. Whitley in his article "Covenant and Commandment in Israel," *JNES* 22 (1963), pp. 37–43; and repudiated *in toto* by F. Nötscher, "Bundesformular und 'Amtsschimmel,'" *BZ* nf9 (1965), pp. 181–214, and by G. Fohrer in the article cited above, ch. 1, note 10 (cols. 893–897). The best account of the discussion to date is given by D. J. McCarthy in his *Der Gottesbund im Alten Testament* (Stuttgart, 1966), expanded from an article, "Covenant in the Old Testament: The Present State of Inquiry" *CBQ* 27 (1965), pp. 217–240. For a general discussion of the ancient Semitic idea of covenant, see McCarthy, *Treaty and Covenant*, p. 169; J. Pedersen, *Israel: Its Life and Culture*, I–II, pp. 263–310; J. Begrich, "Berit: Ein Beitrag zur Erfassung einer alttestamentlichen Denkform" (1944), included in his *Gesammelte Studien zum Alten Testament* (Munich, 1964), pp. 55–66; A. Jepsen, "Berith: Ein Beitrag zur Theologie der Exilszeit" in *Verbannung und Heimkehr: Festschrift zum 70. Geburtstag von W. Rudolf* (Tübingen, 1961), pp. 161–179 (he, also, denies the relevance of the Hittite treaties, p. 175 fn. 21); and W. Eichrodt, "Covenant and Law," *Int* 20 (1966), pp. 302–321. See also P. Buis, "Les formulaires d'alliance," *VT* 16 (1966), pp. 396–411, and E. Kutsch, "Gesetz und Gnade," *ZAW* 79 (1967), pp. 18–35.

4. The word *torah* is derived from the verb *yrh* which, in the *hiphᶜil*, means most commonly "to teach, direct, instruct" (Exod. 35:34; 1 Sam. 12:23) and is used particularly in connection with the ethical and ritual directions given by the priesthood (Lev. 10:11; Mic. 3:11). It is cognate with the word for "teacher" (*moreh*: Prov. 5:13; Isa. 30:20). The new Jewish Publication Society version of *The Torah* (Philadelphia, 1962) ordinarily translates the word by something like "teaching" or "instruction," sometimes in the plural (Exod. 13:9; 16:4; Deut. 33:4). It was this conception of *torah* as the gracious teaching, or revelation, of a wise, all-knowing Teacher, rather than a collection of arbitrary rules imposed by an omnipotent tyrant, that led the writers of Pss. 19:7–14 (Heb. 8–15) and 119 to think of it as something "sweeter than honey" (Ps. 19:10; 119:103) and "the joy of my heart" (Ps. 119:111). Illuminating discussions of the inadequacy of "law" as a translation of *torah* will be found in M. Buber, *Two Types of Faith*, tr. by N. P. Goldhawk (London, 1951), pp. 56f, and W. Herberg, *Judaism and Modern Man* (Philadelphia, 1951), Meridian ed. pp. 285–303. Although the conception they expound is that of postbiblical Judaism, the germ of it is certainly to be found in the later parts of the Old Testament.

5. G. von Rad, *The Problem of the Hexateuch and Other Essays*, pp. 1–78; M. Noth, *Überlieferungsgeschichte des Pentateuch*, pp. 48–67. See, above, ch. 1, notes 6, 7.

6. A similar historical summary is to be found in Deut. 6:21–24. As is pointed out in the following discussion, neither of these contains any mention of the giving of the law and the establishment of the covenant at Sinai; see above, ch. 1, note 8. The date of these passages is uncertain; von Rad says merely that Deut. 6:21–24 is "based upon tradition" (commentary on *Deuteronomy*, tr. by

D. Barton, Philadelphia, 1966, p. 65); he acknowledges that the more important text in Deut. 26 contains late elements, but believes it shows signs of being constructed about a much more ancient core (*op. cit.*, pp. 158f.; *Problem of the Hexateuch*, p. 4). On the other hand, L. Rost, *Das kleine Credo und andere Studien zum Alten Testament* (Heidelberg, 1965), pp. 11–25, contends that the passage in Deut. 26 is primarily the composition of an individual writer in the age of Josiah, even though it may contain some ancient clichés, and was composed with attention to the peculiar problems of the Deuteronomic age.

7. According to von Rad, this stage in the development of the tradition was anterior, in its general outline, to the time of the Yahwist (*The Problem of the Hexateuch*, p. 58).

8. The modern evidence for the history and culture of the patriarchal age is competently and interestingly presented in J. M. Holt, *The Patriarchs of Israel* (Nashville, 1964); more briefly, by H. H. Rowley, "Recent Discoveries and the Patriarchal Age," *BJRL* 32 (1949–50), pp. 44–79; and by W. F. Albright, *The Biblical Period from Abraham to Ezra*, ch. 1, "Hebrew Beginnings."

9. The belief in creator-gods, of course, long antedates the rise of Israel in the ancient Near East, as is to be seen from the mythologies of Babylon, Egypt and Ugarit, so it is not inherently impossible for her to have believed in Yahweh as Creator from the very beginning. It is evident, nevertheless, that her thinking and her interests did not run along this line. It may well be that the first impulse toward elevating the idea of creation into an "article of faith" came, soon after the entry into Canaan, from the tendency to identify Yahweh with the Canaanite god El who, as the Bible itself testifies, was venerated as the "maker of heaven and earth" (Gen. 14:19; "God Most High" translates *ʾel ʿelyon*). See O. Eissfeldt, "El and Yahweh," *JSS* 1 (1956), pp. 25–37, reprinted in *Kleine Schriften*, III (Tübingen, 1966), pp. 386–397.

10. A good account of the contrasts between the historical religion of Israel and the nature religion of her neighbors will be found in G. E. Wright, *The Old Testament against its Environment*, SBT 2 (Chicago, 1950). For an authoritative general survey of the religious and cultural world-view of the ancient Near East, see H. Frankfort *et al.*, *The Intellectual Adventure of Ancient Man* (Chicago, 1946); the contrast between Israel and her environment is well summarized on pp. 363–373. This work is also published by Penguin Books, minus the section on Israel, under the title *Before Philosophy*.

11. Von Rad believes that the composition of the primeval history and its addition to the older core of "theological" tradition was the work of the Yahwist (*The Problem of the Hexateuch*, pp. 64f., 75).

12. Von Rad denies that the main line of Israelite thought ever embraced an *independent* doctrine of creation; the only evidence, he says, for an emphasis upon creation apart from election is to be found in Pss. 8, 19 and 104, which are of Wisdom inspiration and show foreign influence ("The Theological Problem of the Old Testament Doctrine of Creation," *op. cit.*, pp. 131–143). A needed corrective to this extreme view will be found in P. B. Harner, "Creation Faith in Deutero-Isaiah," *VT* 17 (1967), pp. 298–306.

13. See G. E. Mendenhall, "Mari," and C. H. Gordon, "Biblical Customs and the Nuzu Tablets" in *The Biblical Archaeologist Reader*, Vol. 2, ed. by D. N. Freedman and E. F. Campbell, Jr. (Garden City, 1964), pp. 3–33; also J. M. Holt, *op. cit.*; G. E. Wright, *Biblical Archaeology* (Philadelphia, 1957; rev. ed., 1962),

ch. 3, "The Founding Fathers"; and J. Gray, *Archaeology and the Old Testament World* (New York, 1962), ch. 2, "The Land of the Two Rivers."

14. *ANET* contains translations of the Creation and Gilgamesh Epics (pp. 60–72 and 72–99 respectively) by E. A. Speiser; the Babylonian Flood story is found on pp. 93–95.

15. A special study of the Zion-David tradition has been made by S. Amsler, *David, Roi et Messie* (Neuchatel, 1963). He concludes that it is not antithetical, but supplementary, to the Sinai tradition. See also L. Rost, "Sinaibund und Davidsbund," *TLZ* 72 (1947), cols. 129–134; M. Sekine, "Davidsbund und Sinaibund bei Jeremia," *VT* 9 (1959), pp. 47–57; A. H. J. Gunneweg, "Sinaibund und Davidsbund," *VT* 10 (1960), pp. 335–341, and R. Clements, *Abraham and David, SBT* n.s. 5 (Naperville, 1967).

Chapter 4: *God in the Present*

1. See, for example, Prov. 21:3, 27; Eccles. 5:1 (Heb. 4:17) on the wise men's attitude to the cult; for typical expressions of the prophetic point of view on the cult see Amos 4:4f; 5:21–25; Isa. 1:10–15; Jer. 7:4, 22; for the prophets on the wise men, see Isa. 5:21; 29:14; Jer. 9:23 (though the prophets were probably more concerned with the worldly political advice of the king's councilors than with Wisdom as an educational and religious enterprise; see W. McKane, *Prophets and Wise Men, SBT* 44 [Naperville, 1965]).

2. See particularly: A. Haldar, *Associations of Cult Prophets among the Ancient Semites* (Uppsala, 1945): A. R. Johnson, *The Cultic Prophet in Ancient Israel* (Cardiff, 1944). For general discussion of the modern approach to the study of the prophetic movement, see B. D. Napier, *Prophets in Perspective* (New York, 1963) and J. Lindblom, *Prophecy in Ancient Israel* (Oxford, 1962).

3. See H. W. Robinson, *Inspiration and Revelation in the Old Testament* (Oxford, 1946), pp. 231–261; G. von Rad, *Old Testament Theology*, Vol. I, pp. 434–453; R. N. Whybray, *Wisdom in Proverbs, SBT* 45 (Naperville, 1965). The last-named argues that the conception of cosmic "Wisdom" was a device by means of which the Hebrew wise men attempted to accommodate international Wisdom teaching to Israelite tradition (pp. 92–95).

4. See R. Dussaud, *Les origenes cananéennes du sacrifice israélite* (Paris, 1921), and R. de Vaux, *Ancient Israel: Its Life and Institutions*, tr. by J. McHugh (New York, 1961), pp. 438–441.

5. S. Mowinckel, *Religion und Kultus* (Göttingen, 1953), pp. 73–80; *The Psalms in Israel's Worship* (tr. by D. R. Ap-Thomas; Oxford, 1962), I, pp. 15–22.

6. On the theory of a covenant-renewal festival, see above, ch. 1, note 11. Mowinckel believes that the theme of covenant-renewal was only one element in an elaborate series of ceremonies, mostly taken over from the Canaanites and celebrated in the autumn, which had for their central feature the "enthronement" of Yahweh as King of the universe for the coming year (*Le Décalogue*, pp. 122f.). This theory has been widely debated, but the existence of such a feast is too hypothetical and the problems too complex for it to be discussed here. For further references, see below, ch. 9, note 24.

7. On the significance of the temple in the ancient Orient, see the series of articles by H. H. Nelson, A. L. Oppenheim, G. E. Wright, and F. Filson in

The *Biblical Archaeologist Reader*, Vol. 1 (ed. by D. N. Freedman and G. E. Wright; Garden City, 1961), pp. 145–200, under the general title "The Significance of the Temple in the Ancient Near East."

8. On the idea of sacral kingship, see the references in ch. 1, note 12, above.

9. We have limited our discussion of the postexilic cult to the temple and the rites connected with it. The synagogue, of which we spoke in ch. 1, no doubt has its roots in this period, and many of the characteristic features of synagogue religion were already evident, but its full development belongs to the postbiblical period, when it finally supplants the temple entirely.

10. For a comprehensive treatment of the Israelite cult see H.-J. Kraus, *Worship in Israel: A Cultic History of the Old Testament*, tr. by G. Buswell (Richmond, 1966), R. de Vaux, *Ancient Israel*, Part IV, and H. H. Rowley, *Worship in Ancient Israel* (Philadelphia, 1967).

11. See ch. 4, note 2, above.

12. A. Jepsen, for example, makes a sharp distinction between the ecstatic "nebiim" and the great "writing prophets" (*Nabi: soziologische Studien zur alttestamentlichen Literatur und Religionsgeschichte*, Munich, 1934, pp. 132–142).

13. For possible Wisdom influence on the prophets, see J. Lindblom, "Wisdom in the Old Testament Prophets," Suppls. *VT*, 3 (1955), pp. 192–204; also S. Terrien, "Amos and Wisdom" in B. W. Anderson and W. Harrelson (eds.) *Israel's Prophetic Heritage* (New York, 1962), pp. 108–115; J. Fichtner, "Jesaia unter den Weisen," in his *Gottes Weisheit* (Stuttgart, 1965), pp. 18–26, originally published in *TLZ* 74 (1949), cols. 75–79; and H. W. Wolff, *Amos' Geistige Heimat* (Neukirchen, 1964).

14. For general discussion of the Wisdom Literature, see O. S. Rankin, *Israel's Wisdom Literature* (Edinburgh, 1936); W. Baumgartner, *Israelitische und altorientalische Weisheit* (Tübingen, 1933); J. Fichtner, *Die altorientalische Weisheit in ihrer israelitisch-jüdischen Ausprägung* (Beih. ZAW 62, 1933); J. Rylaarsdam, *Revelation in Jewish Wisdom Literature* (Chicago, 1946); G. von Rad, *Old Testament Theology*, Vol. I, pp. 418–459; H. H. Schmid, *Wesen und Geschichte der Weisheit* (Beih. ZAW 101, 1966).

15. See W. O. E. Oesterley, *The Wisdom of Egypt and the Old Testament* (London, 1927); W. G. Lambert, *Babylonian Wisdom Literature* (Oxford, 1960); R. B. Y. Scott, *Proverbs* (Anchor Bible; Garden City, 1965), pp. xl–lii. On the possible Canaanite origin of much of the Wisdom material, see C. I. K. Story, "The Book of Proverbs and Northwest Semitic Literature," *JBL* 64 (1945), pp. 319–337, and W. F. Albright, "Some Canaanite-Phoenician Sources of Hebrew Wisdom," *Suppls. VT* 3 (Leiden, 1955), pp. 1–15.

16. The Book of Proverbs is divided into sections that certainly belong in part to different periods. This is particularly obvious in the case of a section attributed to the time of Hezekiah (Prov. 25:1); another, entitled "The Words of the Wise," is clearly based on the Egyptian Wisdom of Amen-em-opet (Prov. 22:17–24:22: see *ANET*, pp. 421–425; tr. by J. A. Wilson).

17. The concept of *maat* is discussed by H. Frankfort in his *Ancient Egyptian Religion* (New York, 1948), pp. 53–56, 70–77). See also his contribution to *The Intellectual Adventure of Ancient Man* (above, ch. 3, note 10), pp. 14, 82, 108f., and the illuminating discussion by H. H. Schmid, *op. cit.*, pp. 17–22.

18. The suggestion that in some passages of the Old Testament the moral order is conceived to work in an impersonal fashion was first made by K. Koch, "Gibt es ein Vergeltungsdogma im Alten Testament?" *ZTK* 52 (1955), pp. 1–42.

19. The various possible interpretations of the crucial word translated "master workman" are thoroughly surveyed by R. B. Y. Scott, "Wisdom in Creation: the *ʾĀmōn* of Proverbs VIII 30," in *VT* 10 (1960), pp. 213–223; see also von Rad, *Old Testament Theology*, I, p. 447; and, more recently, R. Whybray, *Wisdom in Proverbs*, pp. 101–103.

20. G. von Rad, "The Joseph Narrative and Ancient Wisdom" in *The Problem of the Hexateuch and Other Essays*, pp. 292–300; also his *Old Testament Theology*, Vol. I, pp. 432, 440; and his commentary on *Genesis*, tr. by J. H. Marks (New York, 1961), pp. 430–434.

Chapter 5: *Digression: God and the Natural World*

1. The Ugaritic text will be found in *ANET*, pp. 130f., tr. by H. L. Ginsberg. For further discussion of the conflict between Yahweh and the chaotic waters, see H. G. May, "Some Cosmic Connotations of 'Mayyim Rabbim,'" *JBL* 74 (1955), pp. 9–21; P. Reymond, *L'eau, sa vie, et sa signification dans l'Ancien Testament* (*Suppls. VT* 6; Leiden, 1958), pp. 182–198; O. Eissfeldt, "Gott und das Meer in der Bibel" in his *Kleine Schriften*, III, pp. 256–264 (art. orig. pub. in 1953).

2. That Old Testament man was on the right track in refusing to make a sharp separation between creation and providence is indicated by J. Macquarrie, *Principles of Christian Theology* (New York, 1966), who, like other contemporary theologians, continues to regard them as simply different aspects of the same process (p. 219).

3. This was certainly one meaning attached by the later Hebrews to the name "Yahweh of hosts," the "hosts" being regarded as the "forces" of the natural world. This was apparently the sense in which the phrase was understood by the Greek translators, who frequently render it either *kurios tōn dunameōn* "lord of powers" (Ps. 24:10; 46:7,11 Eng. = 23:10; 45:8,12 Greek), or *kurios pantokratōr* "lord omnipotent" (2 Sam. 5:10; 7:27).

4. W. F. Albright, "What were the Cherubim?" in *The Biblical Archaeologist Reader*, Vol. I, pp. 95–97.

5. On the idea of the Spirit of Yahweh, see P. Volz, *Der Geist Gottes* (Tübingen, 1910); P. van Imschoot, "L'action de l'esprit de Jahvé dans l'Ancien Testament" in *RSPT* 23 (1934), pp. 553–587, and "L'esprit de Jahvé, source de vie dans l'Ancien Testament," *RB* 44 (1935), pp. 481–501; N. H. Snaith, *The Distinctive Ideas of the Old Testament* (London, 1944), pp. 143–158.

6. O. Grether, *Name und Wort Gottes im Alten Testament und im antiken Orient*, Beih. *ZAW* 64 (Leipzig, 1934), pp. 59–158; H. Ringgren, *Word and Wisdom: Studies in the Hypostatization of Divine Qualities* (Lund, 1947), pp. 157–164.

7. See Ringgren, *op. cit.*, pp. 89–149; J. C. Rylaarsdam, *Revelation in Jewish Wisdom Literature*, ch. 5, "Wisdom and the Spirit."

Chapter 6: *The Being of God*

1. See M. Pope, *El in the Ugaritic Texts, Suppls. VT* 2 (Leiden, 1955), pp. 27–35, 92–104; with which, however, compare J. Gray, *The Legacy of Canaan, Suppls. VT* 5 (Leiden, 1957), pp. 115–118.

2. The story of Kumarbi is related in *ANET*, pp. 120f. (tr. by A. Goetze); a more extended account is given by H. G. Güterbock in S. N. Kramer (ed.), *Mythologies of the Ancient World* (Garden City, 1961), pp. 155–160.

3. E. Dhorme, *Les religions de Babylonie et d'Assyrie* (Paris, 1949), pp. 138–150; H. Schmökel (ed.), *Kulturgeschichte des alten Orients* (Stuttgart, 1961), p. 280f., describes Marduk as an "upstart" (*Emporkömmling*); see also E. O. James, *The Ancient Gods* (London, 1960), pp. 119f., 271.

4. E. Otto, *Religionsgeschichte des alten Orients* (*Handbuch der Orientalistik*, Section I, Vol. 8; Leiden, 1964), pp. 57ff.; see also J. A. Wilson, *The Burden of Egypt* (Chicago, 1951), pp. 130f., and H. Frankfort, *Ancient Egyptian Religion*, p. 22. Frankfort minimizes the political factor.

5. C. H. Gordon, *The Loves and Wars of Baal and Anat* (Princeton, 1943).

6. The "Kenite hypothesis," first proposed by Ghillany in 1862, is still held by many scholars. The evidence is well summarized in H. Schmökel, "Jahve und die Keniter," *JBL* 52 (1933), pp. 212–229. The theory is criticized, and a counter view presented, by T. J. Meek, *Hebrew Origins* (New York, 1936; rev. ed., 1950), pp. 93–118.

7. This is essentially the view of T. J. Meek in the book mentioned in the preceding note (pp. 105–110), although he rejects the opinion that the name YHWH was derived from the Kenites. W. F. Albright has long maintained that it is a *hiphᶜil* formation of the verb *hawah/hayah* with the meaning "[he who] brings into being" (i.e., creates). This view was argued in his early article "Contributions to Biblical Archaeology and Philology," *JBL* 43 (1924), pp. 370–378; in his review of B. N. Wambacq, *L'épithète divine Jahvé Sᵉbaʾoth* (Bruges, 1947), *JBL* 67 (1948), pp. 377–381; and in *From the Stone Age to Christianity* (Baltimore, 1940; Anchor ed., 1957), pp. 258–261 (Anchor). It has been most recently defended by his former students, D. N. Freedman, "The Name of the God of Moses," *JBL* 79 (1960), pp. 151–156, and F. M. Cross, Jr., "Yahweh and the God of the Patriarchs," *HTR* 55 (1962), pp. 250–259. Cross regards the word YHWH as originally an epithet of the Canaanite god El, which somehow became detached from its context and developed into an independent divine name. Whatever may be the facts about the original significance of the name, it is evident that it was neither widely, nor long, understood in a causative sense in Israel. As has been emphasized in the above discussion (see particularly pp. 4f., 61f., and ch. I, note 1, above), the thought of Yahweh as the Creator played a minimal—if indeed it played any—part in early Israelite theology; and the opinion preserved in the Masoretic text that the name YHWH is formed from the *qal* rather than the *hiphᶜil* stem of the verb (so Exod. 3:14) certainly represents a very ancient tradition. The present Old Testament text knows no other tradition. One must conclude that Israel borrowed only the name—not the meaning—and later imposed her own quite different meaning upon it. The view that YHWH was for early Israel "merely a name," with no meaning attached to it is well stated by W. Zimmerli in *Gottes Offenbarung* (Munich, 1963), p.

290. For further discussion of the problem see also R. Mayer, "Der Gottesname Jahwe im Lichte der neueren Forschung," *BZ* nf2 (1958), pp. 26–53, S. Mowinckel, "The Name of the God of Moses," *HUCA* 32 (1961), pp. 121–133, and J. P. Hyatt, "Was Yahweh Originally a Creator Deity?" *JBL* 86 (1967), pp. 369–377.

8. This is the point of view of Eichrodt, *Theology of the Old Testament,* I, pp. 220–227; von Rad, *Old Testament Theology,* I, pp. 210ff.; H. H. Rowley, *From Moses to Qumran* (New York, 1963), pp. 59–63; and T. J. Meek, "The Origin of Hebrew Monotheism" in *Hebrew Origins,* pp. 184–228. W. F. Albright is the principal advocate of the view that monotheism originated with Moses (*From the Stone Age to Chritianity,* Anchor ed., pp. 257–272).

9. On the absence of henotheism in Mesopotamia, see W. F. Albright, "The Ancient Near East and the Religion of Israel," *JBL* 59 (1940), pp. 103f.

10. The special sense in which some theologians and biblical scholars use the term "myth" is thoroughly discussed and defended by J. L. McKenzie, *Myths and Realities* (Milwaukee, 1963), pp. 182–200, by R. A. F. MacKenzie, *Faith and History in the Old Testament* (Minneapolis, 1963), pp. 61–74, and J. Knox, *Myth and Truth* (Charlottesville, 1964). For myself, I would avoid this use of the term as unnecessarily confusing; I would agree with the general viewpoint of A. Richardson, who formerly used the word with a special theological meaning but has since abandoned it (*The Bible in the Age of Science,* Philadelphia, 1961, pp. 151–158, see especially fn. 1, p. 155). Many Old Testament stories and images are derived from pagan mythology, but have been purged of their essential mythological character; the story of creation is theological rather than mythological, while the stories of the fall, the flood, etc., are, in their Old Testament context, geared into the historical sequence and belong, therefore, not to myth, but to legend. See also Y. Kaufman, *The Religion of Israel,* tr. and abr. by M. Greenberg (Chicago, 1960), pp. 60–63, and W. F. Albright, *New Horizons in Biblical Research,* pp. 32ff.

11. The process of the demythologizing of ancient myth in Israel has been subjected to careful study by B. S. Childs, *Myth and Reality in the Old Testament* (*SBT* 27; Naperville, 1960).

12. Modern Israeli Hebrew, unlike the ancient language, has the word ʾelah, the feminine equivalent of ʾel. The formation of the word is so correct and inevitable that its absence in the Bible is all the more surprising.

13. On the bewildering, kaleidoscopic shifts of pattern which characterize the ancient Near East pantheon, see, e.g., Albright, *From the Stone Age to Christianity* (Anchor ed.), p. 264; H. Frankfort *et al., The Intellectual Adventure of Ancient Man,* pp. 65ff., 133f., 168f.; A. L. Oppenheim, *Ancient Mesopotamia* (Chicago, 1964), pp. 194–197.

14. The word *satan* in Hebrew means merely "adversary" and, in the two references in Job 1:6, etc., and Zech. 3:1, designates the function, not the name, of the heavenly being; only in 1 Chron. 21:1, in one of the latest books of the Old Testament, does "Satan" appear as a proper name (i.e., without the definite article). A figure similar to "the adversary" appears fleetingly in 1 Kings 22:21, where he is called "the spirit."

15. *The Torah: The Five Books of Moses* (Philadelphia, 1962).

16. See A. R. Johnson, *The Vitality of the Individual in the Thought of Ancient Israel,* pp. 94–105; J. Pedersen, *Israel: Its Life and Culture,* I–II, pp. 153–155.

17. Many contemporary theologians prefer to describe God in terms of "Being," "Ground of Being," "Ultimate Concern," etc., but most would probably still defend the use of imagery drawn from personal life in speaking of, and certainly to, him. "God is the Personality who speaks, acts, disclosing to us Himself and His will," says E. Brunner in *Dogmatics: Vol. 1, The Christian Doctrine of God*, tr. by O. Wyon (Philadelphia, 1950), p. 139 (the whole of pp. 139ff. is relevant). Paul Tillich says, "The symbol 'personal God' is absolutely fundamental because an existential relation is a person-to-person relation. Man cannot be ultimately concerned about anything that is less than personal . . ." (*Systematic Theology*, I, Chicago, 1951; p. 244). See also J. Macquarrie, *Principles of Christian Theology* (New York, 1966), p. 187, and W. Herberg, *Judaism and Modern Man* (Philadelphia, 1951) Meridian ed., pp. 59–62.

18. The animal gods of Egypt are described at some length by E. Otto in *Religionsgeschichte des alten Orients* (*Handbuch der Orientalistik*, Section 1, Vol. 8), pp. 6–14; he denies the connection with totemism which is, however, affirmed by L. Woolley, *The Beginnings of Ancient Civilization* (London, 1963), pp. 716f. H. Frankfort has a sympathetic treatment of this aspect of Egyptian religion in his *Ancient Egyptian Religion*, pp. 8–14. In the Old Testament, Yahweh is, of course, frequently compared to an animal (e.g. Deut. 32:11; Lam. 3:10; Hos. 13:7f.), but only in a metaphorical sense. The horror inspired in the Israelite mind by Egyptian animal worship is vividly expressed in Wisdom of Solomon 12:24–27; 15:18–16:1.

19. Gen. 2:7 (J) says that Yahweh God "formed" man (using the verb *yatsar* which is also used of a potter's work), whereas Gen. 1:27 speaks of God as "creating" man (using the verb *bara*ᵓ, which can have only God for its subject); in Gen. 15:18 (J) Yahweh "makes" a covenant with Abraham (literally, he "cuts" it, the verb *karat* being the same as that used in Gen. 26:28 of Isaac and Abimelek), but in Gen. 17:7 (P) the verb is "establish" (*heqim*), which is without analogy in the language of human covenant-making. For the sake of variety, P sometimes uses the older, commonplace language also (e.g., Gen. 2:2f.).

20. See the account of El's love-making and the birth to him of Shachar and Shalim (G. R. Driver, *Canaanite Myths and Legends*, Edinburgh, 1956, p. 123), and of Baal's copulation with a heifer (*ibid.*, p. 107, lines 18–21).

21. S. Kramer, in *The Sumerians* (Chicago, 1963), pp. 250–254, has an interesting account of divine courtship and marriage in ancient Sumer.

22. Frequently quoted examples of the toleration of images in popular religion are found in Judg. 8:27; 17:3–5; 1 Sam. 19:13.

23. Ikhnaton's deity, Aton, was pictured only in the form of the sun's disk: J. A. Wilson, *The Burden of Egypt*, p. 222.

24. It must not be forgotten that, according to one strain of Old Testament thought (that of the Priestly Document) God has already created man as an image of himself (Gen. 1:27; 9:6); there must have been some who drew the obvious conclusion that it would be presumptuous of created man to attempt to make a further image. There is a valuable discussion of the theological importance of the prohibition of images in von Rad's article, "Some Aspects of the Old Testament World View" (*The Problem of the Hexateuch*, pp. 146–150).

25. A. R. Johnson, *The One and the Many in the Israelite Conception of God* (Cardiff, 2nd ed. 1961), pp. 28ff.; A. Lods, "L'ange de Yahvé et 'l'âme extérieure'" in *Beih. ZAW* 27 (Giessen, 1914), pp. 263–278; F. Stier, *Gott und sein*

Engel im Alten Testament (Münster, 1934); W. Baumgartner, "Zum Problem des 'Jahwe-Engels'" in his *Zum Alten Testament und seiner Umwelt* (Leiden, 1959), pp. 240–246.

26. A. M. Ramsey, *The Glory of God and the Transfiguration of Christ* (London, 1949); G. von Rad, "Deuteronomy's 'Name' Theology and the Priestly Document's 'Kabod' Theology," in *Studies in Deuteronomy*, tr. by D. Stalker, *SBT* 9 (Chicago, 1953), ch. 3. W. F. Albright, in the ref. mentioned in note 13 describes God's glory as "a refulgent envelope." The Old Testament concept of God's glory is exhaustively treated in B. Stein, *Der Begriff Kebod Jahweh und seine Bedeutung für die alttestamentliche Gotteserkenntnis* (Emsdetten i. Westf., 1939); the discussion in H. Kittel, *Die Herrlichkeit Gottes* (Giessen, 1934), includes also the New Testament and extra-biblical literature.

27. A. R. Johnson, "Aspects of the Use of the Term *panim* in the OT," in *Festschrift Otto Eissfeldt*, H. J. Fück, ed. (Halle a. d. Salle, 1947), pp. 155–159; W. F. Albright, *From the Stone Age to Christianity* (Anchor ed.), p. 298; W. Beyerlin, *Origins and History of the Oldest Sinaitic Traditions*, pp. 100–111.

Chapter 7: *The Character of God*

1. A. Alt believes that the so-called apod(e)ictic (that is the unconditional, mostly negative laws) of the Book of the Covenant (Exod. 20:22–23:19) and some other ancient legal codes are the product of Israel's earliest period in Canaan and her attempt to assert and preserve her identity in the presence of an alien culture; see his essay "The Origins of Israelite Law" (cited above in ch. 1, note 11). Alt's views have, however, been subjected to basic criticism in E. Gerstenberger's *Wesen und Herkunft des "apodiktischen Rechts"* (Neukirchen, 1965). Gerstenberger finds the source of these laws in family or tribal Wisdom rather than in cultic proclamation. An increasing number of scholars is inclined to take seriously the tradition of a Mosaic, or at least very early, origin for the Decalogue: see H. H. Rowley, "Moses and the Decalogue" in *BJRL* 34 (1951–2), pp. 81–118; J. J. Stamm and M. E. Andrews, *The Ten Commandments in Recent Research*, *SBT* n.s. 2 (Naperville, 1967); E. Nielsen, *Die zehn Gebote* (Copenhagen, 1965; he says the Decalogue as a whole is not Mosaic, though the first four commandments may be, pp. 106f.). On the possible proclamation of law as a cultic act in early Israel, see above, pp. 83ff.; also W. Beyerlin, *Origins and History of the Oldest Sinaitic Traditions*, pp. 49–67.

2. R. C. Dentan, "The Literary Affinities of Exod. xxxiv.6f.," *VT* 13 (1963), pp. 34–51. The creed is quoted in whole or in part many times in late literature, e.g. Ps. 86:15, 145:8; Neh. 9:17; Jon. 4:2.

3. On the semantic relationship of roots beginning with the consonants *qts*, *qt* and *qd* (all meaning "to cut"), see E. Kautzsch, *Gesenius' Hebrew Grammar*, 2nd rev. ed., tr. by A. E. Cowley (Oxford, 1910), para. 30h.

4. The word is comparatively rare and is perhaps artificially contrived to provide a necessary antonym for "holy"; see, e.g., Lev. 10:10, where it is translated "common" (i.e., not bound by the rules attaching to holy things).

5. The Hebrew term for "cult prostitute" is *qedesha*; the male prostitute is a *qadesh* (Deut. 23:17, Heb. 18).

6. A later copyist, who apparently thought the slaughter of a mere seventy

was unworthy of the Holy God, added the number "50,000," which seemed to him a more suitable figure. (See 1 Sam. 6:19, American Standard Version; RSV simply omits the ungrammatical addition, but see margin.)

7. It is generally agreed that the most sensitive ethical thought of the Old Testament is to be found in Job 31, Job's "negative confession," with its remarkable emphasis on inner attitudes and positive duties.

8. The most illuminating treatment of the whole concept of holiness is still that of R. Otto, *The Idea of the Holy*, tr. by J. W. Harvey (London, 1923). See also J. Hänel, *Die Religion der Heiligkeit* (Gütersloh, 1931); N. H. Snaith, *The Distinctive Ideas of the Old Testament*, pp. 21–50; H. Ringgren, *The Prophetical Conception of Holiness* (Uppsala, 1948).

9. So in Isa. 5:23 KJV translates "take away the righteousness of the righteous," whereas RSV reads, more idiomatically and intelligibly, "deprive the innocent of his right." Note also the striking difference between KJV and RSV in the translation of the equivalent Greek word *dikaios* in Luke 23:47.

10. In his popular *The Secular City* (Macmillan paperback, New York, 1965), p. 65, H. Cox quotes the Dutch philosopher van Peursen as speaking approvingly of the Hebrew *functional* conception of "truth" as closer to the views of modern times than older "mythical" or ontological conceptions.

11. The present book contains no separate discussion of "the wrath of God," because God's wrath is not a permanent aspect of his character, but only an occasional mode of his action. The phrase is, of course, anthropomorphic, and ordinarily represents God's violent reaction to human disloyalty and disobedience (Exod. 32:10). Yahweh's wrath may be considered either as a manifestation of his holiness, which destroys the unholy (2 Sam. 6:7; cf. 1 Sam. 6:19f.), or of his righteousness, which purges away all that is not "right" (Isa. 10:1–4); or of his jealousy, which will not tolerate that which is alien to his own nature (Nah. 1:2). His wrath is regarded as infinitely less significant than his love and favor (Ps. 30:5; Isa. 54:7f.). See R. V. G. Tasker, *The Biblical Doctrine of the Wrath of God* (London, 1951) and A. T. Hanson, *The Wrath of the Lamb* (London, 1957), pp. 1–40. Only very rarely is the primitive idea of unmotivated divine wrath attached to Yahweh (2 Sam. 24:1); see P. Volz, *Das Dämonische in Jahwe* (Tübingen, 1924). The term "wrath" is used in an impersonal sense, as synonymous with disaster, in 2 Kings 3:27 and 1 Macc. 1:64.

12. N. H. Snaith, *The Distinctive Ideas of the Old Testament* (London, 1944).

13. The standard treatment of the word is N. Glueck's *Hesed in the Bible*, tr. by A. Gottschalk from the German ed. of 1927 (Cincinnati, 1967); a different approach is taken by H. J. Stoebe, "Die Bedeutung des Wortes häsäd im A.T.," in *VT* 2 (1952), pp. 244–254. For Glueck *chesed* is loyalty to the covenant, while Stoebe regards it as the quality of divine condescension that is a precondition of the covenant.

14. The emphasis of the late Holiness Code on the importance of inner attitudes, and upon love as a motivating principle in dealing with other men, is probably also to be attributed to the growing influence of the Wisdom movement. The older codes of law were concerned chiefly with objective acts and external relationships; it was only the wise men who were concerned with what went on in the heart of man. With the breakup of the Israelite state at the exile the codes came to be regarded as standards of desirable conduct rather than as collections of statutory ordinances with the force of civil law; this

changed situation opened the way for the eventual fusion of "torah" and "wisdom." On the subject of Wisdom influence on law, see E. Nielsen, *Die zehn Gebote,* pp. 90ff. On the relation between Wisdom and the Holiness Code, see C. Feucht, *Untersuchungen zum Heiligkeitsgesetz* (Berlin, 1964), pp. 108–112.

Chapter 8: *Digression: The Names of God*

1. J. Pritchard (ed.), *ANET,* tr. by E. A. Speiser, pp. 60f.

2. On the significance of the name in Semitic thought see J. Pedersen, *Israel: Its Life and Culture,* I–II, pp. 245–259.

3. O. Grether, *Name und Wort Gottes im Alten Testament,* pp. 1–58, 159–185; G. von Rad, *Studies in Deuteronomy,* pp. 37–44.

4. On the problem of the original meaning of the tetragrammaton YHWH see above, ch. 6, note 7. For its traditional English pronunciation, see note 5, below.

5. It was the combination of the consonants YHWH with the vowels of ʾadonay (a/e,o,a) that gave rise to the familiar, but entirely illegitimate, pronunciation "Jehovah" (Yehowah); the initial vowel (a/e) fluctuates because of the different character of the consonant (guttural or nonguttural) with which it is associated.

6. On the significance of names compounded with ʾab (father) and ʾach (brother) see M. Noth, *Die israelitischen Personennamen* (Stuttgart, 1928), pp. 66–75. Such names, which are common in the ancient Semitic world, have the function of identifying the god as either the head (ʾab) of the tribe or as one of its members (ʾach). Being a part of Israel's inheritance from an older world, names of this kind have no special importance for Old Testament theology.

7. For L. Köhler, ʾadon is the characteristic and determinative Israelite epithet for Yahweh: (*Old Testament Theology,* Philadelphia, 1957, pp. 30–35). ". . . the statement 'God is the Lord' . . . is the backbone of Old Testament theology" (p. 35).

8. W. F. Albright, *From the Stone Age to Christianity* (Anchor ed.), pp. 213f.

9. The "elohistic" psalter, in which the occurrence of the name ʾelohim for God is far more frequent than YHWH, consists of Pss. 42–83. It is instructive in this connection to compare Pss. 14 and 53, which are, respectively, Yahwistic and Elohistic versions of the same song.

10. The singular form (ʾelah) is normal in Aramaic and Syriac, as in Arabic (ʾilah), where it is combined with the definite article (ʾal) to form a quasi-proper name (ʾallah).

11. See M. H. Pope, *El in the Ugaritic Texts.* The book is largely concerned with ʾel as a Canaanite god, but chs. 1 and 2 are devoted to a consideration of the etymology of the word and its use as an appellative.

12. See Pope, *op. cit.,* ch. 5.

13. On all these names, see Albright, *op. cit.,* 246–248.

14. Pope, *op. cit.,* p. 19, confesses himself agnostic as regards the derivation of the word and prefers to treat it simply as a primitive noun.

15. See the work of B. N. Wambacq listed above in ch. 6, note 7, with the review by Albright; also J. Obermann, "YHWH in Recent Discoveries," *JBL* 68 (1949), pp. 309–314; O. Eissfeldt, "Jahve Zebaoth" in his *Kleine Schriften,* III (Tübingen, 1966), pp. 103–123 (art. orig. pub. in 1950); J. P. Ross, "Jahweh

Seba'ot in Samuel and Psalms," *VT* 17 (1967), pp. 76–92; M. Tsevat, "Studies in the Book of Samuel IV: Yahweh Seba'ot," *HUCA* 36 (1965), pp. 49-58.

16. See above, ch. 5, note 3.

17. O. Eissfeldt, in a widely discussed monograph, *Molk als Opferbegriff im Punischen und Hebräischen und das Ende des Gottes Moloch* (Halle, 1935), maintained that the Hebrew word *mlk* in such passages as 2 Kings 23:10 refers to a type of offering rather than a god, but most scholars continue to believe that, in some instances at least, it represents a divine name. See W. Eichrodt, *Theology of the Old Testament*, I, 149f.; R. de Vaux, *Ancient Israel*, 444f.

18. O. Eissfeldt, "Jahve als König," in *Kleine Schriften*, I (Tübingen, 1962), pp. 172–193 (art. orig. pub. in 1928); V. Maag, "Malkut Jhwh" in *Suppls. VT* 7 (1960), pp. 146–153; J. Gray, "The Hebrew Conception of the Kingship of God," *VT* 6 (1956), pp. 268–285, and "The Kingship of God in the Prophets and Psalms," *VT* 11 (1961), pp. 1–29; E. Lipiński, *La royauté de Yahwé dans la poésie et le culte de l'ancien Israël* (Brussels, 1965); J. de Fraine, "La royauté de Yahvé dans les textes concernant l'arche," *Suppls. VT* 15 (1966), pp. 134–149; R. C. Dentan, "The Kingdom of God in the Old Testament" in *The Interpreter's One-Volume Commentary on the Bible* (Nashville, 1968).

Chapter 9: *God in the Future*

1. The most notable representative of this point of view is H. Gressmann, *Der Ursprung der israelitisch-jüdischen Eschatologie* (Göttingen, 1905), revised edition entitled *Der Messias* (Göttingen, 1929); for a criticism of it, see S. Mowinckel, *He That Cometh*, pp. 127f., 460f., and the literature mentioned there in the notes.

2. The third line of this passage is one of the most famous cruxes of Scripture. The Hebrew, literally translated by KJV and the American Standard Version, reads "until Shiloh come." The RSV reading, given in the text above, is largely determined by the analogy with Ezek. 21:27 (Heb. 32). The new Jewish version of *The Torah* translates, "so that tribute shall come to him."

3. The most persuasive defense of this interpretation is that of G. von Rad (*The Problem of the Hexateuch*, p. 66, fn. 107; *Genesis*, pp. 149f., 155f.), whose argument is based upon the blessing's contextual relationship to the disaster at Babel, with which the immediately preceding primeval history ends; a universal curse, he argues, must be healed by a *universal* blessing.

4. On the Moabite Stone, Mesha, King of Moab, reports that Moab had been humbled before Israel because Chemosh, the god of Moab, "was angry with his land" (*ANET*, p. 320, tr. by W. F. Albright).

5. The present conclusion of Amos' book (9:8b–15) consists of a series of passages expressing strong confidence in Yahweh's favor toward Israel in the future. In contrast to the critical orthodoxy of the Wellhausen school, which regarded these as obvious postexilic additions to the book, some recent commentators have taken the position that they are authentic (G. A. Danell, *Studies in the Name Israel*, pp. 133–136; G. von Rad, *Old Testament Theology*, II, p. 138, at least as respects vv. 11f.; J. M. Myers, *Layman's Bible Commentary*, Vol. 14, Richmond, 1959, pp. 146–149). The view that denies them to Amos still seems the most probable; the arguments *pro* and *con* are well presented in R. S.

Cripps, *A Critical & Exegetical Commentary on the Book of Amos*, 2nd ed. (London, 1955), pp. 67–77.

6. S. Mowinckel, *He That Cometh*, p. 145; *The Psalms in Israel's Worship*, I (tr. by D. R. Ap-Thomas; Oxford, 1962), pp. 118ff.

7. G. von Rad, "The Origin of the Concept of the Day of Yahweh," *JSS* 4 (1959), pp. 97–108; *Old Testament Theology*, II, pp. 119–125.

8. The event is recorded in 2 Kings 17:5f. and in the annals of Sargon II: *ANET*, pp. 284f., tr. by A. L. Oppenheim. See Y. Kaufman's remarks on the fall of Jerusalem, which are also largely applicable to the fall of Samaria, in his *Religion of Israel*, pp. 401f.

9. C. C. Torrey, *The Second Isaiah* (Edinburgh, 1928), pp. 20–55; J. D. Smart, *History and Theology in Second Isaiah* (Philadelphia, 1965).

10. S. B. Frost's *Old Testament Apocalyptic: Its Origin and Growth* (London, 1952) contains useful discussions of all this material.

11. Much of the specific ideology and imagery of apocalyptic is believed to derive from Persian sources; see, e.g., Frost, *op. cit.*, pp. 72–76; S. Mowinckel, *He That Cometh*, pp. 264ff., 273–277; R. C. Otto, *The Kingdom of God and the Son of Man* (tr. by F. V. Filson and B. L. Woolf; Grand Rapids, n.d.), pp. 20–33.

12. S. Mowinckel, "Psalms and Wisdom" in *Wisdom in Ancient Israel and in the Ancient Near East* (M. Noth and D. W. Thomas, eds.; Leiden, 1955); = *Suppls. VT* 3), pp. 206–217.

13. Sirach 39:1 states explicitly that the wise man "will be concerned with prophecies," while Wisdom of Solomon 8:8 explains that Wisdom "has foreknowledge of signs and wonders and of the outcome of seasons and times." The argument that apocalyptic has its origin in Wisdom teaching is fully stated by von Rad, *Old Testament Theology*, II, pp. 303–308.

14. It is almost universally agreed that the Book of Daniel in its present form is a product of the Maccabean persecutions of 168–165 B.C. (1 Macc. 1:10–64). See N. W. Porteous, *Daniel* (Philadelphia, 1965), p. 20.

15. Although the figure of "the son of man" in its present context is unambiguously identified with the Jewish people, it has been plausibly argued that, in an older form of the story, he was an individual saviour of heavenly origin. See S. Mowinckel, *He That Cometh*, pp. 350–353; A. Bentzen, *Daniel* (*Handbuch zum Alten Testament* 19; 2nd ed., Tübingen, 1952), pp. 62f.

16. The so-called "Isaiah Apocalypse" (Isaiah 24–27) is almost unanimously regarded as the latest part of the book. For a comprehensive discussion of the date and other problems, see O. Eissfeldt, *The Old Testament: An Introduction* (3rd ed., tr. by P. R. Ackroyd; New York, 1965), especially pp. 325ff. Eissfeldt is inclined to date it in the third century B.C.

17. On the basis of 25:10, Eissfeldt would identify it with some disaster that had befallen the capital of Moab (*op. cit.*, p. 326).

18. S. Mowinckel, *He That Cometh*, p. 273; R. Martin-Achard, *From Death to Life*, tr. by J. P. Smith (Edinburgh, 1960), pp. 186–222.

19. See Isa. 24:21–23; 51:6; 60:19f.; 65:17; 66:22; Zech. 14:6f.; Enoch 45:4f.; 90:20–27; 91: 15–16; 2 Esdras 5:4–9; 7:30–42; D. S. Russell, *The Method and Message of Jewish Apocalyptic* (Philadelphia, 1964), pp. 280–284.

20. It should be noted that *berit* is also used elsewhere in the sense of "promise," with no sense of mutuality or juridical arrangement, obviously so,

e.g., in Isa. 59:21. Yahweh's promise to Noah (Gen. 8:21f.) is apparently understood as a covenant in *this* sense in Isa. 54:10 and Jer. 33:20–25; the covenant with Abraham in the early source is pure promise, with Yahweh alone passing between the pieces of the animals as a pledge of his future faithfulness (Gen. 15:17f.). It is this aspect of *berit* that is specially stressed by Jepsen in the article mentioned in ch. 3, note 3, above. Kutsch (see the same note) insists that the word *berit* in the Old Testament means *only* solemn promise or imposed obligation, never "relationship" or "mutual agreement."

21. On the idea of the spirit in the Old Testament, see above, chap. 5, note 5.

22. This is, of course, the passage quoted by Peter in explanation of the curious phenomena of Pentecost (Acts 2:16–21).

23. See above, ch. 8, note 18; S. Mowinckel, *He That Cometh*, pp. 143–149, 169–173; J. Bright, *The Kingdom of God* (New York, 1953), pp. 162–170.

24. The connection of the Feast of Booths (or Tabernacles) with Yahweh's enthronement is discussed at length by S. Mowinckel, *The Psalms in Israel's Worship*, I, pp. 118–130; Mowinckel's interpretation has, however, been challenged by N. H. Snaith in *The Jewish New Year Festival* (London, 1947), pp. 195–220 and *passim*.

Chapter 10: *Ancient Israel and the Modern West*

1. It is commonly said that either the author of the J document of the Pentateuch or the author of the "early source" in Samuel and Kings (in case they are not the same person) is the first "writer of history" in the modern sense. See R. H. Pfeiffer, *Introduction to the Old Testament* (New York, 1941), pp. 356–359; von Rad, *Old Testament Theology*, I, pp. 48–56.

2. The contemporary Jewish writer, Erich Fromm, as an example, regards the Old Testament God simply as an objectification of the values Israel derived from her deepest social experiences (*Ye Shall be as Gods: A Radical Interpretation of the Old Testament and its Tradition*, New York, 1966, pp. 61f., 226–229). R. L. Rubenstein believes the traditional idea of God is valid only as providing a focus for man's "ultimate concern" (*After Auschwitz: Radical Theology and Contemporary Judaism*, New York, 1966, p. 238 and *passim*); the biblical "Father-God," the "God of history," is dead, or rather, never lived, since he was merely the projection of certain human ideals and aspirations. Both these men are deeply religious, but whether the values in which they so passionately believe can long survive without any transcendental reference—without the God of the Bible—is something only the future can reveal.

INDEX OF SUBJECTS
AND PERSONS

INDEX OF
SCRIPTURE REFERENCES

References are to the English text (RSV, KJV, *etc.*).